ALCMAN
AND THE COSMOS
OF SPARTA

ALCMAN

and the

COSMOS OF SPARTA

Gloria Ferrari

THE UNIVERSITY OF CHICAGO PRESS

Chicago and London

Gloria Ferrari is professor emerita of classical archaeology
and art at Harvard University. She is the author of *Materiali
del Museo Archeologico di Tarquina XI: I vasi attici a figure rosse
del periodo arcaico* and *Figures of Speech: Men and Maidens in
Ancient Greece*, the latter published by the University of Chicago
Press and the 2002 recipient of the James R. Wiseman Book
Award from the Archaeological Institute of America. Her articles
have been published in a range of scholarly journals, including
Opuscula Romana, Metis, and *Classical Philology.*

The University of Chicago Press, Chicago 60637
The University of Chicago Press, Ltd., London
© 2008 by The University of Chicago
All rights reserved. Published 2008
Printed in the United States of America
17 16 15 14 13 12 11 10 09 08 1 2 3 4 5
ISBN-13: 978-0-226-66867-3 (cloth)
ISBN-10: 0-226-66867-3 (cloth)

The University of Chicago Press gratefully acknowledges the generous
support of Harvard University's Loeb Fund of the Department of the
Classics toward the publication of this book.

Library of Congress Cataloging-in-Publication Data

Ferrari, Gloria, 1941–
   Alcman and the cosmos of Sparta / Gloria Ferrari.
      p.   cm.
   Includes bibliographical references and index.
   ISBN-13: 978-0-226-66867-3 (hardcover : alk. paper)
   ISBN-10: 0-226-66867-3 (hardcover : alk. paper)
      1. Alcman—Criticism and interpretation. 2. Cosmology, Ancient.
   3. Theater—Greece—Sparta—History—To 500. I. Title.
   PA3862.A5F47 2008
   884′.01—dc22

                                                          2007041681

CONTENTS

ACKNOWLEDGMENTS

This study grew out of the 2004 James W. Poultney Lecture, sponsored by the graduate students of the Department of Classics at Johns Hopkins University. It is a pleasure now to thank my hosts—Helene Coccagna, Gareth Driver, and Gregory Jones in particular—for their gracious reception and a memorable seminar. Since then, many friends and colleagues have provided helpful comments and aid of all kinds. I think with gratitude of Carmen Arnold Biucchi, Mehmet-Ali Ataç, Natasha Bershadski, Anton Bierl, Kevin Clinton, Marcel Detienne, Nancy Felson, Hallie Franks, Thomas Jenkins, David Pingree, Mark Schiefsky, Nikola Theodossiev, and Kathryn Topper.

I owe a large debt to those who have commented extensively on one or more drafts of the book. Alan C. Bowen's advice on astronomy, ancient and modern, allowed me to correct mistakes and improved my understanding of Alcman's text at several points. John C. Franklin introduced me to a tradition of music-cosmology reaching back to the Bronze Age and Mesopotamia that may fill in the background of Alcman's cosmic sirens. It was especially valuable to have Gregory Nagy's views on the manuscript, since his work deeply informs my thinking on the nature of the performance of poetry in archaic Greece. Brunilde Sismondo Ridgway offered a wealth of references and suggestions on the last section. I am grateful to Mary Ebbott for her comments on the first, which include an observation that led me to focus on the strain of lament in the song. Dimitrios Yatromanolakis's advice on issues of philology, literary criticism, and ritual has been immensely helpful, particularly at the early stages of writing. Leslie Kurke, one of the readers for the Press, gave the manuscript an extraordinarily attentive reading that included many suggestions for corrections and improvements. Probing questions from the other, anonymous reader helped me think more clearly about the role of the chorus in performance. At every step Laura M. Slatkin provided the intellectual support a difficult project needs in order to move forward. Her studies of allusion in Homer and particularly of the concept of measure in Hesiod and the Presocratics have shaped my interpretation of the cosmological elements in the *Partheneion*. Just as important have been her responses to this study as it took shape—unfailingly generous, illuminating, and substantial. From the title page to the last footnote, her presence is writ large on the pages that follow.

For their assistance in the final preparation of the manuscript I thank Teresa T. Wu, Ivy Livingston, Jennifer L. Ferriss, and Melissa A. Haynes. I gratefully acknowledge a grant toward the cost of photographs and editorial assistance from the Clark Fund of Harvard University, and a generous publication subsidy from the Loeb Fund of the Department of the Classics.

Finally, thanks are due to Susan Bielstein, Executive Editor at the University of Chicago Press, for supporting this project from the start; to Anthony Burton; and to Sandra Hazel, whose courteous, attentive editing greatly improved the manuscript.

INTRODUCTION

In a society where music, song and dance are all-pervasive,
at all public and private occasions, in all cults and festivals, folk-art
and high art blend and pass into each other with no
sharp dividing line.

Extant texts of ancient Greek choral lyric are the bare bones of productions that fused poetry and music with dance.[1] The songs came alive in performance, which included much else that is not in the text, namely, setting, costumes, props, and lighting. The element of spectacle, which was as integral to choral lyric as it was to drama and a vital part of the audience's experience, is all but lost to us. We especially register the loss in the case of the earliest substantial example of the genre, Alcman's Louvre *Partheneion*, composed in the late seventh century BCE for a Spartan festival.[2] The text consists of a long fragment preserved in the "Mariette Papyrus," P. Louvre E 3320, which remains our principal source for the poem and its accompanying scholia. Little survives of the first part, which presumably contained the invocation to the Muses and at least two mythical narratives, one of which

---

Epigraph. Dale 1969, 157.

1. Over the past thirty years studies of Greek poetry concerned with the nature and context of its performance have made us sharply aware of this fact. Most relevant to the topic of this study are Calame 1977; Herington 1985; Nagy 1990b, 1996; D. Clay 1991; Stehle 1997; Peponi 2004. See also Dale 1969, 156–69 ("Words, Music and Dance"). After Henrichs (1994–95, 94n23) I too occasionally borrow the term "dance-songs" (*Tanzlieder*) from Wilamowitz-Moellendorf 1886, 76.

2. Alcman 1 *PMGF* (= 3 Calame). On the date of Alcman see West 1965, 188–94; Calame 1983, xiv–xvi. The lyric genre to which the song belongs is an unresolved question; see Calame 1977, 2:149–76. *Partheneion* has become the traditional title for Alcman 1 *PMGF* and I continue to use it in a purely conventional sense. But there is no evidence that it was included among the songs of Alcman that were classified as *partheneia*, "maiden songs." In any case, we know essentially nothing regarding either the subject matter of such songs or the occasion for their performance, beyond that they were songs composed for choruses of maidens.

involves the saga of the Spartan prince Hippocoon and his sons. For five of the eight partially preserved stanzas, representing half the estimated maximum length of the poem,[3] the chorus gives what amounts to an ecphrasis of its own performance that repeatedly appeals to the sense of sight. Not only do the singers describe their own appearance and actions, but they emphatically point to what they see and turn to the audience with direct questions, eliciting ocular responses.[4] The issue of what the original audience would have seen, along with the audiences that followed through centuries of repeated performances, is crucial to the interpretation of this difficult text and one that has never been satisfactorily answered.

Taking my cue from the chorus's invitation to visualize what it does and see what it sees, I open this study of the *Partheneion* not by turning directly to the text but by presenting an image—one that comes from another time and place but ultimately appeals to the same conceit. This is a picture painted on four sides of an Early Classical Athenian vessel from the workshop of Sotades, molded in the shape of an oversized *astragalos*, a knucklebone (plates 1–4).[5]

The mouth of the container opens onto one of its long sides (plate 1). The opening may be an integral part of the figural scene that unfolds to its right, since its irregular contour suggests a rock formation or the mouth of a cave. Next to it a man confronts a file of maidens or nymphs engaged in a ring dance, holding one another by the hand. There are three of them, but the third figure's being partially cut off by the edge of the vessel asks us to imagine that the chorus extends beyond the picture field.[6] The man is decidedly unheroic in

3. Page (1951, 1–2) put the total length at ten stanzas of fourteen verses each, as did Robbins (1994, 7), while Calame (1983, 311–12) envisioned the possibility that the poem in its entirety consisted of eight stanzas only.

4. Ocular deictics in the *Partheneion* are the subject of Peponi 2004.

5. British Museum E 804; *ARV*[2] 765.20; *Beazley Addenda* 286. For a summary of interpretations, see Hoffmann (1997, 107–12), who reads the scene as that of a shaman placing his female followers in a state of mystical levitation. Henrichs (1996b, 29) has already pointed to the analogy between the image of the Pleiades in the *Partheneion* and the dancers suspended in midair on the Sotades Painter's *astragalos*.

6. Curtius 1923, 10. F. Hauser (in FR 3:91) was the first to suggest that the opening represents the mouth of a cave, from which the man has emerged; he identified the female figures as

type, a caricature: thin and bent, with a snub nose and a sparse beard, and a cloak tied around his waist. He motions with his right arm toward the dancers while his extended left arm points emphatically upward, directing their attention to a second chorus, ten maidens who dance suspended in the air (plates 2–4). These appear on the other three sides of the *astragalos* in various dance steps, some in slow motion, others twirling with arms extended and the sleeves of their dresses billowing like wings, the way maenads sometimes do when they dance.[7] The picture thus juxtaposes an ethereal chorus to one with its feet firmly on the ground and, by the man's gesture, invites us to draw a relation between the two. But who is he, and who are the dancers? Stackelberg, who first published the vase in 1837, identified the airborne dancers as stars, namely, the Pleiades and the Hyades.[8] For this he offered no explanation, trusting, perhaps, that his reasoning would be plain to anyone familiar with classical texts.

Indeed, the picture on the *astragalos* may be unique, but the idea that the constellations in the night sky are dancing choruses of maidens is commonplace in Greek thought and literary imagery.[9] The Pleiades in particular are archetypal dancers. They were the inventors of the choral dance and the *pannukhis*, performed at night under the starlit sky, when they were maidens and before they were placed in the heavens.[10] There they continue to dance. Together with their sisters, the Hyades, they figure in the picture of the sky on the shield of Achilles in Euripides' *Electra*:

ἐν δὲ μέσωι κατέλαμπε σάκει φαέθων
κύκλος ἀλίοιο
ἵπποις ἂμ πτεροέσσαις
ἄστρων τ' αἰθέριοι χοροί,

---

dancers, "wie die attischen Nymphen drei Mädchen im Reigentanz." See also Robertson 1992, 188–90.

7. Prudhommeau (1965) attempts to identify the dance steps (captions to figs. 353, 355–58, 832).

8. Stackelberg 1837, pl. 23.

9. For an overview, see J. Miller 1986, 19–80.

10. Scholium to Theocritus *Idylls* 13.25 Wendel: πρῶτον δ' αὗται χορείαν καὶ παννυχίδα συνεστήσαντο παρθενεύουσαι.

Πλειάδες Ὑάδες, †Ἕκτορος
ὄμμασιϯ τροπαῖοι·

In the center of the shield
the sun's bright circle
was shining on winged horses,
and the heavenly choruses of stars,
Pleiades, Hyades,
bringing defeat to the eyes of Hector.

(464–69)

Among the poets, Euripides is particularly fond of this figure, to which he turns again in the *Ion,* where the chorus thinks of the newcomer at the Eleusinian night ritual:

ὅτε καὶ Διὸς ἀστερωπὸς
ἀνεχόρευσεν αἰθήρ,
χορεύει δὲ σελάνα.

When Zeus's star-eyed sky
has begun its choral dance
and the moon dances.

(1078–80)

But the cosmic dance, of which the Sotades Painter gives a playful picture and which Euripides uses to dramatic effect, is more than a decorative flourish. It is grounded in a particular archaic cosmology, attached in Greek tradition to the fabulous name of Pythagoras: the notion that the movements of the heavenly bodies produce sounds in musical concordance. There is, incidentally, no better candidate for the identity of the shabby choreographer painted on the *astragalos* than Pythagoras himself.[11] Legend has it that he made his home on

---

11. Early Classical vase painting offers other examples, comparable in tone, of famous poets and thinkers caught in a defining moment. One thinks of the representation of the cowherd in the company of the Muses on a pyxis in the Museum of Fine Arts, Boston (98.887; *ARV*[2] 774.1: "Hesiod? or rather Archilochus?"; *Beazley Addenda* 287. Identified as Archilochus by D. Clay [2004, 55–57]), and the vignette of Aesop and the fox in the tondo of a cup in the Vatican (Museo Gregoriano Etrusco 16552; *ARV*[2] 916.183; *Beazley Addenda* 304).

Samos in a cave, where he spent much of his days and nights.[12] For his disciples, we are told, he composed hymns and melodies, but "he alone could hear and understand, so he indicated, the universal harmony and concord of the spheres, and the stars moving through them, which sound a tune fuller and more intense than any mortal ones."[13] Our figure finds a match not in that Pythagoras, the object of wonder and veneration for all ages, but in the caricature of the Pythagorean on the Athenian comic stage: the unkempt, malnourished vegetarian in a threadbare cloak, engaged in abstruse pursuits.[14]

The Pythagoreans are widely credited with the theory that "the movement of the stars produces a harmony," in Aristotle's words.[15] As for so much else, our best sources are Athenian and Classical in date. A fragment of Critias vividly evokes the cosmogonic context of the dance of the stars:

σὲ τὸν αὐτοφυῆ τὸν ἐν αἰθερίῳ
ῥύμβῳ πάντων φύσιν ἐμπλέξανθ᾽,

---

12. Iamblichus *On the Pythagorean Way of Life* 27; Porphyry *Life of Pythagoras* 9, citing an otherwise unknown Antiphon, author of the treatise *On Men Excelling in Virtue*. Burkert (1972, 97–109) has a helpful discussion of Iamblichus's sources.

13. Iamblichus *On the Pythagorean Way of Life* 64–65; trans. Dillon and Hershbell 1991. See also Porphyry *Life of Pythagoras* 30; scholium at *Odyssey* 1.371.

14. On the *puthagoristai* of Middle Comedy, see Burkert 1972, 198–200. Diogenes Laertius's biography of Pythagoras (*Lives of the Philosophers* 8.37–38) reports that Cratinus ridiculed them in the *She-Pythagorean* and the *Tarentines*, as did Aristophon in the *Pythagorean* (*PCG* frag. 12). Whether or how far Pythagoras himself provided the model for Aristophanes' satire of Socrates in the *Clouds* is a debated issue; see Melero Bellido 1972; Burkert 1972, 291n73.

15. Aristotle *On the Heavens* 290b12–23:

It is clear from these points that the thesis that a *harmonia* occurs when the stars move, on the grounds that the sounds arising are concordant, though it is elegantly and strikingly stated by those who enunciate it, is nevertheless not true. For it seems inevitable to some people that when bodies that are so large move, sound must occur, since it does with bodies in our region, which do not have bulk equal to theirs and do not move with so great a speed. When the sun and the moon and the stars, so great in number and magnitude, are moving with so swift a motion, it is impossible, they say, that there does not arise a sound extraordinary in magnitude. Taking these claims as assumptions, and assuming also that from the distances between them the speeds acquire the ratios of the concords, they say that the sound produced by the stars as they travel in a circle is harmonic. (Trans. Barker 1989, 33)

The Pythagoreans are named at 291a8. Franklin (2006, 53–63) traces the development of a "pre-Pythagorean" music cosmology to Bronze Age and Mesopotamian sources.

ὃν πέρι μὲν φῶς, πέρι δ᾽ ὀρφναία
νὺξ αἰολόχρως ἄκριτός τ᾽ ἄστρων
ὄχλος ἐνδελεχῶς ἀμφιχορεύει.

(*I call on*) thee, the self-made, who hast woven
the nature of all things in the aetherial whirl,
round whom Light, and dusky Night
with shimmering colour, and the innumerable
throng of the stars, for ever dance.[16]

Plato gives us the fullest and most striking statements of this concept. In the *Timaeus* the stars and the planets are divine living creatures and their movements choral dances (*khoreiās*).[17] In the *Republic*, the myth of Er imagines the cosmos in the shape of a whorl spun by *Anankē*, Necessity. The whorl itself consists of eight concentric circles, each endowed with its appropriate motion:

> Up on top of each of the circles rides a Siren, carried around with
> its revolution, each giving out a single sound, a single pitch [*tonos*]:
> and from these sounds, eight in all, is made the concord of a single
> *harmonia*. Round about at equal distances are seated three others,
> each on a throne, the Fates, daughters of Necessity, clothed in white
> and with garlands on their heads.[18]

Observing that eight notes make up a complete diatonic scale, M. L. West argued that "the Sirens appear as part of the astronomical scheme only because the musical scale has been enshrined in the heavens."[19] The idea was later current in Pythagorean thought but it must be older than Pythagoras, since the melodious Sirens already appear in Alcman's Louvre *Partheneion*. Indeed, in the last, fragmen-

16. Critias, frag. 4 *TrGF*. Trans. Freeman 1948.
17. Plato *Timaeus* 40c. See also *Epinomis* 982e: "And thus the nature of the stars is the fairest to behold, for they dance the fairest and most magnificent procession and choral dance of all the choruses in the world . . . and accomplish whatever is needed for all living creatures." Trans. J. Miller 1986, 41. Tarán (1975, 273) dismisses the image as meaningless in that it is "poetical" and "a commonplace."
18. Plato *Republic* 617b–c; trans. Barker 1989, 58.
19. West 1967, 12; 1992, 224.

tary lines the chorus compares its song to that of the Sirens, which is superior:

ἀ δὲ τᾶν Σηρηνίδων
ἀοιδοτέρα μὲ[ν αὐδά],
σιαὶ γάρ

[the song] of the Sirens indeed more harmonious, for they are goddesses.[20]

Although he found other correspondences between Alcman and the Pythagoreans in Alcman's "cosmogony" (Alcman 5 *PMGF*), West saw no further reference to the music of the spheres in the *Partheneion* beyond the use of the Sirens' perfect melody as a term of comparison for the chorus. In the chapters that follow I hope to show that cosmic imagery is not so limited but runs through Alcman's song and governs its staging.

In being concerned with the conditions of the performance in its cultic setting, my approach is in line with much recent work that addresses ancient Greek choral lyric in terms of ritual poetics. The current trend emphasizing the context of production in all of its dimensions owes much to Claude Calame's pioneering study of the morphology and function of the lyric chorus, one that was centered precisely on Alcman's Louvre *Partheneion*. The two volumes of *Les choeurs de jeunes filles en Grèce archaïque*, published in 1977, boldly turned the spotlight onto the choral dance as "social act," that is, onto the ritual and social circumstances surrounding the performance. The study produced an illuminating and influential definition of the structure of the lyric chorus. In the interpretation of the text, however, it failed to put to rest crucial questions. In the past thirty years lively debate has continued regarding the identity of the divinity presiding over the festival; the relevance of the myth of Hippocoon to the gnome that follows it and to the rite performed by the chorus; and the logic of the series of metaphors—if that is what they are—stringing

---

20. Alcman 1.96–98 *PGMF*; West 1967, 11, 14–15. I follow West's reading of these lines in adopting Von der Mühll's supplement αὐδά at 97 and understanding Σηρην[ί]δων as a possessive genitive. Hutchinson (2001, 100–101) also leans toward this reading.

together figures of horses, stars, and birds, with which the performers describe themselves and what they see.[21]

It is a truism that the subject of the *Partheneion* and its ritual function, far from being recondite or riddling, were familiar and, at some level, perfectly accessible to the entire audience for which the song was composed. The point is nevertheless worth stating because it calls attention to the fact that that audience, the participants in a festival, was potentially the entire citizenry of Sparta. We should therefore assume that the imagery and sentiments with which the text confronts us were part of the cultural patrimony of the community at large, in which they will have had currency in various forms—visual as well as verbal, and across artificial distinctions drawn between high and low art. A comprehensive account of that kind of local knowledge is beyond our grasp. There is, however, much to suggest that Alcman's Spartan audience was conversant with currents of thought and artistic movements that operated on a Panhellenic scale. Literary and archaeological sources paint a picture of Sparta in the seventh century and the first part of the sixth as a prosperous, outward-looking intellectual and artistic center, very different from the proverbially austere city of the centuries that followed. As regards its material culture, excavations have revealed a late-blooming but vigorous Orientalizing phase in the seventh century, marked by an increase in the production of luxury goods, such as bronzes and ivories, as well as painted pottery.[22] Their distribution allows us to map their reach across the Mediterranean, from the Black Sea to Spain, documenting a taste for things Laconian. As one might expect, concentrations of pottery occur at sites linked to Sparta by direct or indirect ties of colonization, such as Taras and Cyrene. Yet the large quantity of Laconian pottery, in addition to ivories and bronzes, recovered in the excavations

21. See, e.g., the series of questions posed by D. Clay (1991, 48–50) and the characterization of the poem by Tsitsibakou-Vasalos (1993, 129) as "cryptic" and "dark and at places impenetrable." Peponi (2004, 295) aptly compares our position vis à vis the text to being confronted with "riddling statements from a first-person speaker who persists in anchoring her poetic message to a communication situation irrevocably inaccessible to us."

22. See Förtsch 2001 for an exhaustive analysis of this phenomenon; a succinct overview in Förtsch 1998. For a general account of the quality of Spartan material culture in this period, see also Cartledge 2001.

on Samos points to the "special relationship" between the two cities, which Cartledge has painstakingly reconstructed.[23] The tradition that Lycurgus brought from Samos the Homeric poems, which he obtained from the corporation of rhapsodes descended from Creophylus, is but one indication of the emergence of Sparta onto the international stage.[24] West writes: "In the light of the evidence at our disposal, Lesbos and Sparta stand out as the great centres of musical excellence in the seventh century."[25] At the head of the long list of songwriters from other Hellenic cities who were active in Sparta at that time is Terpander of Lesbos, to whom are attributed the pathbreaking invention of the seven-string lyre and the establishment of the citharodic nomes.[26] Both his name and that of the legendary Arion are tied to the celebration of the great Spartan festival of the Karneia, in which they competed, contemporary with the Twenty-sixth Olympiad (676–673).[27] Thaletas of Gortyn delivered Sparta from a plague with his songs, according to one source. According to another he instituted choral performances that put an end to civil strife in the city.[28] Legend has it that Pythagoras, who visited Sparta to study its laws, used to sing the paeans of Thaletas in the belief that they engendered serenity.[29] And since at least the fourth century BCE scholars have debated whether Alcman himself was Laconian or a Lydian from Sardis.[30]

While the specific Spartan institutions and the festival, ritual, and historical circumstances constituting the context of performance of the *Partheneion* demand our attention, we should be attentive as well

23. Cartledge 1982.
24. Aristotle frag. 611.10 Rose; Plutarch *Lycurgus* 4; see Nagy 1990b, 74. On recitations of Homer in seventh-century Sparta, see Gostoli 1988, 232–33.
25. West 1992, 334. See also Calame 1977, 2:33–37.
26. See D. A. Campbell 1988, 2:294–313. Nagy (1990b, 86–90) argues that the traditions concerning Terpander's inventions reflect a process of "Panhellenization" of lyric poetry.
27. Hellanicus *FGrHist* 4F85, by way of Athenaeus 635e; on the fame of Arion, the inventor of the dithyramb in Corinth, see Herodotus 1.23.
28. *PMG* 713 (iii); Plutarch *Lycurgus* 4.1–2; see pp. 115–16 of the present text.
29. Porphyry *Life of Pythagoras* 32, 33.
30. Apparently Aristotle believed that Alcman was Lydian; see P. Oxy 2389, scholium IV to Alcman 16 *PMGF* (= 8 Calame). On this old controversy see Page 1951, 168–70 and Janni 1965, 96–120.

to this other context: the live stream of song-making within which Alcman composed, consisting of his predecessors and his competitors, with whom his audience would be equally acquainted.[31] These poetic traditions were arguably Panhellenic in character. I use the term in the sense developed by Nagy to mean traditions of poetry, song, and myth that arise in the eighth century and are part of a pattern of integration at the level of cults and festivals among the Hellenic city-states. With regard to the development and diffusion of both epic and lyric poetry he writes,

> By Panhellenic poetry, then, I mean those kinds of poetry and song that operated not simply on the basis of local traditions suited for local audiences. Rather, Panhellenic poetry would have been the product of an evolutionary synthesis of traditions, so that the tradition that it represents concentrates on traditions that tend to be common to most locales and peculiar to none.[32]

By virtue of the fact that allusions to it are far removed from one another in space and time (Alcman at Sparta, the Pythagorean teachings on Samos or in Magna Graecia, Plato at Athens), the mention of the song of the Sirens at lines 96–98 stands to be a fragment of precisely such an overarching tradition. A first premise of this study is that the *Partheneion* addresses the particular requirements of the Spartan ritual within a broader Panhellenic frame in terms of formal features, mythic narratives, and sets of beliefs.[33] Like the song of the Sirens, other elements of Alcman appeal to enduring and widespread notions and images; these range from philosophical treatises to the imagery, inspired by festivals and songs, that appears on painted vases.

A second premise of this study concerns the dramatic dimension of choral performances. With one exception, interpreters of the

31. Kurke (2005, 82) warns against privileging the ritual context in the interpretation of choral lyric over poetic traditions.

32. Nagy 1990b, chaps. 2 and 3, the quotation from p. 54; 1999, 7. The phenomenon was identified mainly on archaeological grounds in Snodgrass 1971, 419–21, as one of "intercommunication."

33. Hinge (2006, 324–48) argues that the language of Alcman is Panhellenic in terms of "deep structure," although epichoric at the level of performance.

Partheneion have assumed that here the actor and her role are one and the same, in other words, that the chorus "speak of themselves as themselves":[34] Spartan maidens engaged in a particular Spartan ritual. This is in line with the longstanding belief that, whereas the choruses of Athenian tragedy, comedy, and satyr play enact specific and fictional personae, "members of a civic chorus, by contrast, present themselves in their own person."[35] The introduction of stage costumes—the mask in particular—is accordingly viewed as a new development, taking place in the late sixth century BCE, and as a major difference between Athenian drama and the choruses of ritual. In the case of the *Partheneion*, this perspective has had the effect of identifying the chorus members, the sentiments they express, and the actions they describe with actual historical persons and practices. From the start, the chorus's hyperbolic praise of the beauty of individual members and of Hagesichora and Agido has been taken as the expression of personal erotic feelings and has prompted comparisons with Sappho and the *thiasos* over which she allegedly presided.[36] That is to say, the song would be not only sung *by* maidens, but first and foremost *for* and *about* maidens.

That all performance fundamentally entails mimesis invites scrutiny of this shaky tenet. Evidence that lyric choruses could, and did, play the part of mythical or epic characters is in fact both abundant and well known. One might begin with the statements in Plato's important treatment of the dance in the *Laws* that "the choric art

34. R. Parker, cited in Carter 1988, 98.

35. Lonsdale 1993, 7; note, however, that elsewhere Lonsdale freely admits of mimesis in choral performance: "Many dance performances were themselves representations, and it is often impossible to distinguish for certain between fiction and real performance" (11). See also pp. 17, 31, 98–99. Calame 1994–95, 137: "[in the choruses of drama] the *khoreutai* are no longer only addressing the gods in a cultic action and representing particular members of the community, they are also masked actors playing out scenes of a heroic action onstage." But, as Kowalzig (2004, 41) observes, the relationship of dramatic choruses to the lyric ones is an unresolved question.

36. See, e.g., Diels 1896, 352–53; Wilamowitz-Moellendorf 1897, 260; and lately Hutchinson 2001, 92–94. Page (1951, 65–67) takes a more skeptical view. The analogy was elaborately restated by Calame (1977, 2:86–97; 1997, 207–63), who sought to ground the function of the lyric chorus in general (and the production of the *Partheneion* in particular) in female rites of initiation. See also Clark 1996. Stehle (1997, 30–39, 87–88) argues against the view that the chorus maidens express erotic feelings for one another; rather, they would represent themselves as desirable potential brides for the young men in the community.

[khoreiā] as a whole consists of dance and song" and that "what is involved in choric performance [khoreiās] is imitations of characters [mīmēmata tropōn], appearing in actions and eventualities of all kinds which each performer goes through by means of habits and imitations [mīmēsesi]."[37] The Homeric hymn to Delian Apollo offers a prime example of mimesis in khoreiā. The singer evokes a great festival of the Ionians on Delos and describes the choral dance of the kourai Dēliades, a phrase which is usually translated as "Delian Maidens" but can equally appropriately yield "Delian Nymphs." These are historically well-attested cult attendants of Apollo and Artemis on Delos, whose main duty was the performance of the dance-song honoring the two gods.[38] But what the singer, who himself wears the mask of Homer, describes is not just a troupe of skilled dancers. The Deliades are a "great wonder," mega thauma, whose "glory," kleos, is immortal. They enchant the tribes of men and know how to reproduce the voice and clattering speech of all men: "each would say that he himself were singing, so perfectly harmonious is their beautiful song."[39] These prodigious qualities properly belong to the divine archetype, which seasonally recurring performances reenacted: the dance-song

37. Plato Laws 654b, 655d; trans. Barker 1984, 1:141, 143. On this passage see Lonsdale 1993, 31–33, who concludes that "the participants in archaic rituals, with or without the help of masks and costume, behave as if they were the 'other'—as if they were gods or animals."

38. Bruneau 1970, 36–37; Henrichs 1996a, 56–59. Calame (1997, 104–10) calls the Deliades a group of "professional dancers," implying that they are fundamentally different in nature from the civic choruses sent by the Ionian cities and Athens to perform in the Delian festival. It is preferable to think of them as cult personnel and, in that sense, as equally "professional" as the Delphic Pythia, paid servants of the god, who took on and performed an ancient role.

39. Homeric Hymns 3.156–64. Most scholars take mīmeisth' at line 163 (162–64, πάντων δ' ἀνθρώπων φωνὰς καὶ βαμβαλιαστὺν // μιμεῖσθ' ἴσασιν, φαίη δέ κεν αὐτὸς ἕκαστος // φθέγγεσθ', οὕτω σφιν καλὴ συνάρηρεν ἀοιδή) to mean that the Deliades are capable of "imitating" all languages of mankind—one at a time. See Barker 1984, 40n4; A. M. Miller 1986, 59–60; Nagy 1990b, 43–44; Calame 1997, 104. There is but one song, however, and a better sense is obtained by understanding that the maidens sing a universal harmony that contains within itself all voices and forms of speech and comes across to each hearer in his own tongue. That is also the sense of the translation in Evelyn-White 1936: "Also they can imitate the tongues of all men and their clattering speech: each would say that he himself were singing, so close to truth is their sweet song." With Evelyn-White I retain the reading βαμβαλιαστύν at line 162, and take it to mean that the Deliades sing in all languages, including those of foreigners. Burkert (1987, 54) sees in mīmeisth' an indication of mimetic elements in the performance of the choral lyric.

of the Delian Nymphs, *Numphai Dēliades*. We learn from Callimachus's *Hymn to Delos* (255–58) that these were present at the birth of
Apollo, where they performed "with far-sounding voice the holy song
of Eileithyia," which the brazen vault of the sky echoed back.[40]

In the written sources, evidence of costumes for the lyric chorus
is scant but not entirely lacking. Plutarch, citing the Atthidogra-
pher Demon, describes the procession at the Athenian festival of the
Oschophoria as a reenactment of Theseus's return: the two youths at
the head of the procession were dressed in women's clothes, impersonating the two boys whom Theseus had substituted for two of the
girls he took to Crete. Female characters called *Deipnophoroi* impersonated (*apomīmoumenai*) the mothers of the boys and girls destined
for the Minotaur. Led by the two youths, the chorus performed songs
called *ōskhophorika*, which were akin to, or a subset of, *partheneia*.[41]
One can only speculate as to what kind of costume was involved in
the performance of what Plato (*Laws* 815c) calls Bacchic dances, in
which the chorus impersonated (*mīmountai*) Nymphs, Pans, Silens,
and Satyrs.

Costumed choruses performing to the *aulos* are the subject of a
good number of Athenian painted vases from the mid-sixth century
onward—"knights" riding men dressed as horses, "Scythians" on
stilts, heroes riding dolphins, and more. Such pictures now are called
predramatic, a label implying that they anticipate later developments
and, therefore, represent deviations from the normal practice in the
staging of choral lyric.[42] There are two examples, however, which can
be identified as representations of costumed choruses and are much
too early in date (670–660 BCE) to be dismissed as mere anticipa-
tions. These are two Middle Protoattic stands, allegedly from a tomb

40. On the Delian Maidens as archetype, see Nagy 1996, 56–57, 73; Henrichs 1996a, 57. See
pp. 125–26 of the present text.

41. Plutarch *Theseus* 23.3–4; Photius *Bibliotheca* 322a, 318b, 320a, 321a; see Calame 1997,
125–28.

42. Webster 1970, 11, 20–21, 93; these are collected and analyzed in Green 1985; Steinhart
2004, 8–31. Csapo (2003) argues that in visual as well as literary representations, dolphins and
Nereids are quintessentially dancers and that the latter in particular are associated with the
performance of the dithyramb in Dionysiac ritual.

on Aegina, which were once in the collection of the Berlin Antiquar-ium.[43] Webster recognized in the scene on the conical body of the first, A 41, a representation of a choral performance. It shows a file of nine men, all in the same pose, each holding a staff, dressed in elabo-rately patterned tunics and mantles. The two figures at the head of the procession, of which only the lower part remains, are identified as a lyre player and an *aulos* player.[44]

Berlin A 41 has a companion piece in the second stand, Berlin A 42 (plate 5). The similarities are plain to see, in spite of the fact that in the latter the composition is abbreviated and includes no musicians. The main scene shows a procession of five men, identical in hairstyle (long locks falling onto their shoulders), beard, dress, and stance, each holding a spear. The row of evenly spaced figures is interrupted by a large bird (of which only part of the feet remains on the baseline), above which is a painted inscription giving the name of Menelaus in Doric dialect: *Menelās*. On an Athenian vase, the Doric spelling calls for an explanation. Assuming that this is a "label" for the figure it pre-cedes (or follows), scholars have hypothesized that either the painter came from Aegina, where Doric was spoken, or the series of vases in the Protoattic Black and White style, to which the stand belongs, was made on the island rather than Athens.[45] An explanation exists, however, that accounts at once for the use of Doric dialect and for the choruslike appearance of this sequence of figures. Rather than a label, the inscription belongs to a genre that, although less common, is nevertheless well attested on Athenian painted vases: phrases that introduce into the figured scenes excerpts of dialogue or song, entire lines as well as single words. A late sixth-century psykter by Oltos, to give just one instance here, has a file of dolphin riders, each uttering *epidelphinos*, which may be the title of the play to which the chorus

43. Berlin, Antiquarium A 41 and A 42, both destroyed in World War II. *CVA* Berlin 1, Germany 1 (1938), 23–24, pls. 30; 34 (A 41) and 24–25, pls. 31–33 (A 42). On the provenience, see Morris 1984, 7, 45; C. Dehl-von Kaenel in *CVA* Berlin 6, Germany 53 (1986), 13–14.

44. Webster 1970, 9; R. Eilmann and K. Gebauer, *CVA* Berlin 1, Germany 1 (1938), 23–24, also identify the fragmentary figures as musicians.

45. Jeffery (1949, 26) raised the issue. For a review of the debate, see Morris 1984, 91–92n2; Ferrari 1987, 180. Morris vigorously argued the case for an Aeginetan production.

belongs.[46] Likewise on Berlin A 42 the dipinto *Menelās* should be understood as a quotation, the title, as it were, of the song the chorus performs. And the form is Doric for the same reason that at Euripides' *Rhesus* 257 the chorus sings *heloi Menelān*: the use of the non-Attic long alpha is required by the poetic genre, that is, choral lyric.[47] Compositionally, bird and inscription mark a break in the orderly sequence of the figures. Visually, they take the place of the *aulos* player and, like him, introduce into the picture the notation of sound.[48]

The Menelas stand gives a picture not of a procession of Homeric heroes but of a chorus performing a song on a heroic theme. This genre of lyric is best known to us from the poems of Stesichorus, of which large fragments survive.[49] That it was in existence at least by the seventh century, however, is made clear by the notorious story in Herodotus of the attempt made in the early sixth century by Cleisthenes, tyrant of Sicyon, to deprive the hero Adrastus of the ancestral honors that were traditionally accorded to him. These included the performance of "tragic choruses" (*tragikoisi khoroisi*) that corresponded to, or represented, his sufferings (*pros ta pathea*).[50] The importance of the Menelas stand and its relevance to an investigation of the role of the chorus in Alcman's *Partheneion* have to do with the fact that this is not simply an ensemble of citizens in festival garb.

46. New York, Metropolitan Museum of Art L.1979.17.1; *ARV*² 1622–23.3*bis*; *Beazley Addenda* 163; Green 1985, 101. On this type of painted inscription, see Kretschmer 1894, 90–93; Immerwahr 1965, 153; Ferrari 1987, 181.

47. Ferrari 1987; Snodgrass 1998, 102–3; Steinhart (2004, 21) expresses skepticism of this hypothesis. Wachter (2001, 26, AIG 1) lists the dipinto as Aeginetan, although he doubts that the vase itself was made on the island.

48. The function of the bird remains unexplained. Note, however, that a large swanlike bird appears in other representations of choral performances, e.g., on a Geometric fragment from Argos, next to a striding figure, who may be the *aulos* player (Webster 1970, fig. 1). On an Attic amphora of the 560s BCE in Athens, National Museum 559, an *aulos* player performs in the presence of the bird and two listeners; *ABV* 85.1; *Beazley Addenda* 23. Papaspyridi-Karouzou (1938, 495–501) identifies the musician as the mythical *aulos* player Olympus.

49. Downplaying the Herodotean story, Burkert (1987, 45, 51–54) understands the emergence of lyric poems with a myth-epic theme as an innovation of Stesichorus.

50. Herodotus 5.67.5; Nagy (1990b, 43) emphasizes the mimetic character of the song-dance for Adrastos by translating *pros ta pathea* as "corresponding to his sufferings." Likewise Lonsdale (1993, 252–54) understands the Sicyonian choruses as "reenacting through mimetic representations the heroic actions and sufferings of Adrastos" (252).

The spear is an element of costume that gives them a role, that of a chorus of "Spearmen," one that is eminently suitable to the theme of their song. Casting about for parallels, one thinks of the Myrmidons, who are characterized as "spear fighting" at *Odyssey* 3.188, and probably constituted the chorus in Aeschylus's tragedy by that title; or the troop of Abantes, fierce spearmen with long hair on their shoulders (*Iliad* 2.542–43).

As to Sparta itself, the historian Polycrates, writing in the second century BCE, details choral performances at the Spartan festival of the Hyakinthia that include high-girth tunics for the boys, as well as a parade on caparisoned horses and specially decorated wicker cars for the maidens.[51] The performance of Bacchic choral dances is attested by a gloss of Hesychius that identifies the *Dumainai*—the name of a chorus that also performed songs of Alcman—as maenads, *bakkhai*, and "choral dancers," *khoritides*, in Sparta.[52] A fragment of a song of Alcman, which describes a female character milking a lion on a mountaintop, strongly suggests a Dionysiac theme and might have been performed precisely by a chorus impersonating *bakkhai*.[53] The excavation of the sanctuary of Artemis Orthia unearthed thousands of fragments of terracotta masks, amounting to hundreds of complete examples, which range in date from about 650 BCE to the fifth century.[54] They represent youths and young warriors and several grotesque types, including the satyr.[55] That these masks represent characters of choral performances is a matter of conjecture,[56] but at the

51. *FGrHist* 588F1 (in Athenaeus 139e); on this passage see Nagy 1996, 53–54.

52. Hesychius s.v. *dumainai*; Calame (1997, 154–56) argues that Hesychius's identification of the dancers as *bakkhai* is erroneous. The chorus of *Dumainai* is mentioned in Alcman frag. 10 (b) 8–9 *PMGF* (= 82a Calame) and Alcman frag. 5.2, col. I, 24–25 *PMGF* (= 81 Calame, col. 2, 24–25).

53. Alcman frag. 56 *PMGF* (= 125 Calame); see Webster 1970, 53; Calame 1983, 520–26. On Dionysiac dances in Sparta, see Constantinidou 1998, particularly pp. 21–23.

54. Dickins 1929; Carter (1987) points to the similarity between the Spartan masks and Near Eastern "prototypes," to suggest that the cult of Orthia may have been founded by Phoenicians.

55. The satyr mask is not one of the twenty-five complete examples recovered from the seventh-century levels but is well represented in sixth-century contexts; see Dickins 1929, 182.

56. Dickins 1929, 175, "dancing masks." Bosanquet (1905–6, 338–43) identified one of the grotesque types as "Old Woman" and connected it to a Laconian dance mentioned by Hesychius,

very least they attest to the fact that since the seventh century Spartans were well acquainted with the use of masks in a ritual context. In the chapters that follow I argue that, just as the Deliades reenact in seasonal performances the dance-song of the Delian Nymphs, the chorus of the *Partheneion* too take on the role of archetypal dancers, in their case a chorus of stars. At the heart of the argument is the identification (chapter 2), in the cluster of astral notations at lines 60–63, of a momentous event in the night sky: the cosmical setting of the Pleiades and the Hyades. Its significance, widely recognized from Hesiod to Aratus, is that it marks the beginning of winter. On the occasion of a major state festival celebrating the cycle of the seasons, the chorus dances the Hyades and points to the Moon, Dawn, and Night. Although it is performed by maidens, the *Partheneion* is not about maidens but about *kosmos*, both in the sense of political order—the constitution of the state—and in that of the order of the universe.

Within this frame of reference, it becomes possible to explain the role of the mythical narratives, which are the subject of the first part of the *Partheneion*. The interpretation offered in chapter 1 hinges on the identification at lines 15–19 of broken but unmistakable references to the path of the Sun and the myth of Phaethon. From this I conclude that in addition to the saga of Hippocoon the first, largely lost, five stanzas also narrated the fall of Phaethon. Each is a myth of succession, in which an illegitimate son claims his father's function. The two are brought into confrontation with each other as paradigmatic exempla of disintegration of the established order—one in the polis, the other in the heavens.

The structure of the song rests upon the homology established between the two realms. Chapter 3 explores the ways in which a belief in the correspondence of these two orders of things, such that one

---

s.v. *brullikhistai*, which was performed by "men who donned the masks of ugly women and sang hymns." As Carter (1987, 356) points out, however, the masks in question do not seem to be female. Projecting the possibility of a connection between poetry and masks before the advent of tragedy, Carter (1988) proposed that Alcman's *Partheneion* staged a sacred marriage of Orthia, in which the chorus played the part of Orthia's attendants. Naerebout (1997, 254–55) is skeptical about the use of the masks in dances.

mirrors the other, informed Spartan ritual practice and the very constitution of the city. This notion is fleshed out in the chorus, which
is at once the embodiment of harmony in the community and the
emblem of the harmony of the heavens. The self-dramatization of the
chorus, marked by heavy use of ocular deictics, is a theatrical strategy,
which calls attention to its cultic role in the performance of a rite of
passage.

1
THE MYTHS

*For if I am by birth immortal and ageless, so that I shall share
in life on Olympus, then it is better to endure the reproaches . . . but
if, my friend, I must indeed reach hateful old age and spend my life
among short-lived mortals far from the blessed gods, then it is much
nobler for me to suffer what is fated than to avoid death and shower
disgrace on my dear children and all my race hereafter—
I am Chrysaor's son.*

HIPPOCOON AND HIS SONS

The first thirty-five surviving lines of the *Partheneion* are too badly broken to allow the reconstruction of a continuous text. The fragment opens with a list of names, followed by a moralizing commentary (1–21):

] Πωλυδεύκης.
οὐκ ἐγω]ν Λύκαισον ἐν καμοῦσιν ἀλέγω
Ἔνα]ρσφόρον τε καὶ Σέβρον ποδώκη
]ν τε τὸν βιατὰν
] . τε τὸν κορυστάν   5
Εὐτείχ]η τε Ϝάνακτά τ᾽ Ἀρήϊον
]ά τ᾽ ἔξοχον ἡμισίων

]ν τὸν ἀγρόταν
] μέγαν Εὔρυτόν τε
]πώρω κλόνον   10
]ᾳ τε τὼς ἀρίστως
] παρήσομες
]αρ Αἶσα παντῶν
] γεραιτάτοι
ἀπ]έδιλος ἀλκά.   15
ἀν]θρώπων ἐς ὠρανὸν ποτήσθω
]ρήτω γαμῆν τὰν Ἀφροδίταν
Ϝ]άναϲϲαν ἤ τιν᾽
] ἦ παίδα . . . κω
Χά]ριτες δὲ Διὸς δόμον   20
]ϲιν ἐρογλεφάροι

Epigraph. Stesichorus *Geryoneis*, frag. 11 PMGF; trans. Campbell 1988.

] Polydeuces.
I do not count Lycaethus among the heroes
  ] and Enarsphorus and Thebrus swift of foot
  ] and mighty
  ] and the helmeted   5
and lord Euteiches and Areius
  ] and best of demigods

  ] and the hunter
  ] and mighty Eurytus
  ] battle-rout   10
  ] and the most valiant
  ] [we shall not] pass over.
  ] measure of all
  ] most ancient
  ] unfettered might.   15
  ] of mortals fly to the sky
  ] to marry Aphrodite
  ] mistress
  ] or child
  ] Graces the palace of Zeus   20
  ] love-glancing.

In the first line there is mention of one of the Dioscuri, Polydeuces, followed by a roster of the dead. The first is Lycaethus, whom the scholium identifies as a son of Derites, adding that Alcman here mentions by name Derites' other sons.[1] The other names belong to sons of Hippocoon: Enarsphorus, Thebrus, Areius, Euteiches, and Eurytus. Evidently the preceding text dealt with the feud between Tyndarids and Hippocoontids. The function of this myth within the economy of the *Partheneion* and its relevance to the gnome that follows at lines 13–21 continue to be the subject of speculation. Moreover, it has proved difficult to reconcile the blood and gore these names evoke with the seemingly lighthearted spirit of the second half of the song.

1. Scholium A 1. Apollodorus 3.10.5 includes Lycaethus among the Hippocoontids. All we know of Derites is that, like Oebalus, he was a grandson of Amyclas (Pausanias 7.18.5).

The widely shared assumption that the Hippocoontids, in contrast to the Tyndarids, here have the role of transgressors who are eventually brought to justice overlooks a more complex state of affairs and runs against the grain of the text. The epithets lend their names an epic tone and pathos rivaled only by the roster of the Persian dead in Aeschylus's *Persians*:[2] ποδώκη, swift-footed; βιατάν, mighty; ϝάνακτα, lord Areius; ἔξοχον ἡμισίων, supreme among the heroes;[3] and the untranslatable κορυστάν. The effect of Alcman's song is to confer *kleos*, glory, upon these ancient warriors.[4] The historical truth of their heroic status is attested by the fact that, on a par with the Dioscuri, they were individually honored with shrines.[5] As in other cases, the commemoration of the fallen heroes signals that their struggle was a foundational event in the myth-history of Sparta, one that had political import in the present of the seventh century. For this reason, the myth of Hippocoon and his sons deserves full attention, once more.

The earliest representation of the myth known to us, after Alcman's, occurred on the lost Throne of Apollo at Amyclae, whose figural decoration included the combat of Tyndareus with Eurytus (Pausanias 3.18.11). In Euphorion's *Thrakis* the Hippocoontids had the role of "rival suitors," *antimnēstēres*, of the Dioscuri.[6] In itself, such a rivalry implies no misconduct on the part of the Hippocoontids. Intimations of violence, however, surface in the story that Tyndareus entrusted the young Helen to Theseus, fearing that one of them, Enarsphorus, would rape her (Plutarch *Theseus* 31.1). A connected narrative is not attested until Roman times. The focus is on Heracles' exploit—the cause of the feud, the wound that Heracles received,

2. Aeschylus *Persians* 302–30; on the implications of *kleos* in this passage, see Ebbott 2000; Hutchinson (2001, 80) notes the relevance of this passage to the roster of fallen Hippocoontids.

3. Calame (1983, 316) notes the epic connotations of the expression. In Homer, as well as Hesiod and Simonides, *hēmitheoi* refers to the generation of the heroes; see West 1978, 191; J. S. Clay 1996; Currie 2005, 64. On the promise of death and immortality after death that this term implies, see Nagy 2005, 83–89.

4. D. Clay 1991, 53. Too (1997, 10) sees irony in the use of epic epithets in reference to men undeserving of *kleos*. On the exclusion of Lycaethus from the heroic status accorded the Hippocoontids, see pp. 109–11 of the present text.

5. See p. 122 of the present text.

6. Euphorion frag. 29 Powell.

the slaughter of the offenders.[7] Diodorus (4.33) relates the following myth. Tyndareus, son of King Oebalus, was expelled by his brother Hippocoon and went into exile. Some time later, the sons of Hippocoon, twenty in number, killed Oeonus, a young cousin of Heracles, who then mounted an expedition against them that included various allies, of whom only Iphicles, the Arcadian king Cepheus, and his seventeen sons are specifically mentioned. In the fight that followed, Hippocoon died together with ten of his sons and a "multitude" (pamplētheis) of other Spartiates. Having conquered Sparta, Heracles placed Tyndareus on the throne, to be held by his descendants until a descendant from Heracles would claim it. Heracles' conquest of the city thus laid the groundwork for the claim of the Heraclidae to the Spartan kingship, which they wrenched from Tisamenus, the last king of the line of Pelops.

Pausanias is our most valuable informant, because he had access to the local tradition. He specifies his source (3.1.1) at the very beginning of his compendium of Spartan history, which is structured according to the king lists of the two royal houses. King Oebalus married the Argive Gorgophone, daughter of Perseus, and had a son from her, Tyndareus, as well as a daughter, Arene (4.2.4). Hippocoon contested Tyndareus's succession after the death of Oebalus, arguing that he himself was the rightful heir, because he was Oebalus's eldest son. With the aid of Icarius and his partisans, he made Tyndareus fear for his life and forced him into exile (3.1.4). Heracles' hostility toward Hippocoon and his sons came about as the result of their refusal to purify him for the murder of Iphitus and was compounded by their assault on Oeonus (3.15.3–5).[8] Oeonus was attacked by a dog as he passed the palace of Hippocoon. When he struck the dog dead with a stone, the sons ran out and clubbed him to death. Heracles immediately attacked the Hippocoontids, apparently by himself, but was wounded and fled. He was healed at the temple of Asclepius Cotyleus

7. Detailed analyses of the myth are in Davison 1938; Page 1951, 30–33; Calame 1977, 2:52–59; Robbins 1994, 12–14.

8. Apollodorus (2.7.3, 3.10.5) omits the reference to the murder of Iphitus and adds a third possible reason for Heracles' wrath, namely, that the Hippocoontids had sided with Neleus. He assigns Hippocoon twelve sons, whom he names.

(3.19.7; cf. 3.20.5). In time (Apollodorus 2.7.3), he returned with an army to exact his vengeance.

None of these versions exactly matches the cast of characters as it survives in lines 1–12 of the *Partheneion*, but that is not enough reason to conclude that Alcman offered a substantially different account or a reworking of the myth.[9] Given the state of the text, not much can be made of the fact that Heracles' name does not appear. Moreover, we learn from Clement of Alexandria and his scholiast that Sosibius, the Laconian commentator of Alcman, mentioned that Heracles was wounded by the Hippocoontids, and so did Alcman in the first book of his songs.[10] This suggests that the narrative of the *Partheneion* did not substantially diverge, as regards the sequence of events, from the one we find in Pausanias. Mention of the sons of Derites and, most of all, the sons of Tyndareus, with Polydeuces, may point to greater emphasis on Spartan heroes and internal strife, as one might expect in local tradition.[11] The sons of Derites, however, can easily be accommodated in the "multitude" of other Spartiates mentioned by Diodorus. And it may be passed over as a given that Tyndareus and his sons joined Heracles' armada, which would bring them to power.

No one is in a position to claim the moral high ground in this tale—not the Dioscuri, cattle rustlers and themselves abductors of brides.[12] The disproportionate violence with which the Hippocoontids respond to the killing of their dog is no more reckless than the bloodbath to which Heracles subjects the city in revenge for the death of one man. What permeates the myth is the force of destructive *eris*,

9. Davison (1938, 443) suggested that emphasis on Heracles in later sources is tied to a desire to strengthen the Heraclid claim to the kingship, while in Alcman's treatment Tyndareus and his sons played major roles. Since, however, by the time of Alcman the Heraclids were safely installed on the throne, it is hard to see why a need to justify their rule would not arise until Hellenistic times. A radically different version is proposed by Robbins (1994, 12–16), who imagines that the myth told in the *Partheneion* is the rape of the Leucippides by the Hippocoontids, with the Dioscuri in the role of gallant rescuers.

10. Clement of Alexandria *Protrepticus* 36.11–12 Marcovitch (= Sosibius *FGrHist* 595F13) with scholia.

11. Davison 1938, 441–43.

12. For some reason, most interpreters cast the role of the Dioscuri in their feud with the Apharetids and the rape of the daughters of Leucippus in a positive light; see, e.g., Calame 1997, 187–91; Robbins 1994; Gengler 1995.

strife that brings about bitter feuds and then war, first arising over the apportionment of the kingship. Like the Theban legend of Eteocles and Polynices, the myth confronts the issue of legitimate succession. Neither Pausanias nor any of our other sources address the merit of Hippocoon's claim, but every narrative implies that Tyndareus was the rightful heir. The question of Hippocoon's legitimacy is central to understanding the nature of the conflict he unleashes. Why should he find himself fighting for the kingship? As the eldest son, according to Spartan custom he should succeed his father without question. The problem lies with Hippocoon's pedigree. Apollodorus reports conflicting traditions. In one, Tyndareus, Icarius, Aphareus, and Leucippus are all sons of Perieres and Gorgophone, while the other makes of Perieres the father of Oebalus, who, in turn, begets Tyndareus, Hippocoon, and Icarius by a Naiad nymph called Batia.[13] Pausanias's genealogy is in substantial agreement with yet another one, reported in the scholium to *Iliad* 2.581 and the scholium to Euripides *Orestes* 457. There Tyndareus, Icarius, and Arene are Oebalus's legitimate children, while Hippocoon is *nothos*, the bastard son born of a certain Nicostrate. The fact that Pausanias's elliptical narrative only mentions Tyndareus and Arene as the children of Oebalus and his wife Gorgophone indicates that his source, too, made Hippocoon the child of a different mother.[14]

Illegitimacy explains why Hippocoon's position is problematic. His situation is like that of the Trojan prince Bucolion, so described at *Iliad* 6.23–24:

Βουκολίων δ' ἦν υἱὸς ἀγαυοῦ Λαομέδοντος
πρεσβύτατος γενεῇ, σκότιον δέ ἑ γείνατο μήτηρ

Bucolion was the son of brilliant Laomedon,
the eldest by birth, but his mother bore him *skotios*.

13. Apollodorus 1.9.5, 3.10.3, 3.10.4. On the various genealogies of Hippocoon and Tyndareus, see Frazer 1921, 20–21.

14. Calame (1987, 170) notes the matter of Hippocoon's illegitimacy, albeit as an incidental element in the saga. I am unable to verify the statement that "Gorgophone gives Oibalos three sons who will be in conflict the moment the problem of their father's succession arises." No source, to my knowledge, gives Gorgophone as the mother of Hippocoon.

The scholia explain that *skotios*, "dark" or "in the dark," is the term used for bastards, children conceived in secret without the benefit of wedding torches. What these lines imply is that, although he is the eldest, Bucolion can never be king. In her penetrating study of this metaphor, Ebbott has shown that *skotios* signifies not only the unrecognized nature of the union that brings a *nothos* into existence, but the overarching quality of his existence, in the shadows.[15] Identified with his mother, the bastard is "obscure" in the sense that he lacks the capacity to come of age and become a citizen, and so to emerge onto the public stage of the political realm with the "brilliance" of his father. But Hippocoon is "a bastard who thinks he is legitimate," as Phaedra's nurse says of Hippolytus (Euripides *Hippolytus* 309). By claiming that he can succeed his father, he violates a fundamental principle of political order, which is therefore thrown into chaos and can only be reestablished after he and his descendants are destroyed.

The possibility of conflict might have arisen again with the twin sons of Tyndareus, Castor and Polydeuces, who form a pendant of sorts to Tyndareus and Hippocoon. While the latter two had the same father but different mothers, making the one legitimate and the other a *nothos*, the former have the same mother but different fathers, making one divine (and a *nothos* among the immortals) and the other mortal. In their case, the possibility of conflict is defused by their sharing one life between them, alternately spending one day beneath the earth and the other among the living.[16] This arrangement, a kind of shared rule, prefigures the ultimate solution to the problem: the Spartan dual kingship.[17] The prospect of strife, pitting brother against brother, flares up with a vengeance in the succession of Aristodemus, the first Heraclid on the Spartan throne. He died shortly afterward, just after his wife Argeia had given birth to twin

15. Ebbott 2003, chap. 1, particularly pp. 20–21.
16. Homer *Odyssey* 11.298–304; Pindar *Nemean* 10.55–56; Apollodorus 3.11.2.
17. According to the Laconian tradition reported by Pausanias 3.1.5, the Dioscuri reigned at Sparta before Menelaus. On the Dioscuri as the model for the Spartan kings and their protectors, see Carlier 1984, 298–301.

boys. Herodotus (6.52) tells the following story, specifying that this was the Lacedaemonian version of events and no one else's. Argeia wants both boys to be king. Knowing that the elder would be chosen, she pretends not to know who was born first, which leaves the magistrates in a quandary. They turn to the oracle at Delphi. The Pythia pronounces that both boys should be king, but the first should receive special honors. By a stratagem, it is discovered that Eurysthenes, from whom the Agiads would descend, was the firstborn; Procles, the head of the Eurypontid dynasty, came second. The twins were bitter enemies all their lives, but their mutual hatred had no dire consequences for the city.

The relevance of the myth of Hippocoon to Alcman's Sparta resides in the position it occupies in the etiology of that uniquely Spartan institution, the dual kingship, which would be enshrined in the Great Rhetra of Lycurgus.[18] Within that tradition, its function is that of a paradigmatic exemplum of the disintegration that would follow the accession of a bastard in the hereditary chain of succession to the throne. In so doing, the myth articulates the belief of a direct connection between the legitimacy of the king's birth and the integrity of the state, a belief that remained fundamental to the Spartan ideology of kingship throughout the city's history. In what Carlier expressively calls *la chasse aux bâtards* in the royal houses, the charge of bastardy was leveled at several contenders for the throne, thereby barring them from power.[19] In 491 Demaratus was accused of being *nothos* (falsely, according to Herodotus 6.63–70) and deposed; at the end of the century, Leotychidas was excluded from the succession for the same reason (Xenophon, *Hellenica* 3.3.2); in 243–42 King Leonidas II was removed on the grounds that he had married an Asian woman, with whom he had two children—something that a Heraclid was forbidden from doing.[20]

18. Plutarch *Lycurgus* 6. On the political import of the myth, see Calame 1977, 2:53.

19. On the Spartan obsession with the purity of the royal lines, see Carlier 1984, 292–96; Ogden 1996, 252–62.

20. Plutarch *Agis* 11; see Carlier 1984, 294–95; Richer 1998, 172–76. See p. 107 in the present text.

The third surviving stanza of the *Partheneion* presumably concerns a different myth featuring a combat:

]ἔβα. τῶν δ᾽ ἄλλος ἰῶι
] μαρμάρωι μυλάκρωι
] . εν Ἄιδας
] αυτοι
˙]πον. ἄλαστα δὲ
ϝέργα πάσον κακὰ μησάμενοι.

] of whom one with the arrow
] with marble millstone
] in Hades
] they
] things never to be forgotten
they suffered for the evils they plotted.

(30–35)

Not enough remains to identify the battle with certainty, but the choice of weapons and the cast of multiple offenders point to the battle of the Gods and the Giants.[21] In this regard one should grant particular authority to the evidence of the lost Throne of Apollo at Amyclae, which is our only Archaic source, not far removed in date from the *Partheneion*, as well as our only Spartan source. On it Pausanias (3.18.11) saw and described all too briefly, as though they were placed side by side, Heracles' fight with Thurius in the Gigantomachy and that of Tyndareus with Eurytus, one of the Hippocoontids named by Alcman. The pairing may be significant, if it also occurs in the *Partheneion*.

The foregoing interpretation of the myth of Hippocoon makes the relevance of the gnome that follows it in the *Partheneion* even more problematic. In what sense does the warning "not] to fly to the sky" and the reference to a marriage to Aphrodite (16–17), together

21. Following Diels (1896, 346–47), Page (1951, 43) admitted the possibility that these lines refer to the Gigantomachy; see also Farina 1950, 20–21. Calame (1977, 2:65–66; 1983, 320–21) leans toward the myth of Otos and Ephialtes, following Janni 1965, 68–71. Gengler (1995) identifies in the combat the quarrel between the Dioscuri and the sons of Aphareus.

with the mentions of "allotment" or "measure," *aisa*, and "path," *poros*, constitute the moral of this story? In an attempt to reconcile the sentiment expressed in these lines with the myth of the sons of Hippocoon, scholars have argued that Alcman emphasized the amorous rivalry pitting the Hippocoontids against the Tyndarids.[22] We know a parallel story, that of the contest between the Dioscuri and the two sons of Aphareus over the daughters of Leucippus, which ends with the death of both Apharetids and of Castor. If the quarrel was over women, the argument goes, the warning about not marrying above one's station becomes less obscure. The erotic subtext of the quarrel would bring the spectacle of the heap of corpses, which the first extant lines present us, in line with the tone of the second part of the song, and provide a useful and relevant contrast to the feminine grace that pervades the latter. But the argument is weak. There are, for one thing, too many Hippocoontids to the two Tyndarids, and to the former one should add the sons of Derites. There is moreover no evidence that any of them ever attempted to marry a goddess, let alone fly to the sky. As Page put it (albeit to argue that the vanished myth was that of the rivalry in love), since nothing in the story of the sons of Hippocoon makes this moral appropriate, "we admit the likelihood that a different story, of which fragments are to be found, and with which the moral can easily be reconciled, formed the theme of this part of Alcman's *Partheneion*."[23]

PATH AND SIGN

The missing story, to which the moralizing reflections at lines 13–19 apply, is the myth of Phaethon, as I hope to demonstrate by a somewhat laborious analysis of the wealth of allusions these lines contain:

]αρ Αἶσα παντῶν

] γεραιτάτοι

22. Page 1951, 30–33; Calame 1977, 2:52–57; Robbins 1994, 11–16; and, more warily, Tsitsibakou-Vasalos 1993, 133–35. Hutchinson (2001, 80) considers a "romantic motivation" for the feud unlikely.
23. Page 1951, 33.

ἀπ]έδιλος ἀλκά.   15
ἀν]θρώπων ἐς ὠρανὸν ποτήσθω
]ρήτω γαμῆν τὰν Ἀφροδίταν
ϝ]άναϲϲαν ἤ τιν'
] ἢ παίδα...κω

The text mentions *aisa*, "allotment" or "measure," at line 13, and the lost
part of line 14 or 15 contained the word *poros*, "path," a word the scholium glosses with a reference to Hesiod's *khaos*, in connection with
"oldest."[24] With the exception of the fable in Plato's *Symposium* (203b),
Page's commentary of 1951 knew of no other instance of *poros* as a
personification or an agent that could be called oldest. He explained
its mention in the *Partheneion* in relation to the fate of the Hippocoontids: a moralizing reflection on the fact that their allotted time
had come to an end.[25] In this view, *poros* and *aisa* are two words for
roughly the same concept. Since then *poros* has made another appearance, once more in Alcman, in the company not of *aisa* but of *tekmōr*.
In 1957 the publication of P.Oxy 2390 produced a new fragment consisting of brief citations contained in an extensive commentary:

col. II

[a. . . . .] .λίσσομαι π[αντ]ῶν μάλιστα [·] τὰς Μο]ύσας ὑπερ.[. . . .] ματρός·
τῆς τ[ῶν   ]ντιδων φυλ[. . . χ]ορός (ἐστι)
Δύμα[   ]τρα Δυμα[. . . · ἐν δ]ὲ ταύ-   25
τηι τῆι ὠι[δῆι Ἀλ]κμὰν φυσ[ιολο(γεῖ)· ἐ]κθη-
σ[ό]μεθα δὲ [τὰ δ]οκοῦντα ἡ[μῖν μ]ετὰ τὰς
τῶν λοιπῶ[ν πεί]ρας. Γῆς. [μὲν] Μούσα[ς
θυγατέρας ὡς Μίμνερμ[ος.] τας ἐγε[νεα-

24. Scholium A 3 to line 14, ὅτι τὸν πόρον εἴρηκε τὸν αὐτόν τῶ<ι> ὑπὸ τοῦ Ἡσιόδο(υ)
μεμυθολογημένωι χάει. Page's identification of *aisa* and *poros* as personifications (1951, 33–37),
indeed divinities, rests on no firm evidence but has gained wide acceptance. See, e.g., Calame
1983, 318; Most 1987, 14:"Poros, that dread and ancient god." Voelke (1981, 22) argued that *poros*
and *tekmōr* are divinities because one of them is called *presgus* in Alcman frag. 5 *PMGF*.

25. Page 1951, 36–37.

col. III

[λόγησε]

. . . .

.ν.[1

πάντων ...[

τις [b. ἐκ δὲ τῶ π[   ] τέ-

κμωρ ἐγένετο τ[

μο[.] ἐντεῦθεν ει .[5

πόρος ἀπὸ τῆς πορ. [..]. [

ὡς γὰρ ἤρξατο ἡ ὕλη κατασκευα[σθῆναι

ἐγένετο πόρος τις, οἱονεὶ ἀρχή· λ[έγει

οὖν ὁ Ἀλκμὰν τὴν ὕλην πάν[των τετα-

ραγμένην καὶ ἀπόητον· εἶτα [γενέ-   10

σθαι τινά φησιν τὸν κατασκευά[ζοντα

πάντα, εἶτα γενέσθαι [πό]ρον, τοῦ [δὲ πό-

ρου παρελθόντος ἐπακολουθῆ[σαι] τέ-

κμωρ· καὶ (ἔστιν) ὁ μ(ὲν) πόρος οἷον ἀρχή, τὸ δὲ τέ-

κμωρ οἱονεὶ τέλος. τῆς Θέτιδος γενο-   15

μένης ἀρχὴ καὶ τέ[λ]ο[ς ταῦτ]α πάντων ἐ-

γένε[τ]ο, καὶ τὰ μὲν πάντα [ὁμο]ίαν ἔχει

τὴν φύσιν τῆι τοῦ χαλκοῦ ὕληι, ἡ δὲ

Θέτις τ[ῆι] τοῦ τεχνίτου, ὁ δὲ πόρος καὶ τὸ τέ-

κμωρ τῆι ἀρχῆι καὶ τῶι τέλει. [c. πρέσγ[υς]   20

δ(ὲ) ἀν(τὶ) τοῦ πρεσβύτης. [d. καὶ τρίτος σκότος [·]

διὰ τὸ μηδέπω μήτε ἥλιον μήτε σε-

λ]ήνην γεγονέναι ἀλλ᾽ ἔτι ἀδιάκριτ[ο]ν (εἶναι)

τ]ὴν ὕλην· ἐγένοντο οὖν ὑπο. [.] ... πό-

ρος καὶ τέκμωρ καὶ σκότ[ος ...]. [[e. ἅμαρ   25

τε καὶ σελάνα {καὶ τρίτον σκότος} τὰς [

μαρμαρυγάς]· ἅμαρ οὐ ψιλῶς ἀλλὰ

σὺν ἡλίωι· τὸ μὲν πρότερον ἦν σκότος μό-

νον, μετὰ δὲ ταῦτα διακριθέ[ντο]ς αὐτοῦ

Col. II

In this song (25), Alcman speaks about nature. We shall set forth
our interpretation after the attempts of all others. He (calls) the
Muses the daughters of Earth, giving them the same genealogy as
Mimnermus.

Col. III, 3–29

[**b.** From the *p*[   ]*tekmor* came into being [   ] thence (5)
[   ] *poros* from [   ] for when matter began to be formed a *poros* came
into being as a first principle. Alcman therefore says that the matter
of the universe was chaotic and unformed, and that then someone
came into being (10) who gave form to the universe, next *poros* came
into being, and *tekmōr* followed closely upon the appearance of *poros*.
And *poros* is in the nature of *arkhē*, *tekmōr* in that of *telos*. Once Thetis came into being (15) such *arkhē* and *telos* of the universe came into
being, and the nature of the universe is analogous to the material of
bronze, that of Thetis to that of the craftsman, and that of *poros* and
tekmōr to *arkhē* and *telos*. [**c.** *Presgus*: instead of *presbutes* (old) (20).
[**d.** And third darkness: because neither sun nor moon had come into
being but matter was still undifferentiated. There came into being
[   ] *poros* and *tekmōr* and darkness [   ] [**e.** And day and moon and
third darkness the bright-gleaming: day not by itself but with the sun.
First there was only darkness, afterwards this having been separated . . .[26]

Extricating Alcman from his commentator is not an easy matter.
Evidently by the second century CE this text presented its readers
with difficulties and had been the subject of repeated exegeses. Since
this commentator announces that he will put forward one of his own,
we should look here for a novel interpretation, one that had escaped
previous interpreters. The argument, contained in the commentary to
the first lemma (III, 3), is structured into four steps, each repeating

---

26. Lobel et al. 1957, 52–55; text cited after Calame 1983 (Alcman frag. 81 Calame [= 5
PMGF]).

with further elaboration the information given in the preceding one. It begins with what seems to be a paraphrase in the fragmentary lines III, 3–6, which introduce *tekmōr* and probably included an etymology of the word *poros* (III, 6). There follows a first level of elucidation (III, 7–8), locating the emergence of "a *poros*," *poros tis*, in the context of the differentiation of primal matter, *hulē*, and explaining that this *poros* is an *arkhē*. Together with *telos*, which is mentioned in the lines that follow, *hulē* and *arkhē* belong to the Aristotelian terminology, and we should expect them to be used in their specific sense of "unformed matter," "efficient cause," and "final cause." All we can infer from the commentary so far is that Alcman's text included mentions of *poros* and *tekmōr*.[27] It is uncertain whether there was as well a term that could be interpreted as *hulē*. If there was, it may have have been some inflection of *panta*, which is equated with *hulē* below (III, 17–18). This line of thinking leads on to the amplification of III, 8–15, where it is argued ("therefore," λ[έγει] οὖν ὁ Ἀλκμάν) that what Alcman says is that in the beginning there was primal matter, then came a demiurge who fashioned the universe, then came *poros*, followed by *tekmōr*. Like that of *poros* at III, 8 (πόρος τις, "a certain *poros*"), the identity of the demiurge at first is left unspecified, the masculine gender being used in the unmarked sense that accommodates the feminine as well: "someone who shaped all things," τινά φησιν τὸν κατασκευά[ζοντα] πάντα (III, 11–12). The commentator reveals the identity of the demiurge in the next and final interpretive move (III, 15–20), which may be where his original contribution lies: in the poem, the figure of Thetis as bronze worker is an allegory for the cosmogony he has just ferreted out of the text.

Most has shown beyond doubt that this interpretation belongs to the tradition of allegorical readings of archaic poetry. This approach, which purported to uncover a philosophy of nature underneath the mythical narrative, was applied to Homer in particular, and was favored by writers and scholiasts of Roman imperial date.[28] We may be

27. As Ricciardelli Apicella (1979, 19–20) notes, *poros* and *tekmōr* were certainly mentioned in the poem, although the commentator's definition is probably his own. On the Aristotelian cast of the commentator's phraseology, see West 1967, 4–5; Calame 1983, 441–43. Steiner (2003) argues that the language is Stoic.

28. Most 1987, 6–9, 18–19; see also Penwill 1974, 13.

sure that the text of the poem mentioned bronze working and probably Thetis. But no part of the cosmogony that the commentary outlines can be assigned to Alcman with any confidence.[29] In the end, the definitions of *poros* and *tekmōr* it offers may be no more deserving of our trust than the equation of *poros* with Hesiod's *khaos* proposed by scholiast A on line 14 of the Louvre *Partheneion*.[30] In addition, Most rightly notes that the poem's inclusion in the first two books of the Alexandrian edition of Alcman, which contained what we call "*partheneia*," and its being a choral song lead us to expect that a mythical narrative will follow the invocation to the Muses, as it does in the Louvre *Partheneion*.[31] It is one thing, however, to say that the subject of the song was not a cosmogony but a myth and quite another to exclude the possibility that that myth might have cosmological implications.[32] In early Greek poetry myth and philosophy are not so easily disentangled. One thinks of the legend of Phaethon, for instance, or the role of the Heliads in the proem of Parmenides' philosophical poem *On Nature*, both of which will be discussed later. In Alcman 5, reference to a cosmogony is discernible, not in the commentary but in the scraps of text it preserves, namely, in the troubled lines III, 25–27:

ἄμαρ

τε καὶ σελάνα καὶ τρίτον σκότος· τὰς̣ [

μαρμαρυγάς

And Day

and Moon and third Darkness the [

bright-gleaming[33]

29. This was already Page's conclusion immediately following the publication of the papyrus (1959, 21).

30. West (1963, 155) and Most (1987, 13) point out the parallel.

31. Most 1987, 6.

32. This is what Most's notion of "straightforward myth" as opposed to a cosmogonic narrative seems to imply (1987, 11).

33. This passage is riddled with difficulties. The τρίτον σκότος was mentioned above (III, 21) and may be an interpolation here, as Calame (1983, 449) and others believe, although Page (1959, 20) put forward good reasons to think that it belongs here. The grammatical relationship of τὰς μαρμαρυγάς to the rest of the sentence is obscure; but the word probably appeared in the poem, since, as Penwill (1974, 32n19) observes, it explains nothing and is itself in need of a gloss. The commentator takes μαρμαρυγάς to refer to the sun (falsely, according to Calame 1983, 450),

That Darkness figures in the poem in close proximity to Day and Moon points to the primordial division of day from night that is a fixture of Greek and Babylonian cosmogonies.[34] In this scenario, *poros* and *tekmōr* have their place, and so does *aisa*.

In both literal and figurative usage, *poros* is "pathway"—course, ford, way. *Tekmōr* has the obviously interrelated meanings of "boundary," "fixed point," and "sign."[35] The logic binding *poros*, "the path," and *tekmōr* is complementary: *tekmōr* is a fixed landmark along the path.[36] Both words are used in the description of astral phenomena, *poros* to denote the daily course of sun and moon and the fixed stars, *tekmōr* of the stars as signs in the sky.[37] The only path involved in the alternation of night and day is the one marked by the fixed stars, along which the sun and the moon travel. Another fragment of Alcman, a singleton, probably refers to this as well: "narrow the path and merciless *Anankē*," which evokes the figure of the whorl of *Anankē* with its Sirens.[38] Rather than in a broad conceptual sense, *poros* in association with *tekmōr* or *aisa* should be understood in a specifically astronomical sense to mean what would be identified as the zodiacal belt. Appropriately, in his analysis of Alcman 5 *PMGF*, Vernant cites the cosmogony which Orpheus sings in Apollonius Rhodius's *Argonautica*:

He sang of how the earth, the heavens, and the sea—once upon a time united with each other in a single form—were sundered apart by deadly strife; and how a position fixed [*tekmar*] for eternity in the sky is held by the stars and the journeys [*keleuthoi*] of the moon and the sun.[39]

---

and in this he may be right. μαρμαρυγαί is used of the brilliance emanating from Apollo in the Homeric hymn to Apollo (*Homeric Hymns* 3.203).

34. West 1963, 155–56; Calame 1983, 438–40.

35. Penwill (1974, 17–20, 22–24) analyzes the etymologies and usages of *poros* and *tekmōr/tekmar*; Tsitsibakou-Vasalos (1993, 131–32) reviews previous interpretations of the meaning of *poros* in the Louvre *Partheneion*.

36. Burkert 1963, 827; Calame 1983, 448. See also Detienne 1998, 117–18.

37. Vernant 1970, 46–51; Calame 1983, 447–48.

38. Alcman 102 *PMGF* (= 108 Calame). Both Garzya (1963, 24–25) and Calame (1977, 2:60; 1983, 504) recognized here an echo of the conjoined notions of *aisa* and *poros* in the Louvre *Partheneion*.

39. Apollonius Rhodius *Argonautica* 1.496–500; trans. Hunter 1993, modified.

It is a long way from Alcman to Apollonius Rhodius, but Mesopotamian sources attest that knowledge of the fact that the sun, moon, and planets follow one and the same course through the fixed stars was current well before the late seventh century. Our pair—the "fixed position" and the "path"—finds precise correspondence in the *manzazu* (*nanzazu*), "station," and *harranu*, "path," of which the Babylonian creation myth and astronomical texts speak.[40] In the *Enuma Elish* (5.1–2), Marduk "fashioned the stations (*manzaza*) for the great gods. // The stars, their likeness he set up, the constellations." A prologue to the omens of the *Enuma Anu Enlil* relates how Anu, Enlil, and Ea arranged the sky:

> When Anu, Enlil, and Ea, the great gods,
> heaven and earth built, fixed the astronomical signs;
> established the stellar-positions [*naanzaza*], [se]t fast the stellar-
> locations;
> the gods of the night they [. .]. , divided the paths [*harrani*].[41]

The MUL.APIN, a late eighth-century Babylonian astronomical compendium that incorporates earlier sources,[42] divides the stars into three paths that belong to Anu, Enlil, and Ea, respectively. Across these runs the Path of the Moon, which is also the road that the Sun and the planets travel.[43] The road is defined by the stars "through whose regions the Moon in the course of a month passes and whom he touches"; in other words, it is a path through and past fixed points (MUL.APIN I iv 31–32, 38–39). It is intriguing that Mesopotamian astronomers engaged in mathematical exercises that calculated

40. See *Assyrian Dictionary* 10.1, s.v. "manzazu" (5); 6, s.v. "harranu" (e). On variant names for the Path of the Sun, Moon, and planets, Horowitz 1998, 256–57.
41. Horowitz 1998, 146–47.
42. On the sources and history of the MUL.APIN, see Hunger and Pingree 1989, 8–12.
43. MUL.APIN II i 1–8 Hunger and Pingree. Hunger and Pingree (1999, 67–68) compare the sequence consisting of Stars (Pleiades), Bull of Heaven (or Jaw of the Bull, α Tauri and the Hyades), and True Shepherd of Anu (Orion) in the MUL.APIN star lists to the description of the sky on the shield of Achilles at *Iliad* 18.486, "the Pleiades, the Hyades, and the strength of Orion." On the relation of early Greek astronomy to Babylonian astronomy, see Dicks 1970, 163–75. Note that whether the fact that this text attesting to the notion that the Sun and the planets travel the same path as the Moon means that Babylonian astronomers realized that the path is a circle oblique to the equator is a debated issue, on which see Brack-Bernsen 2003.

distances between constellations, as the Pythagoreans would later be imagined to have done.[44] As in Greek cosmology, the gods presided over the order of the cosmos to prevent transgressions that would plunge the universe back into chaos.[45]

Although its cosmogonic implications are not always in evidence, the image of the path of the sun and moon through the fixed stars occurs in ancient Greek texts and monuments of all periods. There may be mention of the "road of the sky" itself, as in Jocasta's address to the Sun at the opening of Euripides' *Phoenician Women* (1–3):

Ὦ τὴν ἐν ἄστροις οὐρανοῦ τέμνων ὁδὸν
καὶ χρυσοκολλήτοισιν ἐμβεβὼς δίφροις
Ἥλιε, θοαῖς ἵπποισιν εἱλίσσων φλόγα

O you who course heaven's road through the stars,
mounted on a chariot inlaid with gold,
Helius, whirling out your flame with swift mares.[46]

The Sun's journey describes an arc in the sky as the chariot rises to the highest point, then begins its descent toward Ocean. On the same road and by the same means travel Night, Dawn, and Moon.[47]

Horses and chariots dominate the visual as well as the literary

44. The "Hilprecht Text," a Middle Babylonian tablet from Nippur, presents the distances between stars as a mathematical problem; see Horowitz 1998, 179–82. Sources of Hellenistic and Roman date attribute to Pythagoras calculations of distances of the heavenly bodies from one another, in an attempt to determine their harmonic relationship. See, e.g., Pliny *Natural History* 2.83–84; Alexander of Aphrodisias *Aristotle's Metaphysics* 40 (translated with commentary by Dooley 1989, 65–66). These have been dismissed, probably correctly, on the ground that no mathematical astronomy could have existed before Eudoxus; see Burkert 1972, 350–57; Freyburger 1996.

45. In the *Enuma Elish*, V 6–8, the star of Marduk, together with the stations of Enlil and Ea, is charged with maintaining order; in *The Exaltation of Ishtar* 27–30, the Moon and the Sun seem to have the task "to keep all the stars in place as in a furrow, // to make the gods at the fore keep to the path like oxen." See Horowitz 1998, 144–45.

46. On the meaning of τέμνων here as "making your way," see LSJ, s.v. τέμνω VI2b. For a comprehensive survey of literary sources for the course of the Sun, see A. Rapp in *ML* 1.2 (1886–90): 2009–15.

47. *Homeric Hymns* 31.15–16; Homer *Odyssey* 12.380–81. For the chariot of Eos, see *Odyssey* 23.243–46; for that of Selene, *Homeric Hymns* 32.7–11. Pausanias 5.11.8 describes Selene riding a horse among the gold figures on the pedestal of the statue of Zeus at Olympia, and further refers (as nonsense) to a story according to which she rides not a horse but a mule.

imagery of the path of the Sun. What survives of the material record, mainly Archaic and Classical painted vases, presents us with two models for the representation of the succession of day and night. By far the most common is that of the celestial bodies riding in succession, as in the tableaux of the night sky on the tapestry that formed the roof of the festival tent in Euripides' *Ion*. Helius sets, followed by "blackmantled" Night, Moon at her full brilliance, and "lightbearing" Dawn, who chases the stars from the sky:

> Οὐρανὸς ἀθροίζων ἄστρ' ἐν αἰθέρος κύκλωι·
> ἵππους μὲν ἤλαυν' ἐς τελευταίαν φλόγα
> Ἥλιος, ἐφέλκων λαμπρὸν Ἑσπέρου φάος·
> μελάμπεπλος δὲ Νὺξ ἀσείρωτον ζυγοῖς
> ὄχημ' ἔπαλλεν, ἄστρα δ' ὡμάρτει θεᾶι·
> Πλειὰς μὲν ἤιει μεσοπόρου δι' αἰθέρος
> ὅ τε ξιφήρης Ὠρίων, ὕπερθε δὲ
> Ἄρκτος στρέφουσ' οὐραῖα χρυσήρη πόλωι·
> κύκλος δὲ πανσέληνος ἠκόντιζ' ἄνω
> μηνὸς διχήρης, Ὑάδες τε, ναυτίλοις
> σαφέστατον σημεῖον, ἥ τε φωσφόρος
> Ἕως διώκουσ' ἄστρα.

Heaven was mustering the stars in the circle of the sky. Helios was driving his horses toward his final gleaming, bringing on the brightness of Eveningstar. Night, robed in black, was making her chariot, drawn by a pair with no trace horses, swing forward, and the stars were accompanying the goddess. The Pleiades were passing through mid heaven and so was Orion with his sword, while above them the Bear turned its golden tail about the Pole. The circle of the full moon, as at mid month, darted her beams, and there were the Hyades, clearest sign for sailors, and Dawn the Daybringer putting the stars to flight.[48]

In the monumental arts, the sculptures of the Parthenon preserve two instances in which a mythical narrative is inscribed within the

---

48. Euripides *Ion*, 1147–58; trans. Kovacs 1999.

imaginary arc described by the daily course of the sun. On the eastern pediment, the horses of the chariot of the Sun rising above the waves of Ocean, and those of Night plunging downward, frame the scene of the birth of Athena. On the northern metopes the figure of a rising chariot (Eos's or Helius's) at the eastern end and that of Selene setting toward the west enclose the final moments of the sack of Troy.[49] As she normally does in the visual tradition, Selene rides on horseback.[50] What remains in the archaeological record for the most part are pictures that begin to appear on Athenian vases early in the fifth century BCE and extend into the fourth with paintings on Apulian pottery. The sequence of Night, Moon, and Dawn, which the tapestry depicted in the *Ion* presents to us, is reproduced, for instance, on the cover of a Classical pyxis (plate 6).[51] Winged Nyx leads a four-horse chariot at a gallop, and behind her is Selene on horseback, her head turned toward Eos, who follows on a two-horse chariot, wearing a diadem of rays. Stars, rendered as dot-rosettes, shine above Nyx and Selene while the solar disk above Eos's head signifies the light of dawn. The figures race toward a pillar that arises atop a Corinthian column (of which only the upper portion of the capital is visible) in front of a clump of leaves. Like the *terma* of a hippodrome, in this picture the pillar on column marks the turning post in the ethereal racecourse, that is, the point at which the sun appears to reverse the direction of its risings along the horizon.[52] Another pyxis lid shows Eos followed by Helius; before her, Selene on her horse disappears below the arc of

49. Brommer 1979, 52–54, pls. 132, 143; 30–31, pls. 38, 44–45.

50. On the iconography of Selene, see Lacroix 1974, 98–99, 102n3; S. Karusu, *LIMC* 2 (1984): 909–17.

51. Berlin, Staatliche Museen F 2519; *CVA* Berlin 3, Germany 22 (1962), 23, pl. 138; *LIMC* 2 (1984), s.v. "Astra" no. 8 (= 19). The astral disk has led to the identification of the third figure as Helius (Robert 1919, 48; Papaspyridi-Karouzou 1945–47, 30–31; and *LIMC* [above]). The lekythos by the Sappho Painter (plates 10–11), discussed below, where Eos's name is inscribed above the figure, demonstrates that the disk is appropriate to her as well. The figure differs not at all in dress and hairstyle from the preceding one, and nothing indicates that it is male. The sequence of Night and Moon appears also on the cover of the pyxis British Museum 73.9–15.14 (E 776), *LIMC* 2 (1984), s.v. "Astra" no. 9 (= 20).

52. For a fuller discussion of this and other representations of the site of the *tropai heliou*, see below, pp. 140–44. Yalouris (1980, 313–14) relates the column that appears in representations of the astral bodies to Anaximander's conception of the earth as a cylinder, resembling a column drum (frag. 5 D–K).

the sky, her hands raised in a gesture of awe at the dawning light (plate 7).[53] The rising and setting of celestial bodies may be depicted alongside a mythological narrative, in a way that is particularly appropriate on the Blacas krater, where the subject is the rape of Cephalus (plates 8–9).[54] Eos, on foot, pursues the young hunter; above and to the left Selene, on horseback, sinks below the horizon (plate 9); on the other side Helius in his chariot rises above the waves of Ocean (plate 8).

Athenian vases illustrate a second model for the celestial ride, one in which Night, or Selene, and Day, or Eos, do not follow each other but move in opposite directions. The scene painted on a modest Athenian lekythos of the early fifth century offers a clear example. The subject is an adventure of Heracles (plates 10–11).[55] In the area under the handle, arguably the "back" of the vase, the hero crouches on a rocky spur above a cave, which holds a large snarling dog, roasting meat on spits upon an altar. The main picture field is given over to a representation of sunrise: Helius rises in his chariot, while above him, on either side, two more chariots move in opposite directions, emerging from black streamers that reach down to join the outline of the cave. Their drivers are Nyx, on the left, and Eos, on the right. The name of each figure is inscribed and, for good measure, each is surmounted by an astral disk. Iconographically, the scene is related to a short-lived series of representations of the myth of Heracles and the Golden Bowl of the Sun, although, it has been argued, the cave and the dog may point in this case to the capture of Cerberus.[56] The lid of a Classical pyxis in Athens offers a comparable scheme: a winged, astral divinity on a chariot, presumably Eos, looks back at the horse of Selene, which moves in the opposite direction and disappears into a space marked with a triple line. On the other side, Helius rises (plate 12).[57]

53. British Museum 1920.12–21.1; ARV² 1282.1; LIMC 2 (1984), s.v. "Astra" no. 4.

54. British Museum E 446; FR 3:33–36, pl. 126; Lacroix 1974, 104–5, pls. 34–36; LIMC 3 (1986), s.v. "Eos" no. 110 (= "Astra" 22).

55. Metropolitan Museum of Art 41.16.29; attributed to the Sappho Painter, ABV 507.6; ABL 120–24, app. ii, no. 6, pl. 32,1; CVA Gallatin and Hoppin Collections 2 (USA 8, 1942), 93–94, pl. 44, 1; LIMC 2 (1984), s.v. "Astra" no. 3; Cohen 2006, 206–8.

56. Ferrari Pinney and Ridgway 1981.

57. National Museum 17983; ARV² 1282.2; LIMC 2 (1984), s.v. "Astra" no. 7.

These images do not contradict the notion expressed by the more common representation of the cavalcade of celestial bodies in succession, but underscore the point of arrival and departure and their alternation. Access to heaven's road is through a gateway, which both Homer and Hesiod locate at the end of the earth. In the *Odyssey*, 24.11–14, the Gates of the Sun are part of the landscape through which Hermes shepherds the souls of the Suitors on their way to Hades, on the far side of Ocean:

πὰρ δ᾽ ἴσαν Ὠκεανοῦ τε ῥοὰς καὶ Λευκάδα πέτρην,
ἠδὲ παρ᾽ Ἠελίοιο πύλας καὶ δῆμον Ὀνείρων
ἤϊσαν· αἶψα δ᾽ ἵκοντο κατ᾽ ἀσφοδελὸν λειμῶνα,
ἔνθα τε ναίουσι ψυχαί, εἴδωλα καμόντων.

They went past the streams of Ocean and the White Rock,
past the Gates of Helius and the country of Dreams.
Presently they arrived at the meadow of asphodel,
And there the souls dwell, images of the dead.

In the *Theogony* of Hesiod, 744–56, this is the gateway to the House of Night, to which the Sun returns after his day's journey.[58] Moon and Eos moving in opposite directions illustrate the notion that their journeys begin and end, obeying firmly established allotments of time. It is in this regard that the concept of measure, *metra* or *aisa*, is a governing principle in the order of the universe.

MEASURE

In relation to *poros* in the sense of the path of the sun and the moon, *aisa* has a specific meaning and a figurative dimension. A key text in this regard is Parmenides' poem, fragments of which survive under the title *On Nature*. Writing in the early fifth century what would be hailed as a new and revolutionary ontology, Parmenides appeals to the tradition of wisdom poetry represented by Homer, Hesiod,

58. See also Stesichorus frag. S17 *PMGF*.

Epimenides of Crete, and Pythagoras.[59] He does so, to begin with, by writing in hexameters that show a contrived, programmatic use of Hesiodic and, most of all, Homeric diction.[60] The model of Hesiod's encounter with the Muses and, even more, that of Epimenides' dream, in which he converses with the gods and Truth and Justice, stand behind the representation of this inquiry into the nature of knowledge and being as a revelation at the hands of an unnamed goddess.[61] The proem tells the myth of the journey to the place where the revelation occurs, narrated in the first person by the protagonist. He is likewise nameless but characterized as a "youth," *kouros*.[62] What concerns us here is the identity of the path he follows.

The young hero finds himself traveling in a chariot drawn by mares that are "wise," *poluphrastoi* (4), on a road "far removed from the paths that men tread" (27). The road leads through the Gates of Night and Day, which are controlled by Justice. The House of Night figures as well in this landscape, with which we are familiar from Homer's and Hesiod's cosmologies. It is the dwelling from which the Heliads, the daughters of the Sun, best known for their role in the myth of Phaethon, emerge to guide the chariot to its destination. The appearance of the Heliads signals that Parmenides frames his inquiry in mythological terms, conforming to the practice of the natural philosophers who preceded him.[63] In addition the proem holds a wealth of allusions that reveal the mythological, conceptual, and figural background of Parmenides' narrative.[64] The figure of the road recurs insistently. There is

59. See Deichgräber 1958, 634; Guthrie 1965, 10; Detienne 1996, 36–37, 130–34; Burkert 1969, 3, 16–19, 29; Cordero 2004, 14–15.

60. On Parmenidean style and diction, see Mourelatos 1970, chap. 1; Coxon 1986, 7–11, 156–256 passim. Coxon (1986, 11) notes: "in view of Parmenides' Pythagorean associations it is worthwhile to bear in mind the express statement of Iamblichus that the Pythagoreans 'made use of expressions of Homer and Hesiod chosen for the improvement of the soul'" (Iamblichus *On the Pythagorean Way of Life* III, 164).

61. Hesiod *Theogony* 1–115; Epimenides frag. 1 D–K. See Dolin 1962.

62. Confronting the question "why a *kouros?*" Cordero (2004, 24–25) and Conche (1996, 57–59) point to the fact that one's youth is the time for learning. Most other interpreters assume that the characterization is autobiographical. Cosgrove (1974) offers a useful analysis of interpretations.

63. See Slatkin 2004, 26.

64. I use the term *allusion* in the marked sense established by Slatkin 1991: "Allusions . . . are highly charged and repay scrutiny for the myths whose resonance or 'reverberation' they carry

the one imagined as an actual road, albeit divine, on which the youth travels. Metaphors of the road configure in the speech of the goddess the available paths of philosophical inquiry, only one of which leads to Truth.[65] The hypothesis that the road of the youth's journey is the path of the Sun, as a number of scholars have proposed,[66] affords a way to understand the relationship between the narrative and the metaphorical use of this image in the poem, along with its relevance to the cosmological import of "measure," Alcman's *aisa*.

The proem of Parmenides' poem lingers on the features of the chariot and of the road that leads to the goddess:

ἵπποι, ταί με φέρουσιν, ὅσον τ' ἐπὶ θυμὸς ἱκάνοι
πέμπον, ἐπεί μ' ἐς ὁδὸν βῆσαν πολύφημον ἄγουσαι
δαίμονος, ἣ κατὰ πᾶν τατὴ φέρει εἰδότα φῶτα·
τῇ φερόμην, τῇ γάρ με πολύφραστοι φέρον ἵπποι
ἅρμα τιταίνουσαι, κοῦραι δ' ὁδὸν ἡγεμόνευον.
ἄξων δ' ἐν χνοίῃσιν ἵ<ει> σύριγγος ἀυτήν
αἰθόμενος, δοιοῖς γὰρ ἐπείγετο δινωτοῖσιν
κύκλοις ἀμφοτέρωθεν, ὅτε σπερχοίατο πέμπειν
ἡλιάδες κοῦραι προλιποῦσαι δώματα νυκτός
εἰς φάος, ὠσάμεναι κράτων ἄπο χερσὶ καλύπτρας.

The mares, which carry me as far as my spirit might reach,
sped me on, after they brought me and placed me upon the *daimōn*'s
road
of many sounds, which stretched over the world carries the witness
lights.
On this I was carried, for on this road carried me the wise mares,
straining at the chariot, while the maidens led the way.
Ablaze in the naves the axle sent forth the shrill sound of the pipe,
for it was urged on by two rounded wheels at either end,

into the narrative as a whole, signaling a constellation of themes that establish bearings for the poem as it unfolds and linking it continually to other traditions and paradigms and to a wider mythological terrain" (108).

65. On the image of the road in Parmenides, see Cordero 2004, 19–23.
66. Kranz 1916, 1159. See also Gigon 1968, 246–47; Cornford 1952, 118n1; Guthrie 1965, 7; Burkert 1969, 7, 28.

even as the maiden daughters of the Sun hastened to escort me
toward the light, having left the House of Night,
pushing away veils from their heads with their hands.

(Frag. 1.1–10 Coxon)

This translation anticipates conclusions I draw from the argument I am about to present. At present, there is little agreement among scholars as to the direction of the journey and the meaning of epithets such as *poluphēmos* (2) of the road and *poluphrastoi* (4) of the horses. While the latter may be understood in the sense of "wise" or "experienced" to say that the horses know the way, the meaning of *poluphēmos* remains problematic.[67] The third line of the proem in particular has long represented an interpretive stumbling block. At issue are the identity of the *daimōn* whose road this is, and the meaning in line 3 of the cluster that I transcribe as πᾶν τατή. The role that *eidota phōta*—"the one who knows," as the phrase is generally translated—plays in this context is the thorniest problem. If φῶτα is understood to mean "man," "mortal," it can refer only to the young narrator, since we learn later (1.27) from the goddess that this road is "far removed indeed from the step of men." But how can the narrator describe himself as εἰδότα, "one who knows," when he is just on his way to receiving that knowledge?[68] How would this characterization of the road—populated by divine charioteers, full of sound, the way of knowledge—strike an audience able to appreciate its nuances? For it is precisely that common fund of traditional knowledge that Parmenides addresses in a studied manipulation of epic language.

Lexically and grammatically, εἰδότα φῶτα may be two different things. It is either the masculine accusative singular of ὁ εἰδὼς φῶς, "the man who knows," or the neuter accusative plural of τὸ εἰδὼς φῶς, the contracted form of the Ionic and epic φάος. The latter means "light" in general as well as "ray" of the sun or the moon, yielding in this case

67. Coxon 1986, 157: "the way with much discourse"; Tarán 1965, 10: "uttering many things"; Conche (1996, 44) explains the word in light of Parmenides frag. 8.2–3, "on this way there are very many signs." Trans. Coxon 1986.

68. Some scholars (e.g., Bowra 1937, 109–10; Burkert 1969, 5; Coxon 1986, 158–59) take the expression to characterize a religious experience, such as that of the initiate in a mystery cult. Mansfeld (1964, 229–33) and Cordero (2004, 26) believe that the traveler is on his way back from the goddess and that the narrative of the encounter is a flashback.

"the knowing lights."[69] Because they may take identical forms, ὁ φῶς and τὸ φῶς lend themselves to punning wordplay. Take, for instance, Creusa's exclamation, where φῶς signifies both the light of the Sun and the mortal child Ion:

ὦ τέκνον, ὦ φῶς μητρὶ κρεῖσσον ἡλίου

O son, o light dearer to a mother than that of the sun.
(Euripides *Ion* 1439)

While in Attic tragedy the use of the contracted form of φάος is the rule, we expect Parmenides to follow epic usage. He makes exceptions, though, for special effect, the most remarkable of which involves precisely φῶς as the contracted form of φάος.

Parmenides frag. 14 is a singleton that describes the moon:

νυκτιφαὲς περὶ γαῖαν ἀλώμενον ἀλλότριον φῶς

An alien light wandering darkly bright around the earth.[70]

Allotrion, "alien" or "foreign," refers to the fact that the moon produces no light of its own but reflects the light of the sun. "Alien light," therefore, is a correct literal translation of *allotrion phōs*. It fails to acknowledge, however, that the expression pointedly echoes the Homeric formula *allotrios phōs*, which signifies the stranger, as in Penelope's address to her son:

καί κέν τις φαίη γόνον ἔμμεναι ὀλβίου ἀνδρός,
ἐς μέγεθος καὶ κάλλος ὁρώμενος, ἀλλότριος φώς.

One who saw you, some outsider, viewing your size and beauty, would say you were the son born of a prosperous man.[71]

If the Homeric allusion has been recognized by modern commentators, we can be certain that it would not have escaped the audience Parmenides had in mind. Its effect is to characterize the light of the

---

69. So far as I know, only Eisler (1910, 388) translates εἰδότα φῶτα as "all-knowing lights."
70. Parmenides frag. 14; trans. Coxon 1986.
71. Homer *Odyssey* 18.218–19; trans. Lattimore 1965.

moon as alien to it and, at the same time, as a "stranger," an alien presence in the night.[72]

The phrase εἰδότα φῶτα is a comparable exercise in creative ambiguity. εἰδότα may be taken in two distinct but complementary meanings. As a singular qualifying φῶτα in the sense of "man" or "being," it refers to the Sun's capacity as *panoptēs*, "all-seeing," to know or, better, "witness" all that happens on earth.[73] For that reason, Helius is invoked as the witness par excellence, as he is by Lyssa in Euripides' *Heracles*:

Ἥλιον μαρτυρόμεσθα δρῶσ' ἃ δρᾶν οὐ βούλομαι.

I call the Sun to witness that what I am doing I do against my will![74]

Taken as a plural qualifying φῶτα in the sense of "lights," εἰδότα refers to the means by which the Sun sees. For his authority as witness depends on the rays, which reach all things. The Homeric hymn to Demeter makes this explicit. The goddess turns to Helius for help and says, "for you from the bright upper air look upon all things on earth and upon the sea with your rays."[75] What is impenetrable to his light, *phaos*, remains hidden from the Sun—the Cimmerians, for instance, who live under a blanket of fog and clouds (*Odyssey* 11.14–16). Accordingly, Zeus persuades Hera to lie with him in the open on Mount Ida with the following argument:

Ἥρη, μήτε θεῶν τό γε δείδιθι μήτε τιν' ἀνδρῶν
ὄψεσθαι· τοῖόν τοι ἐγὼ νέφος ἀμφικαλύψω

72. Coxon 1986, II, 245: "P.'s phrase ἀλλότριον φῶς is a play on Homer's ἐς μέγεθος καὶ κάλλος ὁρώμενος ἀλλότριος φώς (σ 219), prompted perhaps by the participle ἀλώμενον, since a vagabond is an alien; an ἀλλότριον φῶς is therefore a light not originating in the places through which it travels." See also Diels 1897, 110; Guthrie 1965, 66; Mourelatos 1970, 224–25.

73. Homer *Iliad* 3.277; Hesiod *Works and Days* 267–68; Aeschylus *Prometheus Bound* 91: τὸν πανόπτην κύκλον ἡλίου, "the all-seeing orb of the sun." With regard to Xenophanes frag. 34 D–K, Fränkel notes that the archaic use of *eidenai* fully retains the sense of "knowing by experience" through "having witnessed" something, as is well illustrated at *Iliad* 2.485, where to "know," *eidenai*, means to "be present," *pareinai*. See Fränkel 1968, 335–36; 1975, 342–45.

74. Euripides *Heracles* 858; trans. Kovacs 1998. See also Euripides *Suppliants* 260–61: θεούς τε καὶ γῆν τήν τε πυρφόρον θεὰν // Δήμητρα θέμεναι μάρτυρ' ἡλίου τε φῶς, "calling the gods, the earth, Demeter the torchbearer, and the light of the Sun to witness" (trans. Kovacs 1998).

75. *Homeric Hymns* 2.69–70; see also Hesiod *Theogony* 760.

χρύσεον· οὐδ᾽ ἂν νῶϊ διαδράκοι Ἡέλιός περ,
οὔ τε καὶ ὀξύτατον πέλεται φάος εἰσοράασθαι.

Hera, do not fear that any mortal or any god
will see, so close shall be the golden cloud that I gather
about us. Not even Helios can look at us through it,
although beyond all others his light [*phaos*] has the sharpest vision.[76]

The wordplay that φῶς allows enables the expression εἰδότα φῶτα
to signify both the Sun's power of vision, which resides in his rays,
and his role as quintessential witness. In the latter, absolute sense, one
should also understand the striking reference to sunrise in the Louvre
Partheneion (39–43):[77]

ἐγὼν δ᾽ ἀείδω
Ἀγιδῶς τὸ φῶς· ὁρῶ
ϝ᾽ ὥτ᾽ ἄλιον, ὅνπερ ἇμιν
Ἀγιδὼ μαρτύρεται
φαίνην.

I sing
the light of Agido. I see it
like the sun, whom
Agido summons to appear and
witness for us.

In the proem, the relative clause ἣ κατὰ πᾶν τατὴ φέρει εἰδότα
φῶτα (3)—at once "carries the rays that witness" and "carries the one
who knows"—specifies the sense in which the road belongs to the
daimōn:[78] it is the road he travels with his light. Hesiod's *Theogony*

76. Homer *Iliad* 14.342–45; trans. Lattimore 1951. See also Aeschylus *Prometheus Bound*
796–97: ἃς οὔθ᾽ ἥλιος προσδέρκεται ἀκτῖσιν οὔθ᾽ ἡ νύκτερος μήνη ποτέ, "neither does the sun with
his rays look down upon them, nor ever nocturnal moon."
77. See Page 1951, 84.
78. I follow Kranz 1916, 1159; Gigon 1968, 246–47; Cornford 1952, 118n1; Guthrie 1965, 7 in
identifying the *daimōn* with the Sun and in understanding *hodon* as the antecedent of the pro-
noun that follows. Burkert (1969, 7, 28) also wonders if the road in question is that of the Sun.
Note, however, that the majority of interpreters identify in the *daimōn* the Goddess. See, e.g.,

offers a comparable image in Day holding out to mortals "all-seeing light," φάος πολυδερκές, on the road that crosses the threshold of the Gates of Night and Day.[79] The reading κατὰ πᾶν τατή, which is the one transmitted in all the manuscripts,[80] substantially corresponds to Wilamowitz-Moellendorf's emendation κατὰ πάντα <τατή>.[81] Its sense, "stretched over the world," is an apt characterization of the road of heaven. It is the image of the road of the Sun that in Parmenides frag. 8 structures the metaphor of the way that alone leads to true knowledge—as one "along which are many signs"—with a phrase that evokes the familiar pair of *poros* and *tekmōr*.

Finally, in regard to the road of the Sun, the adjective *poluphēmos* has a particular charge. It occurs twice in Homer, where it unequivocally refers to sound—the "many-voiced" assembly at *Odyssey* 2.150, and Phemius, the singer "of many songs" at *Odyssey* 22.376.[82] Making the road one of "many songs," *poluphēmos*, together with the musical notation of the sound of pipes arising from the axle of the chariot, sets

Untersteiner 1958, lxi; Tarán 1965, 11; Gallop 1984, 49; Coxon 1986, 157; Conche 1996, 44–45; Cordero 2004, 26–27.

79. A comparable expression is used of Eos at Hesiod *Theogony* 451. The commentator of Alcman 5 *PMGF* may have had such an image in mind when he wrote "day not by itself but with the sun" (col. III 27–28); see p. 31–32 of the present text.

80. Coxon 1986 gives the following manuscript readings: πάντ᾽ ἅτη N, πάντάτη L, πάντα τῇ Eς. The erroneous reading πάντ᾽ ἅστη was widely regarded as the most acceptable until Coxon (1968) discovered that it appears in no manuscript; Lesher (1994) reproposes it as an emendation. Analyses of the many emendations that have been proposed may be found in Diels 1897, 48; Untersteiner 1958, lii–liiin4; Pelliccia 1988; Conche 1996, 44–45.

81. Wilamowitz-Moellendorf 1899, 203–4. τατός, "stretched," is applied to membranes in Aristotle *History of Animals* 519a32. There may be an allusion to the road of the Sun in a fragment of Empedocles, 135 D–K: ἀλλὰ τὸ μὲν πάντων νόμιμον διά τ᾽ εὐρυμέδοντος // αἰθέρος ἠνεκέως τέταται διά τ᾽ ἀπλέτου αὐγῆς, "but that which is lawful for all extends continuously through the broad-ruling Air and through the boundless Light." Trans. Freeman 1948. *Teinō* may be said literally of roads, as at Plato *Laws* 763c. For a metaphorical use of this image in reference to Eros, see Plato *Symposium* 186b1–2, ὡς μέγας καὶ θαυμαστὸς καὶ ἐπὶ πᾶν ὁ θεὸς τείνει. In philosophical texts, *to pān* means "the whole" in the sense of universe, world; see, e.g., Aristotle *On the Heavens* 268a10–11: καθάπερ γάρ φασι καὶ οἱ Πυθαγόρειοι, τὸ πᾶν καὶ τὰ πάντα τοῖς τρισὶν ὥρισται, "for, as the Pythagoreans say, the world and all that is in it are determined by the number three."

82. On this point, see Mourelatos 1970, 41. In Pindar *Isthmian* 8.58, *poluphāmos* is the dirge "of many voices."

off powerful reverberations. It is an allusion to the theory, possibly attributed to Pythagoras by this time,[83] that the movements of the heavenly bodies produce sounds that result in musical harmony. The allusion is not surprising. Parmenides' engagement with Pythagorean doctrine is attested by Sotion's testimony and by references to it in other fragments of the poem.[84]

Next in the proem (11–14) comes the arrival at the Gates of Night in a passage that obviously looks back on the following description in the *Theogony*:

καὶ Νυκτὸς ἐρεμνῆς οἰκία δεινὰ
ἕστηκεν νεφέλης κεκαλυμμένα κυανέῃσι.
τῶν πρόσθ' Ἰαπετοῖο πάις ἔχει οὐρανὸν εὐρὺν
ἑστηὼς κεφαλῇ τε καὶ ἀκαμάτῃσι χέρεσσιν
ἀστεμφέως, ὅθι Νύξ τε καὶ Ἡμέρη ἀμφὶς ἐοῦσαι
ἀλλήλας προσέειπον ἀμειβόμεναι μέγαν οὐδὸν
χάλκεον· ἡ μὲν ἔσω καταβήσεται, ἡ δὲ θύραζε
ἔρχεται, οὐδέ ποτ' ἀμφοτέρας δόμος ἐντὸς ἐέργει,
ἀλλ' αἰεὶ ἑτέρη γε δόμων ἔκτοσθεν ἐοῦσα
γαῖαν ἐπιστρέφεται, ἡ δ' αὖ δόμου ἐντὸς ἐοῦσα
μίμνει τὴν αὐτῆς ὥρην ὁδοῦ, ἔστ' ἂν ἵκηται·
ἡ μὲν ἐπιχθονίοισι φάος πολυδερκὲς ἔχουσα,
ἡ δ' Ὕπνον μετὰ χερσί, κασίγνητον Θανάτοιο.

There stands the awful home of murky Night wrapped in dark clouds. In front of it the son of Iapetus stands immovably upholding the wide heaven upon his head and unwearying hands, where Night and Day being on either side of it greet one another as they pass the great threshold of bronze: and while the one is about to go down into the house, the other comes out at the door. And the house never holds them both within; but always one is without the house passing over

83. Bowen (1982) points out that the analysis of how sound is produced in Archytas (frag. B1 D–K) is easily applied to the heavens.

84. Diogenes Laertius *Lives of the Philosophers* 9.21. On Parmenides' familiarity with Pythagorean philosophy, see Tarán 1965, 3, 201; Couloubaritsis 1986, 32–33; Coxon 1986, 11, 15–16, 38–39, 240–42; Cordero 2004, 9–10.

the earth, while the other stays at home and waits until the time for her journeying come; and the one holds all-seeing light for them on earth, but the other holds in her arms Sleep the brother of Death.[85]

While the *Odyssey* (24.11–14) speaks of the "Gates of the Sun," in the *Theogony* the gateway belongs to the House of Night, situated above the chasm that holds the Titans. The "House" of Night figures as well in Parmenides' proem, as the place from which the Heliads emerge (9), and is mentioned, as we shall see, also in the *Partheneion* (73). Since the two are never on the same side of the threshold, the journeys of Night and Day are distinct. Accordingly, they may be spoken of in the plural, *keleuthoi*. There is, however, only one road, the one that leads to the gate.[86] As their paths cross, Night and Day greet each other, moving in opposite directions. This image has caused some perplexity, because it is not easily reconciled with the idea that Night follows Day upon the same path, as Dawn, the Sun, and the Moon are envisioned doing on the monuments and vases mentioned earlier in this chapter. It has a parallel, however, in a passage of the *Odyssey* which describes the country of the Laestrygonians. That is the region near the paths, *keleuthoi*, of Night and Day, "where one herdsman, driving his flocks in hails another, who answers as he drives his flocks out,"[87] so that a man who could do without sleep could earn double wages. The vignette has a proverbial cast. The picture on the Sappho Painter's lekythos that was examined above, not far in date from Parmenides, seems to confirm that the notion of Night and Day trading places had wide currency.

Like Hesiod, Parmenides makes the point that Night and Day are never together on the same side of the threshold but alternate:

ἔνθα πύλαι νυκτός τε καὶ ἤματός εἰσι κελεύθων,
καί σφας ὑπέρθυρον ἀμφὶς ἔχει καὶ λάινος οὐδός,

85. Hesiod *Theogony* 744–56; trans. Evelyn-White 1936. The text is from West 1966, except for line 748, where I prefer the variant manuscript reading ἀμφὶς ἐοῦσαι because, as West notes, it was probably the one known to Parmenides (pp. 366–67). West considers lines 740–45 an interpolation (pp. 358, 365). Parmenides, however, later identifies the house of Night as the dwelling of Day and Night (frag. 1.32).

86. Deichgräber 1958, 667; Vos 1963, 21–22.

87. Homer *Odyssey* 10.82–86; trans. Lattimore 1965. See West 1966, 366.

αὐταὶ δ’ αἰθέριαι πλῆνται μεγάλοισι θυρέτροις·
τῶν δὲ δίκη πολύποινος ἔχει κληῖδας ἀμοιβούς.

There are the gates of the paths of Night and Day, whom lintel keeps
apart and threshold of stone. The gates themselves, reaching to the
sky, are blocked with great doors, of which much-punishing Justice
holds the alternating keys. (1.11–14 Coxon)

The phrase *amphis ekhei* (12) echoes *amphis eousai* at *Theogony* 748,
with the same meaning: the threshold marks the boundary that keeps
Night and Day apart.[88] A second specific allusion to the Hesiodic
passage is *amoibous* (14), which recalls *ameibomenai* at *Theogony* 749.
The same figure is implicit in both. The latter stresses that the figures
exchange one realm for the other by crossing the threshold. κληῖδας
ἀμοιβούς, "alternating keys," is a hypallage, which transfers what properly belongs to Night and Day—alternation—to the keys that open
and close the gates and so let the one in and the other out.[89]

Like the notion that the path of the sun, moon, and planets winds
its way through the signposts of the fixed stars, that of the gateway
through which the sun sets and rises is also well attested in Mesopotamian cosmology.[90] There occurs as well the figure of Justice at the
gate, but as the minister of Šamaš.[91] The task of opening the doors
of heaven belongs primarily to Šamaš himself and, in addition, to
the gods that are the other heavenly bodies.[92] It is noteworthy that
the Greek tradition, upon which Parmenides draws, places the keys
instead in the hands of Justice. It is she and not the Sun who enforces
the rules and threatens punishment. This capacity of Justice with

88. I understand σφας in reference to Νυκτός τε καὶ Ἥματός; see Ferrari Pinney and Ridgway 1981, 142.
89. Deichgräber (1958, 659) notes that *amoibous* can mean only the alternation of opening
and closing in regard to the exchange of Night and Day. For another instance of a transferred
epithet in Parmenides, see fragment 9.4, ἔργα τε κύκλωπος πεύσῃ περίφοιτα σελήνης ("and you
will learn of the migratory deeds of the round-faced moon," trans. Coxon 1986), where the
moon's capacity to move, or revolve, becomes an attribute of her "deeds."
90. Heimpel 1986, 132–40; Horowitz 1998, 266–67; correspondences with the proem of
Parmenides are noted in Burkert 1969, 10, 18; Steele 2002, 584–85.
91. Babylonian "Sunset Prayer"; see Heimpel 1986, 129; Steele 2002, 585–86.
92. Heimpel 1986, 140.

regard to the Sun himself is in evidence in a fragment of Heraclitus, with which these lines of Parmenides are frequently glossed:

Ἥλιος γὰρ οὐχ ὑπερβήσεται μέτρα· εἰ δὲ μή, Ἐρινύες μιν Δίκης
ἐπίκουροι ἐξευρήσουσιν.

The Sun will not transgress his measures; otherwise the Furies, ministers of Justice, will find him out.[93]

Burkert saw that in Parmenides, as in Heraclitus, Justice has the task of keeping Night and Day to the "measures," *metra*, of time allotted to each.[94] He cites a passage of Euripides' *Phoenician Women* that expands on the same point, where Jocasta tries to persuade Eteocles to share the throne with Polynices:

καὶ γὰρ μέτρ᾽ ἀνθρώποισι καὶ μέρη σταθμῶν
Ἰσότης ἔταξε κἀριθμὸν διώρισεν,
νυκτός τ᾽ ἀφεγγὲς βλέφαρον ἡλίου τε φῶς
ἴσον βαδίζει τὸν ἐνιαύσιον κύκλον,
κοὐδέτερον αὐτῶν φθόνον ἔχει νικώμενον.
εἶθ᾽ ἥλιος μὲν νύξ τε δουλεύει μέτροις,
σὺ δ᾽ οὐκ ἀνέξηι δωμάτων ἔχων ἴσον;
[καὶ τῶιδ᾽ ἀπονεῖμαι; κᾆτα ποῦ 'στιν ἡ δίκη;]

In fact, it is Equality that has established measures and weights for mankind and given them number. For Night's rayless eyelid walks an equal portion of the yearly round with the light of Day, and neither of them feels envy when bested. So then, when Sun and Night are subject to measures, will you, having an equal share of the house, refuse to accord it to this man? Where then is justice?[95]

93. Frag. 94 D–K (52 Marcovich), trans. Freeman 1948. See Kranz 1916, 160–61; Untersteiner 1958, lxxvi; Gigon 1968, 246; Conche 1996, 50, 206.

94. Burkert 1969, 10–11. Marcovich (2001, 275–76) understands *metra* in the sense of "spatial measures," "orbit."

95. Euripides *Phoenician Women* 541–48; trans. Kovacs 2002, modified. I print the text in Diggle 1994, which adopts Weil's emendation μέτροις at line 546 for the βροτοῖς of the manuscripts, while both Kovacs and Mastronarde (1994) retain βροτοῖς. Apart from the fact that the

Jocasta's speech holds out the "measures" that ensure the equitable alternation of night and day and the orderly succession of the seasons as the paradigm of the kind of fair apportionment that underpins an orderly society.[96] In the *Partheneion*, it is *aisa* that signifies the cosmic import of "measure." In conjunction with *poros*, the road of heaven, *aisa* has the marked sense of the time allotted to darkness and light, respectively, a set portion that was assigned forever at the moment of their primordial separation. The kind of violation that Heraclitus envisions would throw the universe back into chaos, as would any deviation of the stars from the established path. In mythical thought, that threat to the balance of nature is embodied in Phaethon, who for that reason is an ideal foil for the image of a harmonious universe, such as one finds in Alcman's *Partheneion* and Parmenides' proem. An allusion to Phaethon in the latter has long been recognized in the role assigned to his sisters, the Heliads.[97] The sisters, in one version of the story, yoked the chariot for the fatal ride, and at the end they famously mourned his death. In significant ways, the hero of the proem is cast as an anti-Phaethon.[98] He too is a *kouros*, a youth entering upon manhood, driving a chariot pulled by immortal mares at a gallop, on the road of the Sun. But he escapes Phaethon's tragic fate, because Law and Justice vouch for his legitimacy (1.26–28).

PHAETHON

In the *Partheneion* references to Phaethon, the exemplum of what calamity would ensue should the chariot of the Sun deviate from the prescribed path, follow on the heels of the mention of *poros* and *aisa* (15–19):

passage is all about fair apportionment, *douleuei* has such abject connotations of servitude as to rule out the possibility that it refers to the relationship of divine beings to mortals.

96. See Slatkin's characterization of this concept in Hesiod (2004, 47): "Due measure and right season are invested with an ethical dimension, most fully realized as the basis for the operations of Justice."

97. Bowra 1937, 103–4; Burkert 1969, 7.

98. Cordero 2004, 26: "Phaethon becomes a negative image of the Parmenidean traveler, whose journey does have those elements that were absent from the unfortunate child of the Sun's feckless dash: (1) the guarantee of right and justice . . . and (2) maiden guides who know the right direction."

ἀπ]έδιλος ἀλκά.

ἀν]θρώπων ἐς ὠρανὸν ποτήσθω

]ρήτω γαμῆν τὰν Ἀφροδίταν

Ϝ]άνασσαν ἤ τιν’

] ἤ παίδα . . . κω

Leaving aside, for the moment, the supplements that have been proposed for lines 16–17, I translate:

] unfettered might
] of mortals fly to the sky
] to marry Aphrodite
] mistress or some
] child . . .

The two imperatives at lines 16 and 17 have been interpreted in
terms of sententious moralizing, warning men not to overstep their
bounds. Page, for instance, translates: "The soaring valour of man
must [not] take wing to Heaven, [nor] try to marry Aphrodite,"
and Calame: ". . . la vaine résistance. (Qu'aucun) parmi les hommes
n'aspire au ciel, (qu'aucun) ne tente d'épouser Aphrodite."[99] But flying to the sky and marrying Aphrodite are disparate kinds of transgressions, and the logic according to which they are paired here is
not apparent. Moreover, while there are no tales of men assault-
ing Aphrodite, there are several of Aphrodite abducting or seduc-
ing mortals, namely, Anchises, Adonis, Phaon, and Phaethon. Like
Eos,[100] Aphrodite is predator, not prey, and both goddesses reverse
the familiar paradigm of male gods in pursuit of beautiful and re-
calcitrant youths and maidens.[101] When it comes to sexual matters,
Aphrodite is in charge, and she accounts as well for the mortal loves
of the gods. Phaethon's name does not appear in this extremely lacunose part of the text, but the allusion is as unmistakable as the

99. Page 1951, 21; Calame 1983, 270.

100. On the loves of Eos, see C. Weiss, *LIMC* 3 (1986): 758–79; Stewart 1995, 86. Nagy
(1990a, 246–54) stresses the parallelisms between Eos and Aphrodite.

101. As Wilamowitz-Moellendorf (1883, 441) remarked, mortals cannot marry Aphrodite;
at most it is she who does the marrying. On the mortal loves of Aphrodite and the structural
similarities of the stories of Phaethon, Phaon, and Adonis, see Nagy 1990a passim.

reference to Prometheus would be in the phrase "let no man steal fire or cheat the gods of their share." Only in the myth of Phaethon do flying to the sky and the prospect of marrying Aphrodite coexist.[102] Across variant tellings, the constant elements of the story are as follows. Phaethon is the son of Helius and an Oceanid (or a Nereid, or a nymph). Upon coming of age he claims the right to drive his father's fiery chariot across the sky. But he cannot control the Sun's horses, which veer off the established path and, coming too close to the earth, scorch it with fire. Zeus puts an end to this by striking Phaethon with a thunderbolt. Phaethon plummets into the Eridanus; on its bank, his mournful sisters are turned into black poplars, even now inconsolably weeping tears of amber. There exist two myths of his union with the goddess. In the *Theogony*, Phaethon is the child of Eos and Cephalus, whom Aphrodite carries off in the bloom of his youth to be the keeper of her temple:

αὐτάρ τοι Κεφάλῳ φιτύσατο φαίδιμον υἱόν,
ἴφθιμον Φαέθοντα, θεοῖς ἐπιείκελον ἄνδρα·
τόν ῥα νέον τέρεν ἄνθος ἔχοντ' ἐρικυδέος ἥβης
παῖδ' ἀταλὰ φρονέοντα φιλομμειδὴς Ἀφροδίτη
ὦρτ' ἀνερειψαμένη, καί μιν ζαθέοις ἐνὶ νηοῖς
νηοπόλον μύχιον ποιήσατο, δαίμονα δῖον.

Then to Cephalus she bore a splendid son, strong Phaethon, a man resembling the gods, whom, a boy in the tender bloom of glorious youth, his mind that of a child, laughter-loving Aphrodite seized and carried away. She made him the hidden steward in her divine temple, a divine spirit.

(986–91)

The Hesiodic corpus contains another reference to Phaethon. In a fragment of the *Catalogue of Women*, the so-called *gēs periodos*, the mentions of "amber" and "deep-flowing Eridanus" allude to the

102. Nagy (1990a, 235–55) brings to light the significance of Aphrodite's role in the story of Phaethon and the cosmological implications of this solar myth. Diggle (1970, 4–32) offers a complete survey of sources.

lament of the Heliads over Phaethon's body.[103] *Hēliades* was the title Aeschylus gave to his tragedy about Phaethon, and their myth has no existence outside that narrative. Substantial fragments survive of Euripides' *Phaethon*. There he is the son of Clymene, an Oceanid, and Helius. His impending marriage to Aphrodite is at center stage. Phaethon has been raised in Aethiopia, on the banks of Ocean and not far from the palace of Helius, as the son of Clymene and old King Merops. It is apparent that at the opening of the play (45–62) his mother has told him that his true father is Helius; she now urges him to go to the palace of the Sun and find out the truth of her claim. Phaethon wavers. His decision, it seems, depends on a meeting he will have with Merops. The conversation takes place against the background of preparations for Phaethon's wedding ceremony, which are in full swing. In the *parodos*, the chorus sings of the coming day, in anticipation of the festivities

> ἤδη μὲν ἀρτιφανὴς
> Ἀὼς ἱ[ππεύει] κατὰ γᾶν,
> ὑπὲρ δ᾽ ἐμᾶς κεφαλᾶς
> Πλειά[δων
> μέλπει δὲ δένδρεσι λεπτ-
> ὰν ἀηδὼν ἁρμονίαν
> ὀρθρευομένα γόοις
> Ἴτυν Ἴτυν πολύθρηνον.
> σύριγγας δ᾽ οὐριβάται
> κινοῦσιν ποιμνᾶν ἐλάται,
> ἔγρονται δ᾽ εἰς βοτάναν
> ξανθᾶν πώλων συζυγίαι·
> ἤδη δ᾽ εἰς ἔργα κυνα-
> γοὶ στείχουσιν θηροφόνοι,
> παγαῖς τ᾽ ἐπ᾽ Ὠκεανοῦ
> μελιβόας κύκνος ἀχεῖ.

103. Frag. 150 Merkelbach and West. Diggle (1970, 10–27), attempting to discredit every source which attests that Hesiod knew the Phaethon story, emphasizes the fact that Phaethon's name does not appear in this very fragmentary text. But in this context (a description of the lands over which the Boreads fly in pursuit of the Harpies) one hardly expects the full narrative.

Already Dawn courses over the earth, above our heads the Pleiades
[. . .] and in the trees the nightingale sings her tremulous melody,
mourning at daybreak Itys, Itys much lamented. On the mountains,
shepherds rouse their flock at the sound of the Pan-pipe, pairs of
tawny colts awake to the pasture. Already the hunters, killers of wild
beasts, set out on their pursuits and on the streams of Ocean the
sweet-singing swan wails.[104]

This aubade is laced with dark forebodings.[105] In itself, the space
allotted to the description of dawn breaking draws out the tension
between the chorus's expectation of a day like any other and what the
audience knows is to come. At daybreak, the Pleiades are still visible
overhead, the nightingale sings, men begin to stir, and on the streams
of Ocean the swan utters its cry (63–78).[106] Many have remarked that
the song of the nightingale, a mother mournfully calling her dead son's
name, prefigures Clymene's sorrow.[107] The image of the swan is directly relevant to the present inquiry because it recalls the last surviving lines of the *Partheneion* (100–101):[108] ἐπὶ Ξάνθω ῥοαῖσι // κύκνος,
"on the streams of Xanthus the swan." In Hellenistic and Roman tradition, both literary and visual, we find the swan firmly entrenched in
the Phaethon myth.[109] In Ovid's *Metamorphoses* (2.367–80) Cycnus,
king of the Lygurians, appears in the final scene. He is a kinsman

104. Euripides *Phaethon* 63–78. Numeration and text cited after Diggle 1970, with slight
emendations as discussed below.

105. Reckford 1972, 428n25. Webster (1967, 222–23) and Diggle (1970, 100–104) read no
more into this passage than notations of natural phenomena that signal dawn. Note that the
swan's song is absent from the comparable description of daybreak in the *Rhesus* 528–35.

106. Mention of the Pleiades following the expression "above our heads," ὑπὲρ δ' ἐμᾶς
κεφαλᾶς, at Euripides *Phaethon* 65 suggests that, as at *Rhesus* 529–30 (ἑπτάποροι Πλειάδες
αἰθέριαι ["in their seven paths the Pleiades high in the sky"]), the Pleiades are still visible. This
argues against Diggle's supplement in the line that follows (Πλειά[δων πέφευγε χορός]). The
notations of dawn listed here find partial but significant correspondences in those given in
the *Partheneion*; see p. 100 of the present text.

107. Diggle (1970, 100–101) reminds us that the first to do so was Goethe. See Volmer
1930, 29.

108. See Diggle 1970, 103–4.

109. The earliest extant source seems to be Phanocles frag. 6 Powell. Pausanias (1.30.3)
mentions the metamorphosis of Cycnus into the swan by Apollo, with no reference to Phaethon.
The swan is a fixture of the representation of the fall of Phaethon on Roman sarcophagi; see
LIMC 7 (1994), s.v. "Phaethon" nos. 9, 11, 12, 14–19.

of Phaethon on his mother's side and dear to him, who mourns his death until he turns into the swan. Philostratus the Elder, in the ecphrasis of a painting of the fall of Phaethon, projects the role that the swans of the Eridanus will have in perpetuating the myth:

> For swans scattered about, breathing sweet notes, will hymn the youth; and flocks of swans rising aloft will sing the story to [the rivers] Caÿster and Ister; nor will any place fail to hear the strange story. And they will have Zephyrus, nimble god of wayside shrines, to accompany their song, for it is said that Zephyrus has made a compact with the swans to join them in the music of the dirge.[110]

It is impossible to say whether or not Cycnus had a place in the archaic versions of the legend. Given the fragmentary nature of our sources for that period, an argument from silence is no argument at all against the possibility that it did and that, in the *Partheneion* as in the *Phaethon*, the swan's song is more than a cliché.

The middle of the play is largely lost, leaving us uncertain as to precisely how the action developed after the conversation between mother and son and what determined Phaethon's decision to go to Helius. There remains, however, evidence of a clash between Phaethon and Merops, which may have to do with succession to the kingship and certainly has to do with the marriage. It is clear that Phaethon's wedding is not at the planning stage, but being carried out. The chorus states that "the day is marked for the fulfillment of the marriage" (95) and proclaims, "let there go forth the fulfillment song of marriage" (101). The herald who follows them calls the people to assembly and solemnly announces Merops, stating, "father and son decreeing that marriage shall come to pass upon this day" (116–18). That father and son are in agreement, however, is belied by unconnected fragments of the heated exchange between Merops and Phaethon that follow at some distance:

> (Φα.) ἐλεύθερος δ' ὢν δοῦλός ἐστι τοῦ λέχους,
> πεπραμένον τὸ σῶμα τῆς φερνῆς ἔχων.
> (Μερ.) ἐν τοῖσι μώροις τοῦτ' ἐγὼ κρίνω βροτῶν,

---

110. Philostratus *Imagines* 1.11.2–4; trans. Fairbanks 1931.

ὅστις πατρῷα παισὶ μὴ φρονοῦσιν εὖ
ἢ καὶ πολίταις παραδίδωσ' ἐξουσίαν.
(Φα.) ὡς πανταχοῦ γε πατρὶς ἡ βόσκουσα γῆ.

(*Pha.*) A free man is the slave of the marriage bed,
once he has sold his body for the dowry.
(*Mer.*) This I number among the follies of mankind,
for a man to surrender a father's authority to sons
who are incapable of reason, or power to the citizens.
(*Pha.*) Any land that offers nourishment is a homeland.

(158–63)

It is apparent that Merops has imposed this marriage on Phaethon
and that the latter rebels. When Merops insists on exercising his pa-
rental authority, which is somehow linked to his hold on the throne,
old as he is, Phaethon contemplates finding another homeland. The
plot turns on Phaethon's fatal choice: he can either stay and obey his
father, consenting to a marriage that he finds repugnant; or he can go
and find his other father by subjecting himself to a crucial test that
will establish whether or not he is Helius's true son.[111] The choice
had been laid out at the start of the play, with Phaethon's reply to his
mother's request that he go to the palace of the Sun:

ὅταν δ' ὕπνον γεραιὸς ἐκλιπὼν πατὴρ
πύλας ἀμείψηι καὶ λόγους γάμων πέρι
λέξηι πρὸς ἡμᾶς, Ἡλίου μολὼν δόμους
τοὺς σοὺς ἐλέγξω, μῆτερ, εἰ σαφεῖς λόγοι.

should my venerable father arising from his slumber
come outdoors and speak to me of marriage,
then I shall go to Helius's palace
and I shall find out, mother, if what you say is true.

(59–62)[112]

111. Diggle (1970, 39–40, 159–60) imagines that, feigning acquiescence to Merops's plans,
Phaethon then departs for the palace of Helius, ostensibly in search of his bride.
112. Lesky (1932, 8–9; followed by Diggle 1970, 93–94 and Webster 1967, 222) argued that
ὅταν (59) here is used in a purely chronological sense, as though Phaethon were keeping an

Debate over the identity of Phaethon's bride has centered on a scene near the end of the play. Phaethon's body has been brought to the palace and is presumably onstage. Clymene mourns; then, seeing Merops approaching with a chorus of maidens, she locks the corpse in her husband's treasure-house and departs, denouncing Helius-Apollo (214–26). The chorus sings a formal epithalamium hymning Aphrodite and her "newly-yoked colt," whom she hides in the sky in her starlike palace.[113]

Ὑμὴν Ὑμήν.
τὰν Διὸς οὐρανίαν ἀείδομεν,
τὰν ἐρώτων πότνιαν, τὰν παρθένοις
γαμήλιον Ἀφροδίταν.   230
πότνια, σοὶ τάδ' ἐγὼ νυμφεῖ' ἀείδω,
Κύπρι θεῶν καλλίστα,
τῶι τε νεόζυγι σῶι
πώλωι τὸν ἐν αἰθέρι κρύπτεις,
σῶν γάμων γένναν·   235

ἃ τὸν μέγαν
τᾶσδε πόλεως βασιλῆ νυμφεύεται
ἀστερωποῖσιν δόμοισι χρυσέων
ἀρχὸν φίλον Ἀφροδίτα·
ὢ μακάρων βασιλεὺς μείζων ἔτ' ὄλβον,   240
ὃς θεὰν κηδεύσεις
καὶ μόνος ἀθανάτων
γαμβρὸς δι' ἀπείρονα γαῖαν
θνατὸς ὑμνήσηι.

---

appointment: not *if*, but *when* his father awakes and speaks to him about his wedding, Phaethon will go to the palace of Helius. In view of Phaethon's vehement rejection of his father's marriage plans for him, however, one obtains a much stronger sense by taking this as a conditional clause. ὅταν normally has conditional force (LSJ, s.v.); for a parallel construction in Euripides, in which ὅταν and ἐὰν are used as equivalent terms, see *Iphigenia in Aulis* 928–29: καὶ τοῖς Ἀτρείδαις, ἢν μὲν ἡγῶνται καλῶς, πεισόμεθ', ὅταν δὲ μὴ καλῶς, οὐ πείσομαι.

113. I retain the following readings from the original papyrus, νυμφεύεται (237), χρυσέων (238), μακάρων (240).

Hymen, Hymen! We sing the heavenly daughter of Zeus, the mistress of loves, Aphrodite, who brings nuptials to maidens. (230) Mistress, for you I sing this wedding song, Kypris, the most beautiful of the gods, and for your newly yoked colt, whom you hide in the sky, the offspring of the union that you inspired. (235) The great king of this city Aphrodite weds, to be the beloved master of the gold in her star-faced palace. O king greater in happiness than the blessed ones (240), you will forge a familial bond with the goddess and alone of mortals will be hymned all over boundless earth as kin of the immortals.

Wilamowitz-Moellendorf saw that Phaethon's bride can be no one but Aphrodite.[114] The bride is a goddess, being called *thea* twice (24, 241), and the only goddess named with regard to this wedding is Aphrodite. But for her, the sole mention of the bride in the epithalamium would be the incidental θεάν at line 241.[115] The only obstacle to this identification is that the chorus's address to her refers to the bridegroom as σῶν γάμων γένναν (235), "born of your union." The genitive has invariably been understood as possessive and translated as "the offspring of your marriage" in the sense of "your own son." This would rule out the possibility that "newly-yoked colt" refers to Phaethon. We then must either identify a different and equally unfortunate bridegroom, a son of Aphrodite hidden in the sky, or envision that the chorus with these words addresses Merops—an awkward solution.[116] But a different reading is possible in light of the role that

114. Wilamowitz-Moellendorf 1883, 411–15. Diggle (1970, 155–60) offers an extensive refutation of the argument; he endorses instead a thought briefly entertained by Weil (1889, 327), that Phaethon's elusive bride is one of the Heliads. The difficulty with this hypothesis is not, or not only, that the Heliads are Phaethon's sisters or half-sisters, or that evidence of such a marriage is entirely lacking (as Diggle acknowledges), but that, like Phaethon, the Heliads are as mortal or immortal as he is—not an indifferent point in this play. The conceit of a formal marriage between a god and a mortal is not unique, as Diggle claims; see Carson 1982 on Pindar, *Pythian* 9 (the wedding of Apollo and Cyrene); and Oakley and Sinos 1993, 35–36 (the wedding of Heracles and Hebe).

115. Huddleston (1980, 116; emphasis hers) observes that "a marriage song sung *for* anyone other than the bride or groom is unknown in Greek literature."

116. Diggle (1970, 151) revives the hypothesis of Weil (1889, 324–26) that the "newly-yoked colt" is Hymenaeus, in spite of the fact that the latter is, by most accounts, the son of Apollo

Aphrodite plays in all unions, be they mortal or divine. She is, as the chorus says (230), *gamēlion*, "nuptial." In particular, she is responsible for the mortal loves of the gods—something that the Homeric hymn to Aphrodite strongly emphasizes. Zeus inspired her desire for Anchises:

καί ποτ᾽ ἐπευξαμένη εἴπῃ μετὰ πᾶσι θεοῖσιν
ἡδὺ γελοιήσασα φιλομμειδὴς Ἀφροδίτη
ὥς ῥα θεοὺς συνέμιξε καταθνητῇσι γυναιξὶ
καί τε καταθνητοὺς υἱεῖς τέκον ἀθανάτοισιν,
ὥς τε θεὰς ἀνέμιξε καταθνητοῖς ἀνθρώποις.

Lest laughter-loving Aphrodite should one day softly smile and say mockingly among all the gods that she had joined the gods in love with mortal women who bare sons of death to the deathless gods, and had mated the goddesses with mortal men.[117]

Earth herself bore Typhoeus "through" golden Aphrodite in "loving" intercourse with Tartarus.[118] In Euripides' *Hippolytus* 448–50, Phaedra's nurse explains to another young man who rejects Aphrodite: "everything is generated by her, she is the one who sows [*speirousa*] and gives desire, from which all of us on earth exist."[119] Here too the "sowing," something that in intercourse is a function of the male, is attributed to the goddess. In this sense, all unions that involve *himeros* and *philotēs*, love and desire, are Aphrodite's *gamoi*. And, just as rapes may be called *Pānos gamoi*, the "marriages of Pan," intercourses driven by lust are "the unholy marriages [*gamous*] of lawless Aphrodite."[120] Grammatically, the difficulty is easily resolved by understanding the σῶν in σῶν γάμων as an objective genitive, "the

---

and one of the Muses, and that there is no trace of a story in which he was translated to the sky. Wilamowitz-Moellendorf (1883, 414–15) proposed that, in a switch of addressee, σῶι πώλωι and σῶν γάμων are directed at Merops.

117. *Homeric Hymns* 5.48–52; trans. Evelyn-White 1936.

118. Hesiod *Theogony* 821–22: ὁπλότατον τέκε παῖδα Τυφωέα Γαῖα πελώρη // Ταρτάρου ἐν φιλότητι διὰ χρυσῆν Ἀφροδίτην.

119. Ebbott 2003, 92: "Hippolytos's rejection of Aphrodite is a rejection of sexual reproduction."

120. Euripides *Helen* 190; *Ion* 1092–93: γάμους // Κύπριδος ἀθέμιτος ἀνοσίους. See also *Ion* 887–88.

union you inspired"—that is, the lovemaking of Helius and Clymene, which produced Phaethon and over which, of course, Aphrodite presided. The fact that she is the bride also explains why neither Merops nor the chorus wonders where the newlyweds are. Merops assumes that Phaethon has gone from his palace to the precinct of the goddess.[121]

In this scene Euripides deploys the familiar trope of death as a marriage by evoking the pageantry of the wedding, specifically, the choral dance that was performed in front of the bridal chamber after the newlyweds had entered it and its doors were locked.[122] The chorus approaches just after Clymene has locked Phaethon's body in the treasure-house. Clymene's pointed choice of words on the one hand alludes to the traditional marriage ceremony and on the other anticipates some extraordinary features of Phaethon's marriage that the chorus will mention:

κρύψω δέ νιν
ξεστοῖσι θαλάμοις, ἔνθ' ἐμῶι κεῖται πόσει
χρυσός, μόνη δὲ κλῆιθρ' ἐγὼ σφραγίζομαι.

I shall hide him
in the shiny chambers, where my husband's gold
lies, but I alone seal the doors.

(221–23)

The function of the word *thalamoi* is pivotal, since its semantic range extends from inner room to bridal chamber and, metaphorically, tomb. Here the meaning oscillates between the latter two. Like a tomb, the *thalamoi* hold the corpse of Phaethon; like those of a bridal chamber, these doors are sealed. In front of the closed doors, as one does at a wedding, the chorus sings the epithalamium. Aphrodite

---

121. Euripides *Phaethon* 251: θεᾶς προσελθεῖν τέμενος ἐξ ἐμῶν δόμων; see Wilamowitz-Moellendorf 1883, 413.

122. On this stage of the wedding and its attendant imagery, see Oakley and Sinos 1993, 35–37. Phaethon's end mirrors the popular metaphor that casts the death of a maiden of marriageable age as a wedding in Hades or to Hades himself; on this trope, see Ferrari 2004, 255–60.

"hides" (κρύπτεις, 234) Phaethon in the sky, while Clymene "hides" (κρύψω, 231) him in the chamber. There, he oversees Merops's "gold" (χρυσός, 223), while, as Aphrodite's consort, he is "master of the gold" (χρυσέων, 238).[123]

These figures of confinement, enclosure, and concealment establish an unequivocal link between this Phaethon and Phaethon the son of Eos, whom Aphrodite abducts in the *Theogony*. The latter is also hidden, *mukhios*, "innermost," invisible, and he too oversees the goddess's riches as the "steward" of her temple.[124] The scholium to *Theogony* 990 explains why in the *Phaethon* the youth may be said to be hidden in the sky, in the stellar palace of Aphrodite, by glossing ζαθέοις ἐνὶ νηοῖς as follows: "the morning star who brings the day and Phaethon is Aphrodite." As Wilamowitz-Moellendorf argued and later, on different grounds, Nagy, we have not two different Phaethons but one and the same, whose legend is part of a cosmological construct in which he becomes Eosphorus.[125] That it is mentioned in the *Partheneion* further confirms that Phaethon's union with Aphrodite, by which he disappears, is not an invention of Euripides, although the conceit of a formal wedding may be.

There are substantial similarities between the legend of Phaethon and that of Hippolytus in Euripides' plays.[126] Each is beautiful and willful in his youth, each unjustly, albeit in different ways, forced into exile by his father. Both die in horrific chariot crashes. Like Phaethon, Hippolytus openly loathes Aphrodite and defies her. The two share another trait, which matters with regard to the *Partheneion* because it also establishes a thematic link between the myth of Phaethon and that of Hippocoon: they are the illegitimate children of powerful fathers. Phaethon is a "divine *daimōn*" (*Theogony* 991). As we learn from Socrates in Plato's *Apology*, *daimōn* is also a name for the illegitimate

123. Wilamowitz-Moellendorf (1883, 415) and Huddleston (1980, 117) point to the tragic irony of this juxtaposition.

124. In such a capacity Ion served his father Apollo at Delphi in Euripides' *Ion* 53–56: "guardian of the gold," χρυσοφύλακα, a trusted steward, ταμίαν τε πάντων πιστόν.

125. Nagy 1990a, 258–59.

126. For a comparison of the two myths, see Reckford 1972 and Goh 2004, chap. 3.

(*nothoi*) children of a god and a nymph or some other mortal, comparable to mules, which are the offspring of a horse and an ass.[127] Although they appear strong and beautiful—and Hesiod does call Phaethon "splendid," *phaidimos* (*Theogony* 986)—the fact that they cannot attain adult status and perform their fathers' function reveals their inadequacy and the falsity of their claim.[128] Accordingly, the *nothos* is cast back into the secrecy that surrounded his birth, becoming, in Phaethon's case, hidden and *mukhios* (*Theogony* 991), a creature of interior spaces, out of the sunlight.[129]

If we now return to lines 13–19 of the *Partheneion* with the foregoing analysis in mind, it will be apparent that the moralizing reflections they offer are entirely appropriate to the myth of Phaethon, and indirectly relevant as well to that of Hippocoon. The mention of *poros* and *aisa* in the gnome is highly relevant, since it was the youth's inability to follow the "path" of the Sun and thus keep to the "measure" of the day that resulted in disaster.[130] The section of Euripides' play that narrated the Sun's chariot's derangement from the path is mostly missing. A few lines remain, however, in which Helius instructs his son, and these lines explicitly mention the course and the *tekmōr*, the fixed point toward which he must aim: ἵει δ' ἐφ' ἑπτὰ Πλειάδων ἔχων δρόμον (171), "go keeping the course that leads to the seven Pleiades."[131] In this scenario, the mention of ἀπ]έδιλος ἀλκά at line 15 can be explained in reference to the horses of the Sun, whose "might" Phaethon was unable to control. ἀπέδιλος, "unsandaled," may convey the idea

---

127. Plato *Apology* 27d8–10; see Ebbott 2003, 73–74. Stesichorus frag. S17 *PMGF* offers a glimpse of the Sun's legitimate family, to which he returns after a day's work, back to his mother Night, his wedded wife, and his beloved children.

128. On the metaphor contrasting *nothoi* with *gnēsioi*, legitimate children, in terms of counterfeit versus genuine coins, see Ebbott 2003, 95–105.

129. See pp. 25–26, 63 of the present text and, on this sense of *mukhios*, Ebbott 2003, 25.

130. The idea is conveyed in the ecphrasis of the fall of Phaethon by Philostratus the Elder, *Imagines* 1.11.2: "At his fall the heavens are confounded. Look! Night is driving Day from the noonday sky, and the sun's orb as it plunges toward the earth draws in its train the stars. The Horae abandon their posts at the gates and flee toward the gloom that rises to meet them." Trans. Fairbanks 1931.

131. The Hyades too may have been mentioned here; see scholium to Aratus *Phaenomena* 172; Diggle 1970, 70, 176.

that the horses of the Sun are unshod because they tread on air, not the ground.[132] It is possible, however, that this rare adjective here plays on its etymology from *pedē*, "shackle" or "fetter." In the sense of "unfettered might," the phrase refers to the fateful moment at which, unbidden, the Heliads released the divine horses from their constraints and yoked them to the chariot.[133] Finally, Phaethon's presumption that a *nothos* is his father's true son is no less misguided than his belief that he can escape Aphrodite's desire—something not even the immortals can do. Accordingly, a restoration of lines 16–17 of the *Partheneion* might read:[134]

μή τις ἀν]θρώπων ἐς ὡρανὸν ποτήσθω
μηδ' ὑποτ]ρήτω γαμῆν τὰν Ἀφροδίταν.

Let no] mortal fly to the sky
nor flee from] marrying Aphrodite.

If all this is correct, the first three stanzas of the poem dealt in some fashion with the myth of Phaethon, before turning to the slaughter of the Hippocoontids. There is in Alcman's corpus a line that describes Phaethon's fall into the Eridanos:

χέρρονδε κωφὸν ἐν φύκεσσι πίτνει.

he falls upon the insensible shore among the sedge.[135]

132. Page (1951, 34–35) indeed took the adjective to signify "conveyed through the air." See D. A. Campbell 1987, 67–69 for a detailed analysis of this phrase.

133. Hyginus *Fabulae* 152 A; for the image of divine horses in golden fetters, see Homer *Iliad* 13.36–37. A second occurrence of *apedilos*, also in conjunction with an airborne chariot, at Aeschylus *Prometheus Bound* 135, σύθην δ' ἀπέδιλος ὄχῳ πτερωτῷ, may be understood in the same sense, as a transferred epithet: "unfettered I hastened in a winged chariot."

134. ὑποτρέω, rare outside Homer, normally takes an accusative object (LSJ, s.v.), but the construction with the infinitive is normal for verbs indicating a will not to do something; see Smyth 1956, 443. Webster (1967, 228) perceived the echo of these lines of Alcman at *Phaethon* 227–35.

135. 14c *PMGF* (= 6 Calame). It is debated whether the verse is an iambic catalectic trimeter or prosodiac + reizianum; see Pretagostini 1977, 72–74 and Dale 1969, 178. In scansion it is not incompatible with that of Alcman 5 *PMGF* (= 81e Calame), ἆμαρ τε καὶ σελάνα καὶ τρίτον σκότος; see Calame 1983, 221.

The verse is metrically inappropriate to the *Partheneion*, but suitable to the little that remains of Alcman 5 *PMGF*, the "cosmogony" discussed earlier in this chapter, where *poros* appears again, together with *tekmōr*, and so possibly also the legend of Phaethon. In other ways, the theme of the order of the cosmos, which depends on the Sun's strict observance of *poros* and *aisa*, runs through the *Partheneion*, which contains at least three more allusions to the tragedy of Phaethon.

2
THE CHORUS

Stars around the beautiful moon
hide back their luminous form
whenever all full she shines
on the earth

silvery.

The Travails of the Chorus

The first stanza of the second half of the *Partheneion* opens with a moralizing reflection that suits any and all of the paradigms of misguided ambition that are the subject of the first part:

> ἔστι τις σιῶν τίσις·
> ὁ δ' ὄλβιος ὅστις εὔφρων
> ἀμέραν [δι]απλέκει
> ἄκλαυστος.

> There is such a thing as retribution from the gods.
> Happy is he who, sound of mind,
> weaves through the day
> unwept.

(36–39)

In the sixty-one lines that follow, the chorus sings of itself in the first person, states its identity, describes its actions, and maps its relationship to three other female characters: Agido, Hagesichora, and Aenesimbrota. The singers are maidens, who issue piercing cries in vain, like owls; they are engaged in *ponoi*, "toils," to which the goddess of dawn, Aotis, will put an end:

> ἐγὼν μὲν αὐτά
> παρσένος μάταν ἀπ' [ὠ]ρανῶ λέλακα
> γλαύξ· ἐγὼν δὲ τᾶι μὲν Ἀώτι μάλιστα
> ϝανδάνην ἐρῶ, πόνων γὰρ
> ἄμιν ἰάτωρ ἔγεντο·

Epigraph. Sappho frag. 34 Voigt; trans. Carson 2002.

ἐξ Ἀγησίχορας, δὲ νεάνιδες
ἰρ]άνας ἐρατᾶς ἐπέβαν.

> I would say I myself
> a maiden wail in vain from the sky,
> an owl. But most of all I long
> to please Aotis for she is ever
> the healer of our labors.
> Away from Hagesichora, maidens
> enter upon delightful peace.

(85–91)

The stage is set just before sunrise:

ἐγὼν δ᾽ ἀείδω
Ἀγιδῶς τὸ φῶς· ὁρῶ
ϝ᾽ ὥτ᾽ ἄλιον, ὄνπερ ἄμιν
Ἀγιδὼ μαρτύρεται
φαίνην.

> I sing
> the light of Agido. I see it
> like the sun, whom
> Agido summons to appear and
> witness for us.

(39–43)

The notation of dawn is given once more at line 61, where the chorus describes its performance as occurring when the Pleiades are visible in the sky at daybreak, *orthriai*.

The passage just cited is also the beginning of an elaborate description of the beauty of three characters, who are not necessarily part of the chorus dancing onstage, moving from Agido to the *khorāgos*, "mistress of the chorus," to Hagesichora. Although the three are contrasted with one another, they are not compared in the sense of being ranked, one above the other. The chorus honors with its song the "light" of Agido, but the *khorāgos* denies it the authority to proclaim Agido superior, because the *khorāgos* is herself "preeminent":

ἐμὲ δ' οὔτ' ἐπαινῆν
οὔτε μωμήσθαι νιν ἀ κλεννὰ χοραγός
οὐδ' ἁμῶς ἐῆι.

But the glorious chorus mistress
forbids me to either praise
or blame her.

(43–45)

The descriptions of these three beauties are couched in terms of features that characterize three kinds of horses. The *khorāgos* resembles a powerful steed, which, in turn, is a dream:

δοκεῖ γὰρ ἤμεν αὐτά
ἐκπρεπὴς τὼς ὥπερ αἴ τις
ἐν βοτοῖς στάσειεν ἵππον
παγὸν ἀεθλοφόρον καναχάποδα
τῶν ὑποπετριδίων ὀνείρων.

ἦ οὐχ ὁρῆις;

For she appears to be
outstanding as if
    one placed among a grazing herd
a perfect horse, a prizewinner with resounding hooves,
    one of the dreams that dwell below the rock.

Don't you see?

(45–50)

This vision, then, is qualified as an "Enetic" courser, and in this respect compared to Hagesichora, although she is at first cast in human form:

ὁ μὲν κέλης
Ἐνητικός, ἁ δὲ χαίτα
τᾶς ἐμᾶς ἀνεψιᾶς
Ἀγησιχόρας ἐπανθεῖ
χρυσὸς ὡς ἀκήρατος.

τό τ' ἀργύριον πρόσωπον,
διαφάδαν τί τοι λέγω;
Ἀγησιχόρα μὲν αὕτα·

That one is an Enetic
courser, while the mane
of my cousin
Hagesichora shines forth
like unalloyed gold.
Her face is silver,
Why do I tell you explicitly?
There is Hagesichora herself.

(50–57)

Next, Agido and Hagesichora are likened to horses, which run one
after the other:

ἁ δὲ δευτέρα πεδ' Ἀγιδὼ τὸ ϝεῖδος
ἵππος Ἰβηνῶι Κολαξαῖος δραμήται.

Next will run Agido, her appearance
that of a Colaxian horse following an Ibenian.[1]

(58–59)

1. I follow Garzya (1954, 51–52) and Calame (1983, 330) in taking ἁ δευτέρα in apposition to Agido, who is the subject, and πεδ' as the product of tmesis from δραμήται, yielding the sense "run after." But I understand δευτέρα strictly in a temporal sense, to mean
that Agido follows Hagesichora and is therefore "next," and I read τὸ ϝεῖδος in its unmarked meaning of "appearance" in reference to the figure of the Colaxian horse. For
a discussion of these vexed lines, see D. A. Campbell 1987, 69–71. It would be odd if
the chorus here proclaimed Agido (or Hagesichora) the winner in a beauty contest, after it has declared itself unable to apportion either praise or blame (9–11). See also West
1965, 197.

The precise meaning of this set of comparisons remains elusive in the nearly total absence of information about the attributes and respective merits of Enetic, Colaxian, and Ibenian horses.² Close attention to internal clues, however, may bring the interlocking metaphors in this passage into sharper focus. The first horse is identified in two strikingly different ways: as a dream and as an Enetic courser. There exist two interpretations of the phrase τῶν ὑποπετριδίων ὀνείρων, a partitive genitive that identifies the horse as belonging to a specific group. There is no good reason to look past a literal reading and resist the idea that this is the herd of the *oneiroi*, the divine bearers of dream visions.³ For Hesiod *Theogony* 212, they are likewise a collectivity, *phūlon*, a race. One of the scholia to the *Partheneion* links ὑποπετριδίων to the idea that the *oneiroi* dwell under a rock. The epithet may refer not to a cave but to the topography of the "land of dreams," which Homer (*Odyssey* 24.11–12, cited by the scholium) locates near the entrance to Hades, past the White Rock and the gates of the Sun.⁴ There is one instance in which the *oneiroi* are said to feed like a herd: in Moschus's *Europa*, the princess falls asleep at dawn, when "the race of true dreams is led to pasture."⁵ Page championed the other view, now prevalent, that the beautiful horse is not an *oneiros* but the horse of your dreams.⁶ The proper term for such a vision, the figure that an *oneiros* conjures up, is actually *enupnion*, but it is true that in post-Homeric Greek *oneiros* may mean either the dream itself or what it

2. The *Kolaxaios* horse is generally identified as Scythian, because the name resembles that of the first Scythian king, Colaxaïs (Herodotus 4.5, 4.7); in reference to horses, see Devereux 1965. Diels (1896, 358–59) first proposed that *Ibēnos* means "Lydian" on the basis of an entry in the geographical dictionary of Stephanus of Byzantium (s.v. *Ibaioi hoi kai Ibēnoi*), in which Ibenoi are said to be both Lydian and Ionian.
3. G. Türk in *ML* 3.1 (1897–1902): 902, s.v. "Oneiros."
4. Scholium A 9. Hinge (2006, 278) notes that the suffix -ίδιος is used of places. Nagy (1990a, esp. 223–34) persuasively explains the meaning of the White Rock: "the White Rock is the boundary delimiting the conscious and the unconscious—be it a trance, stupor, sleep, or even death. Accordingly, when the Suitors are led past the White Rock (*Odyssey* xxiv 11), they reach the *dêmos oneirōn* 'District of Dreams' (xxiv 12) beyond which is the realm of the dead (xxiv 14)" (234).
5. Moschus *Europa* 5: εὖτε καὶ ἀτρεκέων ποιμαίνεται ἔθνος ὀνείρων. It is possible, though, that the figure here is used metaphorically, as at Aeschylus *Eumenides* 196–97, where the Furies are a flock that grazes. See M. Campbell 1991.
6. Page 1951, 85–87; followed by Calame 1977, 2:267, 1983, 327.

bears. This interpretation requires taking ὑποπετριδίων as a metathesis for ὑποπτεριδίων, meaning "winged," and postulating an otherwise unattested class of dream visions consisting entirely of horses. In either case, whether it is an *oneiros* or a "winged dream-horse," ours is an imaginary horse, not the kind that mortals breed and ride.[7] The phrase ἐν βοτοῖς, "among a grazing herd," leaves unspecified what kind of herd this is. The word, however, does highlight the specific respect in which the horse dream differs. *Botoi* are beasts that are pastured, the word retaining the full force of *boskō*, meaning "graze."[8] In stark contrast in this particular regard are horses that feed not on grass but on ambrosia, because they are divine. For instance, *Iliad* 5.767–77 describes Hera's arrival onto the plain of Troy on her chariot drawn by winged steeds, to the place where the Simoeis and the Scamander meet. There she unyoked the horses "and for them Simoeis brought forth ambrosia to pasture [*nemesthai*]" (777). In Plato's *Phaedrus* the horses of the divine soul are unyoked and given ambrosia to eat and nectar to drink.[9] Ovid, *Metamorphoses* 4.214–16, makes the opposition of grass and ambrosia explicit: the horses of the Sun eat heavenly fodder, *ambrosiam pro gramine habent* (215). The food they eat is thus an established mark of divine horses, and it is explicitly or implicitly contrasted with the fare of mortal horses. The sense of the proportional metaphor at lines 47–49 of the *Partheneion* is that the *khorāgos* stands out among the maidens of the chorus as much as a divine horse would among his mortal counterparts.[10] The point therefore may be that the *khorāgos* is immortal and the chorus mortal.

When, in the next line, the dream-horse is compared to Hagesichora, it is called an "Enetic courser," one having attributes of an actually existing race of horses—or people. It is debated whether

---

7. Devereux 1965, 176.

8. Chantraine 1999, 185–86; Garzya 1954, 45.

9. Plato *Phaedrus* 247e4–6, ἐλθούσης δὲ αὐτῆς ὁ ἡνίοχος πρὸς τὴν φάτνην τοὺς ἵππους στήσας παρέβαλεν ἀμβροσίαν τε καὶ ἐπ᾽ αὐτῇ νέκταρ ἐπότισεν "when it is there, the charioteer stations his horses at their manger, throwing them ambrosia and giving them nectar to drink"; trans. Rowe 1999.

10. A reverse image, as it were, occurs in the description of the horses of Achilles at Homer *Iliad* 16.148–54, where Pedasus, "mortal as he was, ran beside the immortal horses" (154). Trans. Lattimore 1951.

Paphlagonian or Adriatic Eneti are meant, and in either case, we know nothing at all about the aspect or qualities of their horses.[11] But one can again tease out of the other term of this comparison what specific Enetic features serve as a foil for the beauty of Hagesichora. If Hagesichora is all silver and gold, her opposite in this regard should be dun and dark.[12] Black seems to be the color of Dreams, whom Euripides describes as black winged.[13] As to the Eneti, a nugget of folklore preserved in Pseudo-Scymnus locates them in the final scene of the fall of Phaethon, on the banks of the Eridanus, and pictures them in black. These are the Eneti who migrated from Paphlagonia to the Adriatic:

> Ἠριδανὸς, ὃς κάλλιστον ἤλεκτρον φέρει,
> ὅ φασιν εἶναι δάκρυον ἀπολιθούμενον,
> διαυγὲς αἰγείρων ἀποστάλαγμά τι.
> Λέγουσι γὰρ δὴ τὴν κεραύνωσιν προτοῦ
> τὴν τοῦ Φαέθοντος δεῦρο γεγονέναι τινές·
> διὸ καὶ τὰ πλήθη πάντα τῶν οἰκητόρων
> μελανειμονεῖν τε πενθικάς τ' ἔχειν στολάς.

The Eridanus, which carries the most beautiful amber, which they say is petrified tears, the translucent weeping of black poplars. For they say that it was there that Phaethon was struck down by the thunderbolt. For that reason, the entire multitude of the inhabitants is clad in black and wears the garb of mourning.[14]

Color and degrees of brightness, rather than speed in a race, I will argue,[15] are the points on which the series of equestrian metaphors turns; metaphors that compare the dream-horse to the "mistress of the chorus" on the one hand and to Hagesichora on the other, and also the latter to Agido. But the Eneti also evoke, for the second time

11. On the debate, Page 1951, 87–88.
12. West (1965, 195) likewise takes the epithet Enetic to refer to the color of the horse but understands that Hagesichora is likened to the horse, not contrasted with it.
13. Euripides *Hecuba* 71. See also Ovid *Fasti* 4.661–62: "interea placidam redimita papavere frontem // Nox venit, et secum somnia nigra trahit."
14. Pseudo-Scymnus *Periegesis* 395–401 Müller (= 391–97 Marcotte). On this tradition, see Marcotte 2000, 200.
15. See pp. 93–94 of the present text.

in what remains of the *Partheneion*, the shadow of Phaethon. Their mournful habit is woven into that myth, as we learn from a fragment of Aeschylus's *Heliads*, which speaks of the grief of the women of Adria.[16] The gleam of gold marks as well the beauty of the chorus. In the singers' case, however, it is not intrinsic but rather the effect produced by a battery of ornaments, which are cast as a defensive panoply (60–77):

ταὶ Πεληάδες γὰρ ἇμιν   60
ὀρθρίαι φάρος φεροίσαις
νύκτα δι᾽ ἀμβροσίαν ἅτε Σήριον
ἄστρον ἀυηρομέναι μάχονται.

οὔτε γάρ τι πορφύρας
τόσσος κόρος ὥστ᾽ ἀμύναι,   65
οὔτε ποικίλος δράκων
παγχρύσιος, οὐδὲ μίτρα
Λυδία, νεανίδων
ἰανογ[λ]εφάρων ἄγαλμα,
οὐδὲ ταὶ Ναννῶς κόμαι,   70
ἀλλ᾽ οὐδ᾽ Ἀρέτα σιειδής,
οὐδὲ Συλακίς τε καὶ Κλεησισήρα.
οὐδ᾽ ἐς Αἰνησιμβρ[ό]τας ἐνθοῖσα φασεῖς
"Ἀσταφίς τέ μοι γένοιτο,
καὶ ποτιγλέποι Φίλυλλα   75
Δαμαρέτα τ᾽ ἐρατά [τ]ε Ϝιανθεμίς"·
ἀλλ᾽ Ἁγησιχόρα με τείρει.

For against us the Pleiades contend   60
   at daybreak, carried aloft
like Sirius across immortal Night,
   as we bring the season of the plow.

---

16. Aeschylus *Heliads* frag. 71 *TrGF*, Ἀδριαναί τε γυναῖκες τρόπον ἕξουσι γόων. References to the black robes worn by the inhabitants of the Eridanus shore in mourning for Phaethon also in Plutarch *Moralia* 557d and Polybius 2.16.13–15.

For surfeit of purple
does not help,   65
nor chased golden
snake-bracelet, nor Lydian
tiara, pride
of violet-eyed maids,
nor Nanno's tresses,   70
not even godlike Areta
or Thylacis and Cleesithera,
nor will you go to Aenesimbrota's house and say:
"let Astaphis stand by me,
and let Philylla and Damareta   75
and lovely Hianthemis look upon me,"
but Hagesichora effaces me.

The chorus thus portrays itself as both intimately linked to Hagesichora and helpless before her. Calame has shown how this relationship conforms to a particular model, that of a collectivity, or a sisterly band of maidens of the same age, surrounding one who is patently superior in all respects, chief among them in beauty. This template has its paradigms in mythical and epic representations: Artemis among her nymphs; Aphrodite among the Graces; Thetis and her sisters; and Helen and her companions, as illustrated in the following lines from Theocritus:

Ἀὼς ἀντέλλοισα καλὸν διέφανε πρόσωπον,
πότνια Νύξ, τό τε λευκὸν ἔαρ χειμῶνος ἀνέντος·
ὧδε καὶ ἁ χρυσέα Ἑλένα διεφαίνετ' ἐν ἁμῖν.

Fair, Lady Night, is the face that rising Dawn discloses,
or radiant spring when winter ends;
and so amongst us did golden Helen shine.[17]

The superiority of the leader of the chorus is expressed in terms of precious metals, as at lines 53–55, and in terms of light and radiance. The ultimate paradigm for brilliant light obscuring dimmer lights is,

17. Theocritus *Idylls* 18.26–34; trans. Gow 1953.

of course, the moon among the stars, as in a fragment of Sappho, where the stars are eclipsed by the radiance of the moon:

ἄστερες μὲν ἀμφὶ κάλαν σελάνναν
ἂψ ἀπυκρύπτοισι φάεννον εἶδος
ὄπποτα πλήθοισα μάλιστα λάμπη
γᾶν [

ἀργυρία

stars around the beautiful moon
hide back their luminous form
whenever all full she shines
on the earth

silvery[18]

This image in turn serves as the metaphor on which Sappho relies to describe the girl who stands out among the Lydian women. She "overcomes" them, as the moon does the stars:

νῦν δὲ Λύδαισιν ἐμπρέπεται γυναί-
κεσσιν ὥς ποτ᾽ ἀελίω
δύντος ἀ βροδοδάκτυλος <σέλαννα>

πάντα περ<ρ>έχοισ᾽ ἄστρα.

But now she is conspicuous among Lydian women
as sometimes at sunset
the rosyfingered moon

surpasses all the stars.[19]

The figure of struggle, which περρέχοισ᾽, "overwhelming," implies, structures the double comparison of the chorus with the Pleiades

18. Sappho frag. 34 Voigt; trans. Carson 2002.
19. Sappho frag. 96 Voigt, 6–10; trans. Carson 2002.

on the one hand and with Hagesichora on the other. The metaphor begins with μάχονται at line 63 and comes into full focus in τείρει, strategically placed at the end of the stanza. With few exceptions, modern interpreters understand that τείρω is being used here, as it is elsewhere, in an erotic sense, meaning that the maidens are consumed with desire for Hagesichora, who, they say, "wears me out."[20] Keeping in mind the agonistic connotations of the relationship of the preeminent maiden to her companions, however, the expression may be best understood to say that, by comparison, Hagesichora's beauty makes that of her companions look dim. Burnett points out that Euripides similarly employs the metaphor of combat for the way in which the members of a chorus of maidens vie with one another in beauty.[21] In the *Iphigenia in Tauris*, the chorus wishes it could fly back home along the route of the sun:

> χοροῖς δ᾽ ἐνσταίην, ὅθι καὶ
> †παρθένος εὐδοκίμων γάμων
> παρὰ πόδ᾽ εἱλίσσουσα φίλας
> ματέρος ἡλίκων θιάσους
> ἐς ἁμίλλας χαρίτων
> ἁβροπλούτοιο χαίτας εἰς ἔριν
> ὀρνυμένα πολυποίκιλα φάρεα
>   καὶ πλοκάμους περιβαλλομένα
> γένυσιν ἐσκίαζον.†

> I would take my place in the choruses
> at noble weddings as when, a maiden,
> at my dear mother's feet
> I'd circle with the maidens
> in their dance, I'd join
> that war of loveliness
> where perfumed curls contend,

---

20. Stehle (1997, 81–82n35), who prefers the possible alternative reading τηρεῖ, "guards me," correctly points out that τείρω has harsh connotations of lust that are inappropriate to the situation envisioned here.

21. Burnett 1985, 10, 160.

I'd wear my best embroidered cloak
and let my loosened hair
cast its shadow on my cheek!

(1143–51)

Burnett's translation, quoted above for lines 1146–51,[22] retains the brunt of words like ἀμίλλας, "contests," and the epic-sounding ἔριν, "battle strife," that are analogous to μάχονται at line 63 of the *Partheneion* and, like it, are hyperboles. The maidens of the chorus are comparable to the Pleiades and, accordingly, compete with them.[23] But they cannot endure Hagesichora's brilliance, when she comes near them. Against it their resources—wealth of purple and gold, the handsome tresses of Nanno, the sheer beauty of Areta, or Thylacis, or Cleesithera—are useless. The chorus will withstand the company of other beautiful maidens that Aenesimbrota, who apparently controls its location, may be persuaded to place at its side, such as Astaphis, and Philylla, and Damareta; but, it says, "Hagesichora effaces me." In other words, the entire stanza (64–77) is a priamel, which runs breathlessly to its climax in the last line.[24]

The naming of individual chorus members is highly unusual and calls for an explanation. Does the poem really present us with a playbill of sorts, the roster of historical persons who danced its first performance? That is what most interpreters of the *Partheneion* have assumed until recently, but there are reasons for doubt. It is unclear whether the persons named at lines 70–76 are all members of one and the same chorus. Strictly speaking, the group that is defenseless before Hagesichora consists of Nanno, Areta, Thylacis, and Cleesithera. Astaphis, Philylla, Damareta, and Hianthemis, to whom they wish to be near, may or may not be in their number. There is further the matter of the discrepancy in the quality of the names themselves, as well as the uncertainty regarding the roles to which they are attached. It is

22. Ibid., 160n15.
23. Garzya (1963, 36) and Robbins (1994, 9) also understand μάχονται at line 63 in the metaphorical sense of "compete," "vie." Puelma (1977, 36n66), D. Clay (1991, 58–63), Henrichs (1994–95, 83), and Bierl (2001, 48–49) understand the expression in reference to choric competition.
24. Race 1982, 54–55.

unclear whether the *khorāgos* and Hagesichora are part of the chorus. They are, however, in plain view, since the chorus points them out to the audience (50, 56–57). Agido may or may not be visible to the audience, but she is within sight of the chorus (40). Where is Aenesimbrota? The expression *es Ainēsimbrotās*, "to Aenesimbrota's house" (73), suggests that she is not part of the chorus.[25] The apparent differences in stage presence separating the chorus from these three, in addition to differences as to rank and beauty, are compounded by the different quality of their names. Unlike the nymphlike names of the chorus members, Agido, Hagesichora, and Aenesimbrota are speaking names, designating a particular capacity: Hagesichora, of course, means "leader of the chorus." Agido has suggested to many a connection with the Spartan ruling house of the Agiadai.[26] But it may just be another determinative epithet drawing its meaning from the same stem, *agein*, and meaning "she who comes first" or "leader." And Aenesimbrota may be understood as "she whom mortals praise."[27]

A strong argument in support of the view that these are fictional or mythical rather than historical maidens has to do with the question of the repeated performances of the *Partheneion*. Herington observed that it is unlikely that the text of the song would be preserved for four centuries without the choral performance ever being staged again.[28] There is (admittedly meager) evidence that ancient lyric choruses by Thaletas and Alcman continued to be produced into the Hellenistic age.[29] And a recurring performance entails impersonation of the original cast, who must therefore be more than mere names. Finally, the mention of *thōstēria* (81) firmly embeds the *Partheneion* in the context

25. Aenesimbrota has been variously identified as the *khorāgos* of a rival chorus (Kukula 1907, 212–13); the head of a school for chorus singers (Page 1951, 65–66); the mistress of a circle analogous to that alleged for Sappho on Lesbos (Calame 1977, 2:95–97); a sorceress who could provide the lovesick maidens with love potions (West 1965, 199–200; Puelma 1977, 40–41; Robbins 1994, 11n25); and the mother or teacher of the last four named maidens (D. A. Campbell 1983, 159).

26. See Calame 1977, 2:140–42, with bibliography; Nagy 1990b, 347–48; Hinge 2006, 290–92.

27. Calame 1983, 425–26.

28. Herington 1985, 54–55; see also Naerebout 1997, 200–202.

29. Sosibius *FGrHist* 595F5 (in Athenaeus 15.678b–c); Plutarch *Lycurgus* 28.5. See Hinge 2006, 282–94.

of a festival,[30] that is, a recurring occasion. All of this argues in favor of the hypothesis laid out by Nagy that the named characters act out at the level of ritual the parts of figures which exist at the level of myth.[31] Nagy refers specifically to Agido and Hagesichora, whom he takes to be the two choral leaders, and identifies their archetypes in the mythical Leucippides. Although much of the poem is about them, however, neither Hagesichora nor Agido (not to mention the elusive Aenesimbrota) have speaking parts. It is even unclear whether or not they are onstage. At center stage is the chorus itself, the protagonist, as the attention lavished upon each of its members indicates.[32] What is its role?

PLEIADES, HYADES, AND SIRIUS

The most revealing piece of information about the stage identity of the chorus comes in the most tormented passage of this section of the song:

> ταὶ Πεληάδες γὰρ ἇμιν
> ὀρθρίαι φᾶρος φεροίσαις
> νύκτα δι᾽ ἀμβροσίαν ἅτε Σήριον
> ἄστρον ἀυηρομέναι μάχονται.
>
> (60–63)

The meaning of several words here is in dispute. φᾶρος means either "mantle" or "plow," depending on whether its alpha is long or short

---

30. θωστήρια is glossed ἑορτή, "festival", in scholium A 17; Hesychius, s.v., a lacunose entry, calls it a banquet. On this point, see Calame 1977, 2:113–14. See pp. 114–15 in the present text.

31. Nagy 1990b, 345–49: "I see no justification for treating a text like Alcman PMG 1 as if it were a composition intended for a given group of historically verifiable persons at one and only one occasion in time" (349); 1996, 53–57. Although he leaves the question of the identity of the chorus unresolved, Nagy stresses the dramatic character of the performance: "The presentation through the chorus is the representation that is mimesis. The 'I' of the choral ensemble is not just the collectivization of persons who are singing and dancing at the ritual: it is also the impersonation of characters that belong to whatever myth is being represented in the ritual" (1990b, 369). Hinge 2006, 292: "Der Chorleiter und der Chor eines jährlichen Festes sind folglich keine Individuen, sondern inszenierte Personifikationen festgelegter Rollen."

32. Hutchinson 2001, 77: "The creation of a vivid but generalized character for a chorus, which concerns Pindar's maiden songs too, connects the poem with Athenian drama: choruses of old men, or girls, are obvious examples."

(the meter allows either). If one envisions this as an offering being brought to a goddess, φᾶρος as mantle or veil is the plausible choice, for which parallels exist in literature and ritual.[33] But φάρος, "plow," is textually preferable as *lectio difficilior*, and besides, it has the support of Sosiphanes, cited by one of the scholia.[34] ὀρθρίαι may be a nominative plural in apposition to the Pleiades, meaning "at daybreak"; or it may be dative singular, the epithet of a goddess for whom the veil or plow is intended, perhaps the goddess of Dawn, who is named somewhat more explicitly below with a descriptive epithet, *Aōtis*.[35] Finally, the Πεληάδες may be the constellation by that name. But the word also means "doves" in Dorian, Athenaeus tells us, and many scholars read "doves" here, in reference to Agido and Hagesichora.[36] Others identify in the Pleiades a rival chorus.[37] Which of the possible permutations and combinations one chooses ultimately depends on one's general understanding of the *Partheneion* as a whole.[38] With West, I believe that in a passage that mentions the Pleiades together with Sirius, these are more likely stars than doves and that we should turn our sights to the night sky, as Alcman repeatedly invites us to do.[39] But this raises another difficulty, for the Pleiades are in fact, and moreover are said to be by ancient Greek writers, the dimmest of stars, while Sirius is just as notoriously the brightest. The statement that the Pleiades arise with the brightness of Sirius would give anyone pause.

33. Calame 1977, 2:128–29; Hutchinson 2001, 91; Priestley 2007.

34. Scholium A 13; ἄροτο(ς) is also written above φαρος in the text of the papyrus (sch. A 12); Herodian (*Peri monerous lexeos*, p. 942.9–14 Lentz) confirms that Alcman used φάρος in the sense of "plow."

35. Page (1951, 76–78) lays out our options with great clarity. The reading ὀρθίαι, proposed by scholium A 13, which would open up the possibility of a rite in the cult of Artemis Orthia, is ruled out by the fact that it is metrically unfeasible. See also Bowra 1934, 35; and Calame 1977, 2:119–20 with references.

36. Athenaeus 9.394d; scholium A 13 states that Agido and Hagesichora are being compared to doves. Calame 1983 reads "doves" in reference to Agido and Hagesichora, envisioned in the role of protectors of the chorus ("fight for us"). Onto these lines, Athanassakis (2000) suggestively brings to bear modern folk traditions in Greece, Albania, and Italy, which refer to the Pleiades as hens or doves, and as a chorus of dancing maidens as well.

37. E.g., Kukula 1907, 214: "ein Agon der *Pleiaden* mit den *Hyaden*"; Page 1951, 55–57.

38. Calame (1977, 2:72–73n52) offers a comprehensive bibliography of interpretations concerning the Pleiades up to that date. See further Stehle 1997, 79; Hutchinson 2001, 90–93.

39. West 1965, 197; D. Clay 1991, 60–61; Hutchinson 2001, 90–91.

Ann Burnett made real progress on this front when she proposed that the point of joining Sirius to the Pleiades is not to compare the two, but to point to a specific and important time of year, a turning point in the cycle of the seasons.[40] In her view, the juxtaposition of Sirius and the Pleiades has to do not with brightness but with the fact that they both rise before dawn, giving shape to a particular configuration of the night sky. She identified the moment as the heliacal rising of the Pleiades in early May after an absence of forty days, an event that marks the beginning of summer. To be sure, their role as indicators of major seasonal changes is what makes the Pleiades such an important star cluster. They are small and faint but important, because they signal the beginning of summer and, at the onset of winter, the "coming around of the plow," that is, the time to start plowing. In the words of Aratus:

ἄγχι δέ οἱ σκαιῆς ἐπιγουνίδος ἤλιθα πᾶσαι
Πληϊάδες φορέονται. ὁ δ᾽ οὐ μάλα πολλὸς ἁπάσας
χῶρος ἔχει, καὶ δ᾽ αὐταὶ ἐπισκέψασθαι ἀφαυραί.

[257–63]

αἱ μὲν ὁμῶς ὀλίγαι καὶ ἀφεγγέες, ἀλλ᾽ ὀνομασταὶ
ἦρι καὶ ἑσπέριαι, Ζεὺς δ᾽ αἴτιος, εἱλίσσονται,
ὅ σφισι καὶ θέρεος καὶ χείματος ἀρχομένοιο
σημαίνειν ἐπένευσεν ἐπερχομένου τ᾽ ἀρότοιο.

Near his [Perseus's] left knee all in a cluster the Pleiades are borne along. The space that holds them is not great and they are individually faint to observe. [. . .] All alike they are small and faint, but they are famous in their movements at morning and evening, and Zeus is the cause, in that he authorised them to mark the beginnings of summer and winter and the onset of ploughing time.[41]

Hesiod likewise links the heliacal rising and the cosmical setting of the Pleiades to the farming cycle:

40. Burnett 1964, followed by Gianotti 1978. See also Diels 1896, 359–60.
41. Aratus *Phaenomena* 254–56, 264–67; trans. Kidd 1997, modified.

Πληιάδων Ἀτλαγενέων ἐπιτελλομενάων
ἄρχεσθ᾽ ἀμήτου, ἀρότοιο δὲ δυσομενάων.

When the Pleiades, daughters of Atlas, are rising, begin your harvest,
and your ploughing when they are going to set.[42]

In the context of the yearly cycle and the agricultural calendar, Burnett
pointed out, there is another suggestive parallel in Hesiod's *Works and
Days*, a passage that contains reference to Pleiades, plowing, and the
notation of daybreak, *orthriai*: "when the House-carrier climbs up the
plants from the earth to escape the Pleiades," it is time for the harvest
and work at dawn, for dawn "puts yokes on many oxen."[43]

Burnett's hypothesis points in the right direction, but has its own
difficulties, the principal one being that the heliacal rising of Sirius,
which occurs early in July, is considerably later than that of the Pleiades: when the Pleiades rise at dawn, Sirius is nowhere to be seen.[44]
The answer to the puzzle lies in another passage from the *Works and
Days*, which also deals with a change of seasons, but a different one,
and includes mention of the Pleiades, the "plow in due season," and
the star cluster often mentioned in the same breath as the Pleiades—
the Hyades:

> αὐτὰρ ἐπὴν δή
> Πληιάδες θ᾽ Ὑάδες τε τό τε σθένος Ὠρίωνος
> δύνωσιν, τότ᾽ ἔπειτ᾽ ἀρότου μεμνημένος εἶναι
> ὡραίου·
>
> (614–17)

But when the Pleiades and Hyades and the might of Orion begin to
set, then be mindful of the plow in season.

---

42. Hesiod *Works and Days* 383–84; trans. Evelyn-White 1936.
43. Ibid., 571–81; trans. Evelyn-White 1936. After Burnett, Stehle (1997, 79–83) also
pointed to the nexus between this passage and the mention of the Pleiades in the *Partheneion*,
and explained it in reference to a change of season, the onset of summer.
44. On the date of the heliacal rising of Sirius, see Geminus *Eisagōgē eis ta phainomena*
17.39–41 Aujac, with the calendar (Cancer).

This is the beginning of winter, marked by the cosmical setting of the Pleiades and Hyades, which occurs, then as now, just before sunrise, at the time when Sirius is most visible in the sky—the star of Autumn, in the Homeric phrase.[45]

With their mention of Sirius and the Pleiades at daybreak in lines 60–63, the dancers inscribe themselves into the configuration in the night sky that heralds winter. They are the Hyades, the sisters of the Pleiades and their rivals in the dance, who share with them the task of marking the change of seasons.[46] The phrase "as we bring the plow" (61) is a figure of speech, in which "plow" (φάρος) metaphorically signifies the plowing season and is the equivalent of ἄροτος in the *Works and Days* passage cited above (616–17, ἀρότου . . . ὡραίου, "plowing in due season") and in Aratus's *Phaenomena* (267, ἐπερχομένου τ᾿ ἀρότοιο, "plowing coming around"). Crucial to this reading is the meaning of *auēromenai*, which most take as a middle voice, intransitive form, in the sense of "arising."[47] In fact, it is best understood as passive, to mean "suspended," "hanging," or "carried aloft," as it does in a beautiful passage of Euripides' *Alcestis*. Serendipitously, like the *Partheneion*, these lines describe a Spartan *pannukhis* that celebrates the cycle of the seasons. The chorus sings to the noble Alcestis:

πολλά σε μουσοπόλοι
μέλψουσι καθ᾿ ἑπτάτονόν τ᾿ ὀρείαν
χέλυν ἔν τ᾿ ἀλύροις κλέοντες ὕμνοις,
Σπάρται κυκλὰς ἁνίκα Καρνεί-
ου περινίσεται ὥρα
μηνός, ἀειρομένας

45. Homer *Iliad* 22.25–29. On the terminology for the risings and settings of the constellations, see Dicks 1970, 13 and Evans 1998, 190–97.

46. Kukula (1907, 209–10, 228) came very close to this reading. He saw that its rivalry with the Pleiades identifies the chorus as the Hyades and further recognized in its mention an allusion to the cosmic dance. He stopped short of casting the performance as a representation of the cosmic dance, however. In his view, "Pleiades" and "Hyades" are the names of two competing semichoruses, which would thus be "compared" to the stars.

47. Calame 1977, 2:74–75n55, 1983, 334. Garzya (1954, 54) and Gianotti (1978, 268), however, observe that ἀείρομαι is not used intransitively in archaic poetry.

THE CHORUS / 87

5. Protoattic stand, 680–650 BCE. Formerly Berlin, Antiquarium, A 42. After CVA Berlin 1, Germany 1 (1938), plate 33.

6. Attic red-figure pyxis lid, 430–420 BCE. Antikensammlung, Staatliche Museen zu Berlin, F 2519. Photograph: Johannes Laurentius. Used by permission of Bildarchiv Preussischer Kulturbesitz / Art Resource, NY.

7. Attic red-figure pyxis lid, 430–420 BCE. London, British Museum, 1920.12-21.1. © Copyright the Trustees of the British Museum.

8–9. Attic red-figure calyx-krater (the Blacas krater), 430–420 BCE. London, British Museum, E 446. © Copyright the Trustees of the British Museum.

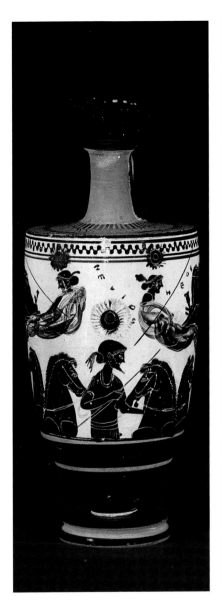

10–11. Attic black-figure lekythos, 490–480 BCE. New York, The Metropolitan Museum of Art, Rogers Fund, 1941. (41.162.29) Photographs © 1980 The Metropolitan Museum of Art.

12. Attic red-figure pyxis lid, 440–430 BCE. Athens, National Archaeological Museum, inv. no. 17983. © Hellenic Ministry of Culture / Archaeological Receipts Fund. Used by permission of the National Archaeological Museum.

13–14. Lucanian volute-krater, 420–400 BCE. Taranto, Museo Nazionale Archeologico, 8263. Whole view of side B and detail. Used by permission of the Soprintendenza Archelogica delle Puglie—Taranto.

15. Acanthus Column, fourth century BCE. Delphi, Museum, inv. nos. 466, 1423, 4851. © Hellenic Ministry of Culture / Archaeological Receipts Fund. Used by permission of the Archaeological Museum of Delphi.

16. Fragment of Attic red-figure vase, 450–440 BCE. Athens, Agora Museum, P 1457. Used by permission of the American School of Classical Studies at Athens: Agora Excavations.

17. Attic Panathenaic amphora, 403–402 BCE. London, British Museum, B 606. © Copyright the Trustees of the British Museum.

18. Silver tetradrachm of Rhodes, ca. 304–189 BC. Silver; 13.39 g. Harvard University Art Museums, Arthur M. Sackler Museum, Loan from the Trustees of the Arthur Stone Dewing Greek Numismatic Foundation, 1.1965.2402. Photograph: Imaging Department © President and Fellows of Harvard College. Used by permission of the Harvard University Art Museums.

19. Metope from the temple of Athena at Troy, third century BCE. Antikensammlung, Staatliche Museen zu Berlin, SK 71-72. Photograph: Juergen Liepe. Used by permission of Bildarchiv Preussischer Kulturbesitz / Art Resource, NY.

20. Apulian volute-krater, 330–320 BCE. Staatliche Antikensammlungen und Glyptothek München, 3297. Detail of the neck. Used by permission of the Staatliche Antikensammlungen und Glyptothek München.

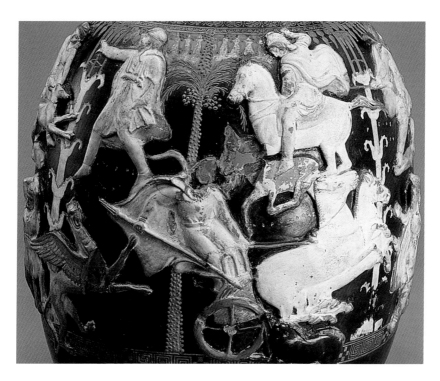

21–22. Attic squat lekythos, 390–380 BCE. Red-figure with added clay, relief, and gilding. St. Petersburg, The State Hermitage Museum, P-1837.2. Whole view and detail. Photographs © The State Hermitage Museum. Used by permission of The State Hermitage Museum.

23. Lucanian bell-krater, 400–380 BCE. Leiden, Rijksmuseum van Oudheden, Rsx 4. Used by permission of Rijksmuseum van Oudheden.

The same combination occurs in the tableaux of the night sky, framed by the chariot of the setting sun on one side and Dawn chasing the stars on the other, in Euripides' ecphrasis of the tapestry that formed the roof of the festival tent in the *Ion*:

> The Pleiades were passing through mid heaven and so was Orion with his sword, while above them the Bear turned its golden tail about the Pole. The circle of the full moon, as at mid month, darted her beams, and there were the Hyades, clearest sign for sailors.[50]

It is possible that, in these ecphrases of the constellations, the pairing of the Pleiades and the Hyades with Orion also has the purpose of identifying their last visible setting at dawn: not just the night sky but the night sky at the onset of winter.[51] In any case, we are left in no doubt as to the importance of these dim star clusters among brighter heavenly bodies.

The Moon and the Stars

The backdrop for the performance of the *Partheneion* is the night sky, animated by the dance of the stars and traversed at a gallop by the sky gods. Within its proper frame of reference the identity of the dancers becomes clear, as does their relationship to astral bodies of a different order, which bear the eloquent names of Agido, Hagesichora, and Aenesimbrota. The chorus impersonates the star cluster of the Hyades, making clear references to the identity of its mythical archetype and to its present ordeal. The Hyades are known to the author of the Hesiodic *Astronomy*, who gives them names comparable to those of our chorus girls, and they are just as well dressed:

---

50. Euripides *Ion* 1152–57; trans. Kovacs 1999. On this passage, see pp. 37–38 of the present text.

51. On the possible significance of the cluster Pleiades, Hyades, and Orion on the Shield of Achilles with regard to the seasons, see Phillips 1980 and Hannah 1994. Goldstein and Bowen (1983, 331–32) note that early Greek astronomy, before Eudoxus, was mainly concerned with the construction of the agricultural calendar on the basis of the observation of the risings and settings of the fixed stars.

νύμφαι Χαρίτεσσιν ὁμοῖαι,
Φαισύλη ἠδὲ Κορωνὶς ἐυστέφανός τε Κλέεια
Φαιώ θ᾽ ἱμερόεσσα καὶ Εὐδώρη τανύπεπλος,
ἃς Ὑάδας καλέουσιν ἐπὶ χθονὶ φῦλ᾽ ἀνθρώπων.

Nymphs like the Graces,
Phaesyle and well-crowned Coronis and Cleeia
and lovely Phaeo and Eudora of the flowing robe,
whom the tribes of men upon the earth call Hyades.[52]

The earliest version of their transformation into stars is the one
attributed to Musaeus by Hyginus.[53] Together with the Pleiades they
formed a group of fifteen sisters, the daughters of Atlas and an Oceanid, whose progeny included a son, Hyas. When Hyas, in the prime
of his youth, was killed in a lion hunt, the five sisters who would be
called Hyades cried for him inconsolably and died of their grief. Zeus
then took pity on them and placed them in the firmament, where
they continue to mourn and weep, their tears reaching the earth as
rain. Notoriously, their cosmical setting, together with the Pleiades,
signaled the start of the rainy season and storms at sea.[54] The image
of maidens engaged in lamentation explains the crying of the *parthe-
noi* that is mentioned at lines 85–87. They cry not from a roof beam,
as the widely accepted but improbable emendation ἀπ[ὸ θ]ράνω proposes, but from the sky. Blass's earlier and rather obvious supplement,
ἀπ᾽ [ὠ]ρανῶ, "from the sky," restores sense to the passage.[55]

Lasko, the verb used of their wailing (*lelaka*, 86), denotes a variety
of animal and human screams, among them the piercing female cries

52. Frag. 291 Merkelbach and West. The mythographic tradition preserves twenty-seven
different names for the Hyades, eight of which occur more than once, although no set is ever
repeated; their number ranges from two to seven. On the variant myths concerning the Hyades,
see P. Weizsäcker, *ML* 1.2 (1886–90): 2752–56; W. Gundel, *RE* 8.2 (1913), s.v. "Hyaden."
53. Musaeus frag. 12 Kinkel (in Hyginus *Astronomy* 2.21). See also Ovid *Fasti* 5.164. Timaeus (*FGrHist* 566F91) gives twelve as the total number of the daughters of Atlas (Pleiades
and Hyades), as does Hyginus in *Fabulae* 192.
54. See Hesiod *Theogony* 615–21; numerous later sources are cited in P. Weizsäcker, *ML*
1.2 (1886–90): 2752.
55. Blass 1870, 195–96. Blass corrected his own supplement in 1878, 23–24. Hutchinson
(2001, 7) prints "ἀπ .. ράνω," adding in the apparatus, "ἀπὸ θράνω legit Blass; ọ placet θ non
multum."

of the formal funeral lament, as seen, for instance, in Sophocles' *Electra* 121–23:

ὦ παῖ παῖ δυστανοτάτας
Ἠλέκτρα ματρός, τίν' ἀεὶ
λάσκεις ὥδ' ἀκόρεστον οἰμωγάν;

O child, child of a most wretched
mother, Electra, why do you always
wail [*laskeis*] this insatiate lamentation?

The verb is used for the lament over the dead in Euripides' *Hecuba* 677–79:

(Ἑκ.) τῆς θεσπιωιδοῦ δεῦρο Κασσάνδρας φέρεις;
(Θε.) ζῶσαν λέλακας, τὸν θανόντα δ' οὐ στένεις
τόνδ'. ἀλλ' ἄθρησον σῶμα γυμνωθὲν νεκροῦ.

Hecuba: Do you bring the body of prophetic Cassandra?
Servant: You wail [*lelakas*] for one who is alive and don't lament this one who is dead. But look upon the body laid bare.

In the same way, in the Louvre *Partheneion* (86–87) the chorus refers to its eternal lament over Hyas as *laskein*: παρσένος μάταν ἀπ' [ὦ]ρανῶ λέλακα // γλαύξ, "I myself a maiden wail [*lelaka*] in vain from the sky, an owl." The adverb *matān*, "to no avail," in conjunction with *laskein* has the same sense as *akoreston*, "insatiate" or "insatiable," has in the passage of the *Electra* quoted above: that of endlessly repeated action that serves no purpose outside itself. Dirges are proverbially "in vain" because the longing they voice for the dead can never be appeased. Athenian writers used *matān* (*matēn*) in reference to the funeral lament so frequently as to suggest that the expression is conventional.[56]

56. See Aeschylus *Libation Bearers* 926: ἔοικα θρηνεῖν ζῶσα πρὸς τύμβον μάτην ("it seems that, though I am alive, I mourn in vain before my grave"), with scholia; Sophocles *Ajax* 852: ἀλλ' οὐδὲν ἔργον ταῦτα θρηνεῖσθαι μάτην ("it is no use to wail in vain like this"), *Antigone* 1252: μάτην πολλὴ βοή ("much crying in vain"); Euripides *Phoenician Women* 1762: τὶ ταῦτα θρηνῶ καὶ μάτην ὀδύρομαι; ("why do I wail and lament in vain?"). See also Plato *Timaeus* 47b5: ὀδυρόμενος ἂν θρηνοῖ μάτην; and, in reference to grief, Aeschylus *Agamemnon* 165: τὸ μάταν ἄχθος, "burden of grief in vain."

The figure of the owl is entirely appropriate to the occasion. As it evokes the somber, relentless quality of the night owl's hooting, it also calls to mind that that sound in fair weather announces the coming of storms and the beginning of winter.[57]

The difference in quality between the nymphlike names of the chorus members and the descriptive quality of those of Agido, Hagesichora, and Aenesimbrota reflects the distance separating the stars from celestial divinities, namely, Dawn, Moon, and Night. The time at which the *Partheneion* is set, as we have seen, is daybreak, and there are intimations of Dawn herself—Eos, or rather, Agido. The name, "she who leads," is analogous to the Homeric *Ērigeneia*, "early born," which is also used as a naming epithet. The course of action the chorus projects offers the strongest support for an identification of it as the star cluster of the Hyades and of Agido as Dawn. The singers refer to their present ordeal as *ponoi*, "labors," which is an odd way to refer to a dance. In an astral sense, however, the term has a precise parallel in a fragment of Mimnermus, where *ponos* means the work of the Sun in his daily track across the sky:

Ἠέλιος μὲν γὰρ ἔλαχεν πόνον ἤματα πάντα,
    οὐδέ ποτ᾿ ἄμπαυσις γίνεται οὐδεμία
ἵπποισίν τε καὶ αὐτῶι, ἐπὴν ῥοδοδάκτυλος Ἠὼς
    Ὠκεανὸν προλιποῦσ᾿ οὐρανὸν εἰσαναβῆι.

Helios' lot is work the whole day long
    nor is there ever any respite
for both him and his horses, from the time rosy-fingered Eos
    climbs up into the sky, leaving Ocean behind.[58]

57. Aristotle frag. 253.15–17 Rose; Theophrastus *On Weather Signs* 52 Sider and Brunschön. For a proverbial expression of the emblematic role of the owl as a sign of winter, see *Appendix proverbiorum* 2.72 Schneidewin-Leutsch. It may or may not be a matter of coincidence that Virgil uses "in vain," *nequiquam*, for the call of the night owl that, as the storm abates, announces fair weather at *Georgics* 1.403: "nequiquam seros exercet noctua cantus"; see Mynors 1990, 85.

58. Mimnermus frag. 12 Allen. Remarkably, the notion that the Sun's course is his labor also occurs in the *Hymn to Šamaš*, 43–46, parts of which may go back to Old Babylonian sources: "To unknown distant regions and for uncounted leagues // You press on, Šamaš, going by day and returning by night. // Among all the Igigi there is none who toils but you, // None who is supreme like you in the whole pantheon of gods." Trans. Lambert 1960, 129.

Like Alcman, Mimnermus presents us with the image of toil and release from toil. If one keeps in mind that the moment the chorus describes is the time of the cosmical setting of the stars just before sunrise, it becomes clear why the singers welcome Dawn and say that Aotis, the dawn goddess, puts an end to their travails, as she always does. Together with the Pleiades, these stars are about to set, that is, to leave the whirl of the dance that is their task, escaping once more the unsustainable brightness of the moon.[59] Hagesichora is the Moon, who may herself be represented as a dancer.[60] As they claim at line 52 of the *Partheneion*, where they call Hagesichora their cousin (*anepsiās*), the Hyades have a tie of kinship with her—although they are mortals and she is a goddess. Pleiades and Hyades are the daughters of the younger Titan Atlas, son of Iapetus.[61] The latter is one of the elder Titans and brother of Hyperion, who is the father of Selene.[62] The best comparison for the chorus's description of Hagesichora's gold hair and silver face (lines 51–54) is contained in the fragment of Sappho quoted earlier in this chapter, in a word detached from the main text that calls the moon "of silver," *arguria*. As for the sun, archaic poetry imagined the rays of the moon as a refulgent mass of hair: she is *euplokamos* and *eukomoios*, "rich-tressed," and, accordingly, described in the last surviving line of the *Partheneion* as "she of the lovely golden hair."[63] The devastating effect that Hagesichora has on the chorus—*teirei*, "wears out, overcomes, effaces"—has already been compared to the way in which, in another

---

59. With Page 1951, 94–95 and Calame 1983, 344, I take ἔγεντο (89) and ἐπέβαν (91) as gnomic aorists.

60. Euripides *Ion* 1078.

61. Hyginus *Astronomy* 2.21 (Musaeus frag. 12 Kinkel), *Fabulae* 192; Timaeus *FGrHist* 566F91.

62. Hesiod *Theogony* 371–74; *Homeric Hymns* 31.4–7; Apollodorus 1.2.2.

63. *Homeric Hymns* 31.6, 32.17–18; Epimenides frag. 2 D–K. On this point see W. H. Roscher in *ML* 2.2 (1894–97): 3132, s.v. "Mondgöttin." Jurenka (1896, 16–18) and Kukula (1907, 208) recognized at lines 51–57 an allusion to the moon. Jurenka argued that in μὲν at line 57, Ἀγησιχόρα μὲν αὔτα, the ε of the papyrus should be read as long (as is the case, e.g., at 43, 44; see Page 1951, 3; Calame 1983, xxviii–xxix). Accordingly, he read, Ἀγησιχόρα μήν(α) αὐτά, "Hagesichora is the moon herself." This conjecture has been dismissed (Page [1951, 89n2] quotes it derisively and Hutchinson [2001] leaves it out of his apparatus). In direct reference to the Moon herself, however, Jurenka's reading points to the possibility of wordplay by allusive homophony.

fragment of Sappho, the moon "overwhelms" the stars.[64] The vehicle for these poetic metaphors is a phenomenon that is easily observed: the concealment of stars that occurs when the moon moves near them and outshines them.[65]

Within this frame of reference, the mention of Aenesimbrota's house at line 73—es Ainēsimbrotās—identifies in Aenesimbrota Night herself. As we have seen, her house, which Hesiod and Parmenides locate beyond the Gates of Night and Day, is a prominent fixture of the topography of the cosmos and the place to which the astral bodies return.[66] Here the stars consider, and dismiss, the possibility of appealing to her in order to escape the proximity of the Moon, once they reach her house (enthoisa, 73). In poetic imagery Nyx is similarly cast as the overseer of the stars. The stars are in Night's domain: they are her ornaments and her attendants,[67] and they are also imagined as her wards, for instance, in Euripides' Electra (54), when Electra calls Night "nurse [trophos] of the golden stars." As the one who has it in her power to arrange and "display" the constellations,[68] in the Partheneion Nyx plays the authoritative role of khorāgos of the dance-song of the Hyades (43–50).[69] She is khorostatis, as she is called

64. See pp. 77–79 of the present text.

65. Alan Bowen has pointed out to me a description of this phenomenon, albeit in regard to the sun, in Theon of Smyrna Aspects of Mathematics Useful for the Reading of Plato 193.6–11 Hiller, where a distinction is made between "occultation" or eclipse (epiprostheitai), and krupsis, "concealment."

66. See pp. 42–43, 48–51 of the present text.

67. See Aeschylus Agamemnon 356, Seven against Thebes 400–401, Prometheus Bound 24; Euripides Ion 1150–51.

68. At Aratus Phaenomena 470, Night "displays," epideiknutai, the brilliant stars to mankind; at 694–98, she "drags down," ephelketai, the constellation of Centaur and "brings down" that of Hydra. Epideiknutai at line 470 may allude to the role of Night as chorus mistress. Nagy (1990b, 344, 364–65, 369, 377) analyzes the use of the largely synonymous verb apodeiknumai to designate the activity of the khorēgos who organizes public choral performances at festivals. In the sense of "making public presentation" of the chorus, the terms may be rendered as "producing."

69. It was debated for years whether the khorāgos mentioned at line 44 is Agido or Hagesichora; see Calame 1977, 2:46–48, with chart facing p. 176. The prevailing hypothesis that it is the latter finds comfort in the etymological analogy of the word khorāgos with the name Hagesichora, both of which mean "leader of the chorus," although they do not necessarily refer to the same role; see Calame (above); Nagy 1990b, 345. Calame's painstaking analysis of the vocabulary of choragic activities (1997, 43–66) is ultimately inconclusive in determining which of two possible meanings khorāgos has here—one who instructs the chorus or one who leads the

below at line 84, the one who "sets up" and instructs the chorus. Her name, "she whom mortals praise," evokes the familiar notion of Night the "giver of sleep," as she is called in Euripides' *Orestes* 175–76. With all this in mind, let us now return to the imagery of peerless beauties and exotic horses at lines 39–59. The image of Night as a dream that is a horse and may be called Enetic and the figures of the Colaxian and Ibenian horses, to which Hagesichora and Agido are likened, are not, strictly speaking, metaphors, but expressions that compound synecdoche with metaphor.[70] The horse images appeal to the notion, amply attested by literary and visual sources, that Night, Moon, and Dawn, like the Sun, cross the sky one after the other, either in a horse-drawn chariot or on horseback, along the path that runs through the constellations.[71] In all three cases, the figure of the horse stands, *pars pro toto*, for the horse-driven celestial body, to which it refers. The ethnic epithets, on the other hand, are indeed metaphors that ask us to visualize the ways in which Night, Moon, and Dawn appear in terms of the differences between Eneti, Ibenians, and Colaxians. In other words, these epithets refer not to breeds of horses but to stereotypical notions about lands and peoples.

In the analysis of the passage earlier in this chapter, I suggested, with regard to the Enetic horse, that the adjective refers to an iconic property of the Eneti themselves, their black robes—black like the color of the dream-horse. But this figure also directly refers to Night, who is *melaina*, "black," and *melampeplos*, "black-robed," like the Eneti.[72] The Enetic-looking horse then becomes a foil for the radiance of Hagesichora and points to the brilliance of the moon against the darkness of the sky. The contrast of Colaxian and Ibenian again hinges on color. If "Ibenian" is a word for "Lydian," it may call up the

---

dance. Late sources attest to the use of the term specifically in Sparta to designate the former; see Athenaeus 14.633a–b; Plutarch *Moralia* 219e (cf. 208d, 149a).

70. Devereux 1965, 177; Robbins 1994, 9.

71. See pp. 37–41, 142–44 of the present text. Burnett (1964, 32) rightly connected the horse images at lines 58–59 with that of Eos traversing the sky by chariot or on horseback. On the chariot and horses of Eos, A. Rapp in *ML* 1.1 (1884–86): 1260–61, s.v. "Eos"; C. Weiss in *LIMC* 3.1 (1986): 748–55 s.v. "Eos." For the Moon, see W. H. Roscher in *ML* 2.2 (1894–97): 3139–44, s.v. "Mondgöttin"; F. Gury in *LIMC* 7.1 (1994): 709–11, s.v. "Selene."

72. See, e.g., Homer *Iliad* 5.310; Aeschylus *Eumenides* 745; Pindar *Nemean* 7.3. Nyx is called *melampeplos* at Euripides *Ion* 1150.

legendary abundance of gold for which Lydia was famous. A "golden" horse aptly matches the metallic beauty of Hagesichora—"unalloyed gold, her face of silver" (54–55). If "Colaxian" is expressive of Scythianness, it may refer to an identifying feature of northeastern barbarians: the red color of their hair.[73] If so, "Colaxian" aptly characterizes the crimson light of Dawn, who is *rhododaktulos*, "rose-fingered," in Homeric and Hesiodic diction.[74] The strength of this interpretation ultimately rests on the fact that it accounts for all the moving parts of the elaborate analogy, in which Agido, Aenesimbrota, and Hagesichora assume on the mythical plane aspects of the natural phenomena they embody. This construction appeals to a fund of concepts and imagery that are both widespread and long-lived. Drawings on Athenian vases, particularly the Berlin pyxis (plate 6) with its representation of Night, Moon, and Dawn riding in succession (briefly considered in chapter 1), afford us a glimpse of the cavalcade of astral bodies. The engraved and gilded figure of Selene riding within the disk of the full moon in the central medallion of a fifth-century silver cup suggestively evokes the golden quality of Hagesichora.[75]

The hierarchical scheme that the poem lays out thus configures the structure of the cosmos in terms of degrees of beauty and allotted tasks and spheres of action. Night yields to Dawn, although they are comparable, because the "measure" of the day must be observed. The Hyades sustain the rivalry of the Pleiades, but are no match for the light of the Moon. Nor can they avoid the Moon by asking Night to place them somewhere else, next to dimmer lights with whom they could compete, as Astaphis, Philylla, Damareta, and Hianthemis presumably are. The result would be to change the fixed position of stars and so to alter the path of the sun and the moon. This is a third, veiled allusion to Phaethon's disaster, which serves as a foil to the restored harmony of the cosmos.

73. Herodotus 4.108–9; Xenophanes frag. 16 D–K; Galen *Mixtures* 2.618. See also the red-haired Scythian on the amphora by the Berlin Painter from the Fleischman collection (J. Paul Getty Museum and Cleveland Museum of Art 1994, 96–98 no. 40).

74. On the epithets for Eos that refer to the reddening sky, see A. Rapp, *ML* 1.1 (1884–86): 1257–58.

75. Sofia, Archaeological Museum; Marazov 1998, 181 no. 116.

Broken as it is, the last stanza of the *Partheneion* holds recognizable allusions to the occasion of the performance and to the measures of the cosmic dance.

τῶ]ι τε γὰρ σηραφόρωι

α[ὐ]τῶς εδ .... ΄

τῶι κυβερνάται δὲ χρή

κἠν νᾶϊ μα ....

ἁ δὲ τᾶν Σηρηνίδων

ἀοιδοτέρα μὲ[ν αὐδά],

σιαὶ γάρ, ἀντ[ὶ δ᾽ ἔνδεκα]

παίδων δεκ .... ει

φθέγγεται δ .... ἐπὶ Ξάνθω ῥοαῖσι

κύκνος. ἁ δ᾽ ἐπιμέρωι ξανθᾶι κομίσκαι

To the trace-horse

to the steersman must
on a ship too [
the song of the Sirens
indeed more harmonious,
for they are goddesses, instead of [eleven]
children ten [
sings . . . on the streams of Xanthus
the swan. She of the lovely golden hair . . .

(92–101)

The passage at lines 92–100 is a priamel,[76] in which two examples of steering and control culminate in the third, that paradigm of orderly

76. The structure of a priamel has long been recognized in lines 92–95. See Dornseiff 1933, 128–29; Van Otterlo 1939–40, 148–53. Whether or not they accept the identification of the passage as a priamel, most interpreters argue that what would be the culminating example in the series is implied rather than stated. See, e.g., Calame 1983, 345; Page 1951, 96: "The trace-horse steers the yoke horses and chariot, the helmsman steers the ship: these are obviously metaphors, or similes, for Hagesichora, who steers and leads the Chorus." Accordingly, the subject that is being compared to the Sirens at line 96 (ἁ δὲ) has been identified as either the chorus itself (e.g., Page 1951, 97–98; Hutchinson 2001, 100–101) or Hagesichora (see Calame 1983, 346, with references), whose performance would be characterized as inferior. Race (1982, 54) saw that, if lines 92–95 are a priamel, the mention of the Sirens that follows (96–100) should be its culmination.

progression that is the movement of the heavenly bodies across the sky. By and large, the sense is clear. At lines 94–95 the mention of the ship's captain in the dative (94) corresponds to that of the trace horse in the dative (92) and establishes the analogy of chariot to ship.[77] The yoke horses, and with them the chariot, must follow the lead of the steer horse; aboard a ship too the crew must heed the steersman's commands; by their timely setting, the constellations obey, as they must, the overarching authority of the Sirens, the chorus that sounds (φθέγγεται) a more concordant harmony.

The superiority of the Sirens is acknowledged in two ways, the first of which requires little explanation: they are goddesses, while the stars of Alcman's chorus are only *paides*—children or girls. The second difference drawn between the two apparently has to do with numbers—eleven versus ten (98–99): ἀντ[ὶ δ' ἕνδεκα] // παίδων δεκ........ει. The import of "eleven" remains elusive, if this word indeed appeared in the text.[78] In the context of the foregoing interpretation, however, and in view of the explicit mention of the Sirens and their melody, it is hard to ignore the special significance that the number ten held in Pythagorean cosmology and harmonics.[79] The doxographic tradition attributes to Philolaus of Croton, a Pythagorean

He left the issue unresolved, however, casting doubt on the available interpretations of lines 96–99 and questioning the relevance of such a climax to the preceding examples. Adopting the supplement μὲ[ν αὐδά] at line 97 (first suggested by Von der Mühl 1958, followed by West 1967, 11), I take ἁ δὲ . . . αὐδά to be the subject of φθέγγεται. On the use of φθογγή for the voice of the Sirens in the *Odyssey*, see Dickson 1995, 196.

77. Van Groningen 1936, 258; Page 1951, 95–96.

78. It is probable that δεκ[α] (or δεκ[ας]) is to be restored at line 99. Page 1951, Calame 1983, and Hutchinson 2001 read αεκ, where Blass (1885, 18) had actually read δεκ. ἕνδεκα, on the other hand, has been inserted in the text entirely on the basis of the scholium A 21 (4–5): ἀλλὰ διὰ τὸ τὸν χορὸ(ν) ὅτε μὲνἐκ ἰᾱ παρθένων, ὅτε δὲ ἐκ ῑ· φη(σὶν) οὐν τὴν χορηγὸν [ἐξελὼν] ἀντὶ ἰᾱ ἀιδειν ῑ, "but because the chorus (consists) sometimes of eleven, sometimes of ten maidens; he therefore says that (subtracting) the chorus-leader ten sing instead of eleven." We owe the suggestion that ἐξελών should be supplied after τὴν χορηγὸν to Brink 1864, 137. "The scholiast is evidently guessing," notes West (1967, 11n4), although he believes that "eleven" actually occurred in the text. It is possible that, in his attempt to explain the meaning of "ten" as a point of comparison, the scholiast sought a number to which it might be contrasted and, as modern scholars would, arrived at eleven by counting the names mentioned in the song—ten, if one does not count the *khorāgos*.

79. See Burkert 1972, 39–40, 72–73, 467–68.

contemporary of Socrates, the earliest and most explicit statement of the idea that the decad informs the structure of the universe:

Φιλόλαος πῦρ ἐν μέσῳ περὶ τὸ κέντρον [. . .], περὶ δὲ τοῦτο δέκα σώματα θεῖα χορεύειν, οὐρανόν, τοὺς ε πλανήτας, μεθ᾽ οὓς ἥλιον, ὑφ᾽ ᾧ σελήνην, ὑφ᾽ ᾗ τὴν γῆν, ὑφ᾽ ᾗ τὴν ἀντίχθονα.

Philolaus maintained that there was fire in the middle of the universe round about its centre. [. . .] Around it move in choral dance ten divine bodies; the sphere of the fixed stars, the five planets, after them the sun and beneath it the moon; beneath the moon the earth and beneath that the counter-earth.[80]

Reflecting on this notion, Aristotle observed:

λέγω δ᾽ οἷον, ἐπειδὴ τέλειον ἡ δεκὰς εἶναι δοκεῖ καὶ πᾶσαν περιειληφέναι τὴν τῶν ἀριθμῶν φύσιν, καὶ τὰ φερόμενα κατὰ τὸν οὐρανὸν δέκα μὲν εἶναί φασιν, ὄντων δὲ ἐννέα μόνον τῶν φανερῶν διὰ τοῦτο δεκάτην τὴν ἀντίχθονα ποιοῦσιν.

Since the decad seemed to be a perfect thing and to comprise within itself the whole nature of number, they [the Pythagoreans] asserted that the planets too were ten, but as only nine were visible they invented the counter-earth as a tenth.[81]

As to the Sirens, we have seen that they appear in Plato's representation of the cosmos as a whorl consisting of eight concentric circles.[82] Each of these carries a Siren sounding a single pitch, and altogether their voices in succession produce a concordant *harmonia*. If Plato's Sirens are eight in number, their connection to the decad with regard to cosmic harmony is established by one well-known Pythagorean precept:

80. Stobaeus *Eclogs* 22.1d (= Aetius 2.2.7; Diels 1879, 336); trans. Philip 1966, 113–14. On the authenticity of this testimony, see Huffman 1993, 395–400.
81. Aristotle *Metaphysics* 986a8–12; trans. Philip 1966, 78. On this passage see further Philip 1966, 97–98n5.
82. Plato *Republic* 617b–c; see p. 6 of the present text.

τί ἐστι τὸ ἐν Δελφοῖς μαντεῖον; τετρακτύς·
ὅπερ ἐστὶν ἡ ἁρμονία, ἐν ᾗ αἱ Σειρῆνες.

What is the oracle at Delphi?
The *tetraktus*, which is the harmony in which the Sirens are.[83]

Postclassical sources represent the *tetraktus* as the central tenet of Pythagorean doctrine. It is a formula, still largely unexplained, consisting of the "tetrad" 1, 2, 3, 4, which in the ratios 4:3, 3:2, 2:1 expresses the basic harmonic intervals. The sum of the numbers is 10. "It is difficult"—writes Burkert—"to relate the ten revolving celestial bodies to music."[84] Yet, it is clear that such a relationship was drawn, and that opens the possibility that the mention of "ten" at line 99 of the *Partheneion* characterizes the perfect song of the Sirens in terms of the perfect number.

In addition to stating that the chorus moves in unison with the order of the universe, the priamel resonates with allusions to Phaethon's disastrous ride, which in the last stanza subtly draw together the mythic and cosmic themes that run through the song. Although the analogy of horses and ships is frequent in lyric, particularly in Pindar, scholars cite as an authoritative precedent for Alcman's use of this figure, and perhaps his source of inspiration, one that would certainly be familiar to his audience as well, the priamel at *Iliad* 23.315–18:

μήτι τοι δρυτόμος μέγ᾽ ἀμείνων ἠὲ βίηφι
μήτι δ᾽ αὖτε κυβερνήτης ἐνὶ οἴνοπι πόντῳ
νῆα θοὴν ἰθύνει ἐρεχθομένην ἀνέμοισι
μήτι δ᾽ ἡνίοχος περιγίγνεται ἡνιόχοιο.

83. Iamblichus *On the Pythagorean Way of Life* 82.12–13; trans. Dillon and Hershbell 1991. On the *tetraktus* see Burkert 1972, 72–73, 186–88, and 166–170 on the antiquity of the tradition of *akousmata*. Philip 1966, 97–98n5, on the contrary, argues that this notion had no currency in early Pythagorean thought.

84. Burkert 1972, 351. John Franklin points out (personal communication, November 15, 2006) that the Pythagorean Nicomachus (via Boethius, *De institutione musica* 1.20 Friedlein) knew a tradition according to which Terpander completed the heptachord in imitation of the seven planets.

The woodcutter is far better for skill than he is for brute strength.
It is by skill that the sea captain holds his rapid ship
on its course, though torn by winds, over the wine-blue water,
by skill charioteer outpasses charioteer.[85]

The Homeric passage lists examples of "intelligent planning," *mētis*, skilled calculations that allow the woodcutter, the ship captain, and, finally, the charioteer, to prevail. But the reverberations that the echo of this passage sets off in the *Partheneion* depend not just on these lines but also on the ones that follow and on their broader context (301–43). The heroes prepare for the chariot race in the funeral games for Patroclus. After Menelaus, Antilochus draws up his chariot. Close by his side, his father Nestor instructs him on the appropriate maneuvers and directs him to the signpost, *sēma*, that marks the turning point. Antilochus's horses are less powerful than those of the other contenders; but the exercise of *mētis* will bring him victory, because, Nestor goes on to say (319–21),

ἀλλ' ὃς μέν θ' ἵπποισι καὶ ἅρμασιν οἷσι πεποιθὼς
ἀφραδέως ἐπὶ πολλὸν ἑλίσσεται ἔνθα καὶ ἔνθα,
ἵπποι δὲ πλανόωνται ἀνὰ δρόμον, οὐδὲ κατίσχει

He who has put all his confidence in his horses and chariot
and recklessly makes a turn that is loose one way or another
finds his horses drifting out of the course and does not control them.

The relevant images here are that of the father pointing out the *sēma* along the racecourse as his son sets out, and that of the charioteer who fails to control his powerful horses and is thrown off the track. We do not know what form the Phaethon myth took in the first, lost part of the *Partheneion*, but the episode in which Helius gives his son directions on the route to follow is as integral to its representation as the young hero's derangement and fall. Long before Ovid's retelling of the story, this image appears, as we have seen, in Euripides' *Phaethon*, where the Sun tells the youth to aim for a particular *sēma* along the

85. Trans Lattimore 1951. See Page 1951, 96n1; Calame 1977, 2:83n71.

celestial *dromos*, the seven Pleiades, and then rides behind him, attempting to guide him at every turn.[86]

These two themes—the dawn that sees the orderly transition from one season to the next and the tragedy of Phaethon—intersect again in the figure of the swan upon the Xanthus (100–101). In the parodos of Euripides' *Phaethon* the swan singing on the streams of Ocean is one of the notations of daybreak, which the chorus sings on the morning of the fatal ride (63–64). The passage opens with the vision of Eos coursing over the earth and ends with the song of the swan:

ἤδη δ᾽ εἰς ἔργα κυνα-
γοὶ στείχουσιν θηροφόνοι,
παγαῖς τ᾽ ἐπ᾽ Ὠκεανοῦ
μελιβόας κύκνος ἀχεῖ.

(75–78)

Already the hunters, killers of wild beasts, set out on their pursuits
and on the streams of Ocean the sweet-singing swan wails.

In addition to signaling the approaching dawn, it was argued above, the swan's mournful song may allude to Cycnus's lament for Phaethon. Both connotations are equally appropriate to the bird's appearance in the *Partheneion*, which is set at daybreak. In the play, however, the river in question is Ocean—understandably, since the great river is the boundary of the land of the Aethiopians, where the action takes place. Ancient sources locate swans on all sorts of rivers,[87] but what determined the choice of the Xanthus in this particular case?

It is significant in this regard that both the swan and the Lycian Xanthus have a strong association with Apollo.[88] The tradition, which represents Lycia as a second homeland to the god, is attested in sources of all periods, beginning with the epic. The *Iliad* repeatedly

86. Euripides *Phaethon* 171–77; see pp. 64–65 of the present text. Ovid *Metamorphoses* 2.122–50.

87. See Page 1951, 100–101.

88. Note especially that the swan is invoked in hymns to the god; see Alcaeus frag. 307 Voigt; *Homeric Hymns* 21.1–3; Callimachus *Hymns* 4.249–55.

proposes a special tie between Apollo and the Lycian heroes Sarpedon and Pandaros; at *Iliad* 4.101 the god himself is called *Lukēgenēs*, "Lycian-born."[89] Patara on the Xanthus was the site of a celebrated oracular sanctuary of Apollo.[90] The city itself, according to Hecataeus (*FGrHist* 1F256), was named for Patarus, the son of Apollo and Lycia, daughter of the Xanthus. Of particular interest here is the tradition according to which Apollo resides in Lycia in the winter months. The legend is explicitly recalled at *Aeneid* 4.143–44:[91]

> qualis ubi hibernam Lyciam Xanthique fluenta
> deserit ac Delum maternam invisit Apollo.

> as when Apollo leaves Lycia, his winter seat, and the streams of
> Xanthus and revisits his mother's Delos.

Virgil's testimony might be dismissed as a late invention, were it not for the fact that the description of the oracle at Patara in Herodotus (1.182) indicates that since the fifth century, at the very least, cult practice conformed to this belief. Although he does not specify the time of year at which the oracle functioned, Herodotus states that the prophetess was active only at certain times, for the oracle was not always available.[92]

89. On this epithet see Chantraine 1999, 650; Bryce (1991, 144–45) argues for the opposing readings "wolf-born" or "born of light." For Apollo and Lycian heroes, see Homer *Iliad* 2.827, 4.119, 16.527–32, 16.667–83; for a direct association between Apollo and the land and people of Lycia, see also *Homeric Hymns* 3.179–81; Bacchylides *Epinician* 12.147–48; Pindar *Pythian* 1.39. Bryce (1991, 144–46) collects and discusses these and other sources in an attempt to discredit their testimony as to the existence of the sanctuary at Patara before the fourth century.

90. See Parke 1985, 185–93.

91. Servius's commentary on this passage specifically mentions the oracular sanctuary at Patara: "nam constat Apollinem sex mensibus hiemalibus apud Patara, Lyciae civitatem, dare responsa [...] et sex aestivis apud Delum." See also Horace *Odes* 3.4.62–64 and 4.6.26: "Phoebe, qui Xantho lavis amne crinis."

92. Herodotus 1.182: καὶ κατά περ ἐν Πατάροισι τῆς Λυκίης ἡ πρόμαντις τοῦ θεοῦ, ἐπεὰν γένηται· οὐ γὰρ ὦν αἰεί ἐστι χρηστήριον αὐτόθι· ἐπεὰν δὲ γένηται, τότε ὦν συγκατακληίεται τὰς νύκτας ἔσω ἐν τῷ νηῷ, "Just as also in Patara of Lycia the woman who is the prophetic mouthpiece of the god whenever the oracle is functioning—for there is not an oracle at all times there—whenever it is functioning, then she is shut in for the night together with him in the shrine." Trans. Parke 1985, 185. Regarding *Aeneid* 4.143–44, Parke (186–87) observes: "The seasonal character of the cult of Apollo in Lycia had already been suggested long before by Herodotus in his emphatic statement that the oracle did not function all the time in Patara, but

If, together, the swan and the Xanthus bring Apollo to mind, the seasonal connotations attached to the god's presence in Lycia illuminate the relevance of this image to the theme of Alcman's song and to the occasion of its performance: it is, I think, an allusion to the fact that Phoebus Apollo resides in Lycia, now that autumn has turned to winter.

---

teasingly he does not make clear during what periods it was active." See also the commentary on the Herodotean passage in How and Wells 1928. The Homeric hymn to Apollo may already contain mention of the sanctuary. The "Pythian" section of the song, which narrates the foundation of the oracle at Delphi, opens with the invocation "O lord, you hold Lycia and lovely Maeonia and Miletus, enchanting city by the sea" (*Homeric Hymns* 3.179–80). Rather than indicate a range of "geographical preferences" (A. M. Miller 1986, 65–66), these names probably refer in synecdoche to the three great oracular sanctuaries of Apollo in Asia Minor: Patara, Clarus, and Didyma. "Miletus" appears in this sense in the list of sanctuaries in Ananius's hymn to Apollo (frag. 1 West), which includes Clarus.

3

RITUAL IN PERFORMANCE

You cannot argue with a song.

The astral configuration the chorus describes is a *tekmar*, a sign, in the sense in which Prometheus uses the word when he describes how he brought culture to mankind. Like writing and animal husbandry, time reckoning was one of his inventions and his gift to mortals:

> ἦν δ᾽ οὐδὲν αὐτοῖς οὔτε χείματος τέκμαρ
> οὔτ᾽ ἀνθεμώδους ἦρος οὔτε καρπίμου
> θέρους βέβαιον, ἀλλ᾽ ἄτερ γνώμης τὸ πᾶν
> ἔπρασσον, ἔστε δή σφιν ἀντολὰς ἐγώ
> ἄστρων ἔδειξα τάς τε δυσκρίτους δύσεις.

They had no sign either of winter or of flowery spring or of fruitful summer, on which they could depend, but managed everything without judgment, until I taught them to discern the risings of the stars and their settings, which are difficult to distinguish.[1]

By enacting the dawn setting of the Hyades in conjunction with the Pleiades and Sirius, and by announcing the coming of the plowing season at the time of the full moon, the chorus conducts a rite of passage that negotiates a turning point in the agricultural cycle regulated by the star calendar.[2] Out of the continuous flow of time as it is perceived, the dance-song produces the moment that separates one season from the next, the point at which things change.[3] As it marks the

---

Epigraph. Bloch 1974, 71.

1. Aeschylus *Prometheus Bound* 454–58 West; trans. Smyth 1922, modified.

2. Van Gennep included calendrical rites in his seminal definition of the rites of passage (1960, 178–84); Chapple and Coon 1942, chap. 21, distinguished "rites of passage," which concern individuals, from calendrical festivals, for which they coined the term "rites of intensification," affecting the community at large. Bell (1997, 102) speaks of "calendrical rites" as a category apart from "rites of passage" that mark social stages of an individual life cycle.

3. Gingrich (1994) explores the relationship between culturally defined and ritually marked concepts of time and the continuous experience of the individual, or "the clear-cut termination of one stellar period and the subsequent beginning of the other" versus periods of "'gap' or

community's observance of this rupture, the performance effectively accomplishes the transition from one state to the other.[4] The day that dawns will be the first day of winter.

Appropriately, then, the song is concerned with cosmic order, which guarantees the timely succession of the seasons, upon which cultivation depends and with it mankind's very existence in the Age of Iron. It seems safe to surmise that the occasion of its performance was a state festival, which had the function of linking the orderly workings of the cosmos to the well-ordered city. The Karneia, which included, among other events, a *pannukhis*, was such a festival, as we learn from the passage from the *Alcestis* quoted in the preceding chapter.[5] A passage in Plato's *Laws* explicitly connects to the welfare of the city knowledge of the heavens, the establishment of the calendar, and the celebration of festivals tied to the rhythm of the seasons. In the ideal *polis*, citizens should learn

> the revolutions of the heavenly bodies—the stars and sun and moon,
> and the various regulations about these matters which are neces-
> sary for the whole state—I am speaking of the arrangements of
> days in periods of months, and of months in years, which are to be
> observed, in order that seasons and sacrifices and festivals may have
> their regular and natural order, and keep the city alive and awake, the
> Gods receiving the honours due to them, and men having a better
> understanding about them.[6]

In no actual *polis* did the observance of astral phenomena play a greater political role than at Sparta.[7] A late source, the *Astrology* attributed to Lucian, even states that the Spartan constitution was modeled on the heavens:

'overlap'" (173), which are times of insecurity and danger."In a way," he writes,"the ritual external-izes the unspoken fear about past and present events as outspoken hope for a new and better period" (174).

4. On the "performative" capacity of ritual in the sense defined in Austin 1962, see Tambiah 1979 and Rappaport 1992, 251.

5. Pettersson (1992, chap. 3) gives a summary of the evidence concerning the Karneia. See pp. 125–33 in the present text.

6. Plato *Laws* 809c–d; trans. Jowett 1953.

7. Richer (1998, chap. 11) examines in detail the role of astrology in the government of Sparta, particularly as regards the ephors.

For the Spartans, Lycurgus drew from the sky his ordering of their whole polity and made it their law never [. . .] to go to war, before the moon should be at her full, for he thought that the potency of the moon is not the same when she waxes and when she wanes, and that all things are subject to her sway.[8]

The veracity of at least part of this statement is borne out by a notorious episode of the Persian wars, which Herodotus (6.106) reports. On the eve of Marathon, the Athenians dispatched Phidippides the herald to Sparta to request aid. The Spartans consented in principle, but could not send an expedition immediately without breaking the law, because it was the ninth day of the month and the moon was not full. "Spartan moons" was proverbial for specious pretexts.[9] Thus the moon in particular—Alcman's Hagesichora—seems to have played a most important role in the Spartan polity. The ephors consulted her oracle at the sanctuary in Thalamae, where she was worshiped as Pasiphae, and she allegedly presided over the full assembly of Spartiates.[10]

HEAVEN AND EARTH

In the *Partheneion* the homology casting the heavens and the state as parallel universes is deployed in two ways: thematically and dramatically. Each in its own sphere, the narrative of Phaethon and that of Hippocoon correspond to each other as examples of catastrophes occasioned by crises of succession. Phaethon's assumption of his father's role throws the astral system into disarray and leads to his destruction. On the civic stage, Hippocoon's ill-founded claim to the kingship tears open a period of murderous strife that leads to the devastation of the city. The restoration of order, with the return of the legitimate heir, Tyndareus, requires that Hippocoon die together with his sons. The correlation between disturbance in the heavens

---

8. [Lucian] *Astrology* 25; trans. Harmon 1936, modified.

9. Diogenianus *Paroemiae* 10.47 Leutsch; see Richer 1998, 174n123.

10. Scholium to Thucydides 1.67.3. Pausanias 3.26.1 identifies Pasiphae as Selene. On the oracle, see Richer 1998, chap. 12.

and the threat of pollution in the royal houses was otherwise drawn at Sparta in the procedure reported by Plutarch on the occasion of the ousting of King Leonidas II in 243/42.[11] Every eight years the ephors trained their sights on the sky on a clear, moonless night and, if a star shot from one part of the vault to another, determined that the king was hateful to the gods and should be removed. In this case, the ephor Lysander testified to having seen the shooting star; Leonidas's impious act was to have fathered a tainted progeny by marrying a foreign woman.

The Gigantomachy, tentatively identified at lines 27–35, would provide the ultimate paradigm of an attempt at usurpation that leads to momentary chaos. The Giants too are marked by their birth as subdivine and ultimately mortal, by virtue of the fact that Earth conceives them from the blood that flows from the castrated member of Uranus.[12] To prevent Earth from bringing her sons back to life with a plant that would revive them, Zeus extinguishes the lights of Dawn, Moon, and Sun and culls the simple himself. This gesture, which Apollodorus's narrative of the myth presents as a mere stratagem, in effect erases the separation of Night from Day and throws the universe back into primordial darkness.

The homology between the cosmos and the state laid out in the mythical narratives of the *Partheneion* is brilliantly developed in terms of theatrical structure. The realization that the dance-song is dramatic mimesis allows us to recognize, in what Clay and others have called "the self-dramatization of the chorus,"[13] the way in which in the second part of the song the performance itself becomes its theme, a feature that also marks many choral odes of Athenian tragedy and comedy. Bierl and Henrichs in particular have called attention to instances in which the chorus members point to their identity as performers, in a metatheatrical turn that makes the spectators aware of the distance

---

11. Plutarch *Agis* 11.4–5; see Carlier 1984, 294–95; Richer 1998, 172–76. Parke (1945) proposed that the same procedure was followed in the ousting of Demaratus. See p. 27 in the present text. Richer (1998, 183–92) argues that the star in question is not a shooting star, as is generally assumed, but Sirius, pointing to Alcman 1.60–63 among other evidence for the prominence of Sirius in Spartan thought.

12. Hesiod *Theogony* 183–86; Apollodorus 1.6.1.

13. D. Clay 1991, 63–64; Peponi 2004, 296.

between the "here and now" of their dance and the "there and then" of the drama being enacted.[14] This phenomenon, which has been termed "self-referentiality," has been interpreted in terms of performative valence, in reference to the ritual function of the chorus in the cultic realm of the festivals of Dionysus.[15] A particularly striking example comes in the second stasimon of Sophocles' *Oedipus Tyrannus*, following the scene in which Jocasta rejects the oracles of Apollo. Faced with the threat of collapse of divine order (909–10), the chorus members, who wear the masks of Theban Elders, ask (895–96): "Why should I dance?" Since nothing in the dramatic action being staged explicitly requires them to do so, "the dancing to which the Theban elders refer," writes Henrichs, "is more properly, and more immediately, a function of their choral identity than it is of their dramatic character—it takes place in the concrete space of the orchestra where they perform, yet it is simultaneously projected into the imaginary past of the dramatic action, as if this chorus were dancing in Thebes as well as in Athens." The effect is not simply to shatter the "dramatic illusion" but to bring to the fore the fact that the chorus has a double role, one that is both "inside the dramatic realm of the play and outside of it in the political and cultic realm of the here and now."[16] This insight of not only a double role for the chorus but, correspondingly, of two distinct stages upon which the performance is projected is a useful starting point for an analysis of the dramatic structure of the *Partheneion* and of its ritual dimension.

In the *Partheneion*, not every element of self-description lends itself to be interpreted as "self-referential" in the sense outlined above. When the chorus states "I sing the light of Agido" (39–40) and "I wail" (86), when its members name themselves and describe their dress, their location, their labors and desires, when they look forward

14. Segal 1982, chap. 7; Bierl 1991, chap. 4; Bierl 2001, 11–64 passim, 308–14; Henrichs 1994–95, 1996. The phenomenon is by no means limited to tragedy and comedy. Fränkel noted some time ago that in choral lyric the description of the performance itself disrupts the illusion that the actor is identical with the character he or she impersonates (Fränkel 1962, 182–83, quoted in Henrichs 1996b, 31).
15. Henrichs 1994–95, 70; Bierl 2001, 32–64, 308–14.
16. Henrichs 1994–95, 67.

to being released from the dance by Aotis (87–89), they remain well within the dramatic persona of the Hyades, beautiful maidens who mourn their brother and dance in the sky till dawn.[17] But in three distinct ways the song forcefully draws attention to the fact and the circumstances of its performance. The first is by a statement whose performative force stems from the authority that the Muses confer on the poet and from the context in which it is uttered.

I refer to the first twelve surviving lines, which open with the statement οὐκ ἐγὼ]ν Λύκαισον ἐν καμοῦσιν ἀλέγω (2), "I do not count Lycaethus among those who struggled (or suffered)," followed by the names of ten sons of Hippocoon, each accompanied by a heroic epithet. The passage closes with τε τὼς ἀρίστως // [. . .] παρήσομες, "the most valiant // we shall [not] pass over" (12).[18] As is generally recognized, the point is not that Lycaethus (and with him the other sons of Derites, who may have been mentioned here) is alive, but that he is excluded from the list. In denying him what he grants the sons of Hippocoon, Alcman's phrase has a precise parallel in an elegy of Tyrtaeus, which defines what it is that makes a man a hero:

> οὔτ᾽ ἂν μνησαίμην οὔτ᾽ ἐν λόγωι ἄνδρα τιθείην
> οὔτε ποδῶν ἀρετῆς οὔτε παλαιμοσύνης,
> οὐδ᾽ εἰ Κυκλώπων μὲν ἔχοι μέγεθός τε βίην τε,
> νικώιη δὲ θέων Θρηΐκιον Βορέην,
> οὐδ᾽ εἰ Τιθωνοῖο φυὴν χαριέστερος εἴη,
>
> [6–9]
>
> οὐ γὰρ ἀνὴρ ἀγαθὸς γίνεται ἐν πολέμωι
> εἰ μὴ τετλαίη μὲν ὁρῶν φόνον αἱματόεντα,
> καὶ δηίων ὀρέγοιτ᾽ ἐγγύθεν ἱστάμενος.

17. Note, however, that Bierl (2001, 54–54) interprets the first-person statement at lines 39–40 as a performative utterance that constitutes ritual action: the maidens worship Aotis (Agido).

18. Following Page (1951, 83), I assume that a negative such as οὐ preceded παρήσομες. Calame (1983, 317) understood the latter in reference to τὼς ἀρίστως in the sense of "we shall pass over the most valiant." In this he is followed by Robbins (1994, 11), who interprets the entire list of names as a *praeteritio*. Hutchinson (2001, 82) observes that "after τὼς ἀρίστως the word cannot be scornful."

I would not mention or take account of a man for his prowess in running or in wrestling, not even if he had the size and strength of the Cyclopes and outstripped Thracian Boreas in the race, nor if he were more handsome than Tithonus in form. [. . .] For no man is good in war unless he can endure the sight of bloody slaughter and, standing close, can lunge at the enemy.[19]

As for the man who does not flinch in the face of death on the battlefield, Tyrtaeus says:

οὐδέ ποτε κλέος ἐσθλὸν ἀπόλλυται οὐδ᾽ ὄνομ᾽ αὐτοῦ,
ἀλλ᾽ ὑπὸ γῆς περ ἐὼν γίνεται ἀθάνατος.

Never do his name and good fame perish, but even though he is beneath the earth he is immortal.

(31–32)

Remembrance denied is a "not taking into account" (οὔτ᾽ ἐν λόγωι τιθείην), the same figure of reckoning that Alcman uses of Lycaethus at line 2 of the *Partheneion*: "I do not count," οὐκ ἐγὼ]ν . . . ἀλέγω, although slightly different in wording.[20] Tyrtaeus and Alcman thus assert their power to withhold or confer glory, *kleos*, since it is song that through the generations will ensure that the name of some will live on, while others are consigned to oblivion.[21] In the *Partheneion* the chorus engages in the apportionment of praise and blame, an operation that has a distinctly social dimension. From Plutarch's *Life of Lycurgus* (8.2), we learn that this was a practice fundamental to the conduct of Spartan society. In Lycurgus's egalitarian state, the blame attached to base deeds and the praise accorded to good ones would be the only source of inequality among the men. The exercise of praise and blame was carried out primarily at festivals, in songs that were

19. Tyrtaeus 12 West, 1–5 and 10–12; trans. Gerber 1999; see Hutchinson 2001, 80.

20. Scholium A 1, 3–4 to the *Partheneion* paraphrases οὐκ . . . ἀλέγω as οὐ συνκαταριθμ(ῶ). See also Pindar *Olympian* 2.78.

21. Detienne (1996, chap. 2) brilliantly demonstrates that the poetics of *kleos* in archaic Greek thought are grounded in the opposition of forgetting and remembering, *lēthē* ("oblivion") and *alētheia* ("truth," expressed as "un-oblivion"), which stand one to the other as silence to speech and blame to praise. He identifies in the phrase οὔτ᾽ ἐν λόγωι τιθείην (Tyrtaeus 12.1) a case in which the poet exercises his power as "master of Blame" (155n51). See further Nagy 1990b, 58–60.

"for the most part praises [*epainoi*] of men who had died for Sparta, calling them blessed and happy; censure [*psogoi*] of men who had played the coward, picturing their grievous and ill-starred life."[22]

By the words "I do not reckon" and "we shall not pass over" the chorus accomplishes a speech act, in which the naming of the action is itself the performance of that action: it numbers the Hippocoontids among the heroes and consigns to oblivion the sons of Derites. Its authority to do so rests not upon its dramatic identity as a chorus of stars, but upon its official role of ritual agent in a cultic setting, before the polity formally assembled.[23] In assigning praise and blame the chorus points to the circumstances of the performance and stresses its choral identity. That authority, however, is denied them on the mythical plane, as they state:

> ἐγὼν δ' ἀείδω
> Ἀγιδῶς τὸ φῶς· ὁρῶ
> ϝ' ὥτ' ἄλιον, ὅνπερ ἄμιν
> Ἀγιδὼ μαρτύρεται
> φαίνην. ἐμὲ δ' οὔτ' ἐπαινῆν
> οὔτε μωμήσθαι νιν ἁ κλεννὰ χοραγός
> οὐδ' ἁμῶς ἐῆι. δοκεῖ γὰρ ἤμεν αὐτά
> ἐκπρεπής

> I sing
> the light of Agido. I see it
> like the sun, whom
> Agido summons to appear and
> witness for us. But the glorious chorus mistress
> forbids me to either praise or blame her.
> For she appears to be
> outstanding.

> (39–46)

22. Plutarch *Lycurgus* 21.1; trans. Perrin 1914. See also 14.3, 25.2. On the role of praise poetry in Spartan society, see Detienne 1996, 45–46; Nagy 1990b, 392.

23. I refer to the definition of the properties of the speech act in the critique of Austin 1962 in Benveniste 1963.

Epainēn and *mōmēsthai*, "to praise" and "to blame," are terms which in Greek lyric belong to a particular "mode of discourse," in Nagy's words—that of *ainos*, praise poetry. *Ainos* is authoritative speech, "a marked speech-act, made by and for a marked social group" (the *polis* in the archaic period), that chastises the base and proclaims the *kleos* of the heroes. The subject of *ainos* is the deeds of mortals; the exercise of it always implies blame, since it involves pronouncing a judgment and ranking some above others.[24] At lines 43–44, the phrase "forbids me to either praise or blame her" refers to the *ainos* that the chorus legitimately performed with regard to the sons of Derites and the sons of Hippocoon. As mortals themselves, however, the Hyades may honor in their song the immortals, with whom they share the heavens, but they lack the authority to rank one above the other.[25] To "sing the light of Agido" honors Eos but, the chorus hastens to add, is not a performance of *ainos*, since it in no way implies disparaging by comparison the powerful beauty of Night, who is "outstanding" herself. The contrast of the two modes of song articulates the two registers along which archaic poetry is deployed: celebration of the gods and praise of the heroes.[26]

A second way in which the song calls attention to the distance between the "here" of the dance of the chorus and the "there" of the dance of the stars is through extensive use of deictic gestures. By using verbs of sight and deictic pronouns and adverbs, the chorus establishes its own spatial relationship and that of its interlocutor to objects, which may be part of the physical context of the performance (ocular deixis) or part of the drama it enacts (fictional deixis).[27] Sorting out which is which requires some knowledge about the mise-en-scène of the dance. To be sure, by reading the poem we cannot see what the festival audience saw

24. Nagy 1990b, 150, 31; see also 147–50, 428–30 and Nagy 1999, 222–24, 250.

25. Insightfully, Hutchinson (2001, 87) notes: "in this instance, the poem, so intensely hierarchical, refuses to rank. That itself is not an unhierarchical feature, just as mortals should decline to rank gods, and not only for prudential reasons."

26. Detienne 1996, 43–45.

27. Bühler (1934, pt. 2, especially 80–81, 121–40) gives the fundamental definition of the three modes of linguistic deixis. Felson (2004) provides an excellent brief introduction to the subject with particular reference to Greek lyric poetry.

in archaic Sparta.[28] But at this point we may hazard an informed guess. If the *Partheneion* was performed before dawn, as the chorus repeatedly states, at a *pannukhis*, the archetype of its dance would have been as present to the audience as the dancers themselves were.[29] What the audience would have seen may be evoked by a fragment of Sappho:

πλήρης μὲν ἐφαίνετ' ἀ σελάν<ν>α,
αἰ δ' ὡς περὶ βῶμον ἐστάθησαν

The full moon shone brightly and
The maidens took their stand around the altar.[30]

The *Partheneion* plays precisely upon such a juxtaposition of moonlit, star-spangled night to dance floor, as would later, at a great remove and in a different vein, the image on Sotades' *astragalos*, with which we began. Against this scenery, readily and endlessly available for each yearly performance, let us consider the dramatic charge of deictics. The chorus points to the dark of night (50), the moon (56–57), and the Pleiades (60–63),[31] all of which are actually visible overhead, but invites the spectators to visualize them in the human form of a dark beauty, a luminous dancer, and a chorus of maidens, respectively. At lines 64–77, the elaborate description of the dancers' appearance and attire both calls attention to the spectacle that is before the audience and projects it onto the stars that are imagined to dance in the sky. These gestures establish correlations between distinct deictic fields, by pointing to objects and actions actually present to the spectators' sight (ocular deixis) but configuring them as objects and actions which the spectators are asked to imagine (fictional deixis). In a continually shifting perspective, the audience is made aware of the chorus

28. D. Clay 1991, 51.
29. Bowra 1934, 40; D. Clay 1991, 52–53, 61. For the view that the *Partheneion* was performed in daylight, see Wilamowitz-Moellendorf 1897, 255; West 1965, 195.
30. Sappho frag. 154 Voigt.
31. On the deictic force of ταί at line 60, see Puelma 1977, 34n64; Calame 1983, 332; Peponi 2004, 303.

as performers immersed in the ritual situation as well, as characters in the drama it enacts.[32]

The metatheatrical turn becomes all the more intense when the chorus turns to the spectators with direct questions.[33] This move, on which the Brechtian *Verfremdung* effect famously relies, invites the audience to reflect on the relation of the performance to the dramatic action it stages. When they dramatically point to Night and Moon—*don't you see?* (50) *why do I tell you explicitly? there is Hagesichora* (56–57)—the dancers do more than expose the seam that joins them as actors to their role. They effectively open "a play within the play." Ubersfeld's graphic definition of this dramatic structure is eminently suited to the case at hand:

> Il y a théâtre dans le théâtre quand il y a deux espaces emboîtés dont l'un est représentation pour l'autre. Il faut donc qu'il y ait des regardants et des regardés, même si les uns et les autres sont regardés par le public.[34]

In the case of the *Partheneion*, the sky itself is a stage, which the full moon traverses and upon which the Hyades dance. On the civic stage of the sanctuary, Alcman's chorus presents the star chorus with a mimesis of itself. The double quality of the performance as spectacle for the heavenly bodies as well as for the Spartan audience is demonstrated by the gesture of the Moon, who must be looking upon the performance, because she applauds it:

οὐ γὰρ ἁ καλλίσφυρος
Ἀγησιχ[ο]ρ[α] πάρ' αὐτεῖ
Ἀγιδοῖ δὲ παρμένει
θωστήρια [τ᾽] ἅμ᾽ ἐπαινεῖ.

---

32. Peponi (2004) perfectly captures this effect, in which the audience's perception "constantly alternates between mere vision and imaginary visualization" (307). She interprets the projections onto the imaginary plane of the drama as a series of metaphors.

33. On addresses *ad spectatores*, see Pfister 1988, 81–83. On the identification of the audience in the addressee of the questions at lines 50 and 56–57, see Puelma 1977, 42n77 and Peponi 2004, 300–301.

34. Ubersfeld 1996, 97; for a general definition of "the play within the play," see also Pfister 1988, 223–30. Rosenmeyer (2002, 9–10) briefly discusses the "play-within" as regards Greek drama. Hutchinson (2001, 78) notes that in the *Partheneion* "a kind of little drama, so to speak, is staged on the edge of the ritual."

Nor does Hagesichora
of the beautiful ankles remain in place
to Agido . . .
and lauds our festival.

(78–81)

It is useful to analyze this dramatic strategy through the focusing
lens of Tambiah's definition of the performative capacities of ritual in
an influential essay that opens with, but never fully develops, precisely
the question of the role of the dance-song in ritual:

> Ritual action in its constitutive features is performative in these
> three senses: in the Austinian sense of performative, wherein saying
> something is also doing something as a conventional act; in the quite
> different sense of a staged performance that uses multiple media by
> which the participants experience the event intensively; and in the
> sense of indexical values—I derive this concept from Peirce—being
> attached to and inferred by actors during the performance.[35]

Its identity as actors constitutes the indexical dimension of the chorus.
When it momentarily steps outside the role of Hyades, it stands revealed in its other role, which is to "represent, reenact, the community
of the polis," to which it has an existential relation.[36] The identification of chorus with *polis*, of dance floor with civic space, was explicitly
made in Sparta, where *khoros* was what the *agora* was called (Pausanias 3.11.9).[37] Plutarch's *Life of Lycurgus* reveals a tradition according
to which choral performances both preceded and embodied the Ly-
curgan laws and constitution, for which the name was *kosmos*. From
his self-imposed exile on Crete, Lycurgus persuaded Thaletas to go
to Sparta. In Thaletas the practices of music and political action are
equated, in that his songs bring strife among the citizenry to an end.
For that reason, "he performed the part of one of the ablest lawgivers
in the world" and "prepared the way for the discipline introduced by

35. Tambiah 1979, 128.
36. Nagy 1990b, 142. For a similar distinction between the dramatic role of the chorus and
its choregic role, see Henrichs 1996b, 56; Bierl 2001, 29; Bierl 2007; Kowalzig 2004, 54–55.
37. Herodotus 1.65.4; Nagy 1985, 40–41; Nagy 1990b, 367–68, followed by Too 1997, 14–15.
On the importance of dance in Spartan society, see Constantinidou 1998, 15–17.

Lycurgus."[38] The reason Thaletas is like a great lawmaker is that, just as laws do, the performance of his choral lyrics enacts social order.[39] The double identity of the chorus in the *Partheneion* enables it simultaneously to embody the harmony of the heavens, signified in the cosmic dance, and the harmony of the state, which it also enacts, as the dancers of the songs of Thaletas had done before.

It is this capacity to represent the *polis* indexically that enables the performative function of the chorus, since performative speech is never a matter of words only. Its efficacy depends on the recognition by all involved that the speaker has the authority to make such a statement and does so in the appropriate circumstances.[40] On the other hand, the dramatic action—the dance of the Hyades—frames and legitimizes the ritual event at the symbolic level in terms of a cosmology that projects the order of the universe and that of the state as analogical structures. The double role of the chorus appears to be a function—again, in Tambiah's perspective—of "ritual's duplex existence, as an entity that symbolically and/or iconically represents the cosmos and at the same time indexically legitimates and realizes social hierarchies."[41] In this case, it does so by staging a confrontation of the order of the cosmos with the *kosmos* of the *polis* such that they are revealed to mirror each other.

38. Plutarch *Lycurgus* 4.1–2. There are significant overlaps between this story and the legends about Pythagoras reported in Iamblichus's *On the Pythagorean Way of Life*: Pythagoras spent time on Crete and in Sparta, "for the sake of their laws" (25); the songs (64, *melē*) he composed had the effect of turning destructive emotions in the members of his community into virtues. Franklin (2004, 244n22) collects references to laws as musical forms. Of particular interest here is the tradition, mentioned by Clement of Alexandria (*Stromata* 1.16.78 Stählin), that "Terpander sang the laws of the Spartans." On the civic function of song in archaic Sparta as regards Terpander, see Gostoli 1988.

39. The story of Thaletas reads like an illustration of Bloch's controversial theses that ritual speech is quintessentially political and that danced lyrics in particular, where stylization is most pronounced, are marked by weak propositional force but high "'performative force'—'not to report facts but to influence people' (Austin, 1962: 234)" (Bloch 1974; the quotation is from p. 67). Bloch's extreme view of ritual as an exercise of political authority and coercion has justifiably come under attack (see, e.g., Tambiah 1979, 151–53; Yatromanolakis and Roilos 2003, 34), but the validity of his characterization of the illocutionary effect of ritual speech is generally recognized; see, e.g., Rappaport 1999, 118, 151, 303.

40. I rely on Benveniste's (1963) more restrictive definition of the speech act, in answer to Austin's (1962) proposal, as well as on Bourdieu's analysis of the speech act in ritual discourse (1982, 103–18).

41. Tambiah 1979, 155.

The Mourning Voice

The correspondences between the *Partheneion* and tragedy do not end with performative self-referentiality. As we have seen, the song as a whole is marked by strong thematic consistency, which centers on the issue of legitimate succession as the guarantee of order, developed through a series of analogies and contrasts. The juxtaposition of bloodshed, heaps of corpses, and Phaethon's crash on the one hand to the feminine grace of maidens' voices on the other dramatizes the tension between the chaos of the past and the harmony of the present.[42] An effective element of continuity—a bridge, as it were, between past and present—is given by a note sounded throughout the text, which has so far gone undetected, that of lament. Indirectly, the lines that seal the mythical narratives and introduce the chorus's self-description refer to funeral lamentations:

ἄλαστα δὲ
ϝέργα πάσον κακὰ μησάμενοι.

ἔστι τις σιῶν τίσις·
ὁ δ' ὄλβιος ὅστις εὔφρων
ἁμέραν [δι]απλέκει
ἄκλαυστος.

things never to be forgotten
they suffered for the evils they plotted.

There is such a thing as retribution from the gods.
Happy is he who, sound of mind,
weaves through the day
unwept.

(34–39)

42. Burnett (1985, 11) perceptively observes, "the ten scented girl-names of the present, when they come, echo the ten blood-soaked masculine names of the mythic past with an effect that is clearly contrived and markedly baroque."

The fortunate man who is "unwept," *aklaustos*, is one whose day does not come to a tragic end that calls for mourning, and he is implicitly compared with the unhappy figures not "sound of mind," who were the subject of the preceding stanzas and for whom formal lamentations were performed. As Nagy observed, the phrase *alasta . . . pason* (36–37) is akin to the epic combination *penthos alaston*, "unforgettable grief."[43] In the latter the epithet *alaston*, which properly applies to the hero's ordeal, is transferred to the grief of those directly affected by his tribulations and, at the level of the community, to the ritual lamentations performed in his cult.

The legendary lament of the Heliads over their brother is not explicitly mentioned in what remains of the *Partheneion*, but there is an allusion to it, I have argued, in the figure of the Enetic horse, which calls up the black robes of the inhabitants of Adria forever mourning Phaethon's death.[44] Cycnus's lament for Phaethon may be evoked as well near the end of the song, by the mention of the cry of the swan at daybreak. The roster of dead Hippocoontids, as we have seen, is explicitly framed in terms of commemoration.[45] In this perspective the expression *en kamousin* (2) takes on its proper significance. Most readers of the *Partheneion* translate it as "among the dead," and *kamontes* may be indeed used in that sense in epic and tragedy.[46] But the primary meanings of *kamnō* are to "toil," "endure," "struggle," and "suffer," while the noun *kamatos* takes on the marked sense of "ordeal," "struggle," in reference to the trials of athletes and the labors of heroes.[47] In marking the difference between Lycaethus and the Hippocoontids, *en kamousin* turns the spotlight on the "sufferings" of the latter. That is what entitles them to be not "passed over" and justifies their heroic status. In the same way, the phrase "suffered unforget-

43. Nagy 1974, 258–60; Nagy 1999, 114 (with chap. 6 for the transformation of the *penthos alaston* of the mourning community into *kleos aphthiton* at the level of epic); Hinge 2006, 238. Calame (1983, 324) interprets *aklaustos* in the active sense as "unweeping."
44. See p. 74 in the present text.
45. See pp. 21–22 in the present text.
46. LSJ, s.v. *kamno* 5.
47. Chantraine 1999, s.v. *kamno*; see Calame 1983, 315; Loraux 1995, 52–53; Nagy 1990b, 138–39, 151. In Pericles' Funeral Oration (Thucydides 2.41.5), *kamnein* signifies heroic death in battle.

table things" (ἄλαστα . . . πάσον, 36–37)—which may apply to all the foregoing mythical transgressors or just to the ones mentioned last—points to the undying memory that is attached to such "sufferings."

How melody, choreography, and dance movements reflected the theme of lament that is embedded in the text of the *Partheneion* is impossible to know, except to say that the performing voice of the chorus is "the mourning voice," as Loraux called it.[48] The Hyades are archetypal singers of the dirge, their catasterism being the result of the insatiable grief for their brother that consumed them. Moreover, they explicitly characterize their song as one of sorrow by calling it a wail (*lelaka*) like the mournful call of the owl.[49] What to make of so explicit a call to grief in a song that celebrates the harmony of the universe as a new season begins? We are in fact very familiar with the marriage of what appear to be incompatible modes—the *paiān* and the hymn with the *thrēnos*—because that is the mark of the choral songs of Athenian tragedy.[50] Most scholars interpret inflections of lament in songs that are not dirges as a new development and the distinctive feature of tragedy, which brought about a synthesis of what had been hitherto distinct lyric genres.[51] That such a synthesis appears already in the earliest lyric we have should be of interest in future inquiries into what tragedy owes the lyric tradition.

As a choral dance-song that commemorates the ordeals of heroes, not on the occasion of a ritual in their individual cults but on the stage of a city festival, the *Partheneion* is not an isolated case. It finds a parallel in the Herodotean story of Cleisthenes' attempt to expel from Sicyon the cult of the hero Adrastus. Herodotus states that the ancestral honors paid to Adrastus included tragic choruses (*tragikoisi khoroisi*) that rehearsed his *pathea*, "sufferings."[52] When the Pythia af-

48. This is the title of Loraux's exploration of the mode of lament in Greek tragedy (2002).
49. Lines 85–87; see pp. 88–89 in the present text.
50. For a review of the rich literature concerning the element of lamentation in Athenian tragedy and its relationship to Homeric epic on the one hand and to ritual laments at funerals on the other, see Dué 2006, introduction and chap. 1. The seminal study of Alexiou (1974, with its second edition published in 2002) remains the standard source on the Greek lament.
51. See, e.g., Segal 1993, chap. 2.
52. Herodotus 5.67.5; see again Nagy 1999, 114.

firmed Adrastus's claim to the city, the tyrant transferred the choruses to the cult of Dionysus. Whatever meaning is to be attached to the use of the term *tragikos* here, what is noteworthy and relevant is Herodotus's narrative implying that the choruses for Adrastus continued to recount and celebrate the hero's *pathea*, albeit in the ritual context of a festival of Dionysus. An even more striking parallel is evoked in the passage of Euripides' *Alcestis* (445–52) that was cited in chapter 2 in reference to the image of the Pleiades suspended in the night sky.

The first *stasimon*, following the episode of Alcestis's death, brings to the fore the inversion of gender roles that runs throughout the play. The part of the hero belongs to Alcestis, who has the courage to confront death itself, while Admetus remains in the house to mourn, taking on a role that normally belongs to women. In these lines "Alcestis reaches heroic status and receives the kind of bardic praise traditionally given to male valor."[53] An epic tone is established at the opening by the chorus's address (435–37): ὦ Πελίου θύγατερ, // χαίρουσά μοι εἰν Ἀίδα δόμοισιν // τὸν ἀνάλιον οἶκον οἰκετεύοις, "O daughter of Pelias, fare-thee-well even as you dwell in the sunless house of Hades." This is one of several allusions to the Trojan epic, an echo of Achilles' address to the dead Patroclus (Homer *Iliad* 23.179): χαῖρέ μοι, ὦ Πάτροκλε, καὶ εἰν Ἀΐδαο δόμοισι, "fare-thee-well, O Patroclus, even in the house of Hades."[54] The chorus goes on to predict that her heroic death will be commemorated in songs, including the "lyre-less hymns" that were performed in the course of a great state festival in the month of Karneios:

> πολλά σε μουσοπόλοι
> μέλψουσι καθ᾽ ἑπτάτονόν τ᾽ ὀρείαν
> χέλυν ἔν τ᾽ ἀλύροις κλέοντες ὕμνοις,
> Σπάρται κυκλὰς ἀνίκα Καρνεί-
> ου περινίσεται ὥρα
> μηνός, ἀειρομένας
> παννύχου σελάνας,
> λιπαραῖσί τ᾽ ἐν ὀλβίαις Ἀθάναις.

---

53. On the play on gender roles in the *Alcestis*, see Segal 1993, 51–86; the quotation is from p. 77.

54. See Dale 1961, 88 and Garner 1988, particularly pp. 60–61.

Poets shall sing often in your praise both on the seven-stringed
mountain tortoise-shell and in songs unaccompanied by the lyre
when at Sparta the cycle of the season of the month Karneios comes
circling round and the moon is aloft the whole night long, and also in
rich, gleaming Athens.[55]

(445–52)

The ritual event that Euripides envisions bears an uncanny re-
semblance to the circumstances surrounding the performance of
the *Partheneion*, as they were reconstructed in the preceding chapters: a *pannukhis* marking the change of seasons. Here too the mode
of lament informs the celebration. The key phrase is ἔν τ᾽ ἀλύροις
κλέοντες ὕμνοις, "conferring glory in hymns unaccompanied by the
lyre." In tragic diction *aluros*, "without lyre," is firmly and exclusively
associated with mourning and specifically with the *thrēnos*.[56] Euripides uses it three more times, each time unequivocally in this
sense: in the *Iphigenia in Tauris*, 146, the heroine's lamentations are
aluroi elegoi; in the *Helen*, 185, Helen's wail is an *aluros elegos*; and
at *Phoenician Women*, 1028, *aluron* qualifies the deadly song of the
Theban Sphinx.[57] The figure of the tragic hymn appears earlier in
Aeschylus's *Agamemnon*, 988–91, where "the heart hymns the lyre-
less [*aneu luras*] threnos of the Erinyes."[58] The point made at *Alcestis*
446–52 is clear: Alcestis will receive the *kleos* bestowed by a genre
of songs that fused praise and lamentation and were traditionally
performed for the heroes at the Karneia. The efficacy of this image
in projecting Alcestis's heroic status depends in no small measure
on knowledge on the part of the audience that the *pannukhis* at
the Karneia included choral songs that celebrated the heroes —
"hymns" in some sense — in the lyre-less mode that also marked the

55. Trans. Kovacs 1994, modified.
56. Loraux 2002, 61–62. In spite of this, interpreters of the *Alcestis* reject the possibility
that *aluros* here has the meaning that it has everywhere else. Dale (1961), followed by Paduano
(1969), takes it to denote poetry spoken with no accompaniment or accompanied by the *aulos*,
contrasted in a technical sense to songs accompanied by the lyre. On the "figure of negated song,"
see Segal 1993, 16–20.
57. See also Sophocles *Oedipus at Colonus* 1221–23; Alexis frag. 1162 PCG.
58. At Aeschylus *Eumenides* 331–33, the song of the Furies is a lyre-less [*aphormingtos*]
hymn, withering to mortals.

thrēnos.[59] The "tragic oxymoron" of tragedy, to quote Loraux again, characterizes as well the Louvre *Partheneion.*

The strain of lamentation in the *Partheneion,* particularly as regards the Hippocoontids, taps into the community's emotional connection to its past.[60] Its resonance with the audience may be gauged by reflecting that hero-shrines of the sons of Hippocoon were prominently located in the Spartan sacred landscape and presumably were the site of periodic observances. Pausanias names the shrine of Alcon, reportedly a son of Hippocoon, at the head of the Dromos, where the athletes trained to his day; near the Platanistas, the Plane-Tree Grove where the violent hand-to-hand combats of the ephebes took place, he notes the shrines of Alcimus, Dorceus, Enarsphorus, and Thebrus, of whom the latter two correspond to names that survive in the text of the *Partheneion.* And between an area called the *Sebrion,* after Thebrus, and a shrine of Helen, not far from the heroon of Heracles that commemorated his fight with the Hippocoontids, Pausanias saw the tomb of Alcman.[61]

Alcman acquitted himself well in the task of grounding the song in Spartan myth-history and ritual practice. But, like the myth of Phaethon, the outer frame of the *Partheneion* is Panhellenic in character. As it throws further light onto the brilliant culture of seventh-century Sparta, therefore, the poem also confirms the city's cosmopolitan character. On the one hand, Alcman's cosmology echoes notions of unfathomable antiquity, which are attested in Mesopotamian sources going back to the second millennium BCE, as well as in Homer and Hesiod. That is the case with *poros,* the road of the Sun with its stellar signposts, which find parallels in the *harranu* and *manzazu* of the

59. Rutherford (1994–95, 121) admits the possibility that the passage refers to actual songs performed at the Karneia. Bierl (2007) shows that the choral song of the Spartan women at the end of Aristophanes' *Lysistrata* pointedly echoes the imagery and wording of the Louvre *Partheneion,* in a way that suggests that at least the educated members of the Athenian audience would be familiar with this genre of Spartan lyric. See also Hinge 2006, 297–99.

60. On the emotional dimension of choral lyric in tragedy, see Loraux 2002 and Dué's perceptive observation (2006, 166): "The distance between the world of heroes in the there and then and the world of the audience in the here and now was bridged by the tragic chorus, who maintained a physical connection to the audience (via their location in the orchestra) and mediated between the two worlds."

61. Pausanias 3.14.7, 3.15.1–3. See Page 1951, 26–27; Calame 1977, 2:54.

Babylonian creation myth. By staging the dance of the Hyades and by its mention of the song of the Sirens, the poem also bears witness to the antiquity of the notion of the cosmic harmony and of the concept of a universe regulated by the musical scale, which later tradition would attribute to Pythagoras.

The importance of Alcman's *aisa* reflects the role that the concept of "due measure," Justice, plays in Hesiod and pre-Socratic philosophers. As Slatkin has shown, that is the principle that keeps the processes and patterns of nature in equilibrium through a cycle of exchanges that mirror the human condition. Likewise, Alcman's is a universe in which stars labor and the Sun itself rises when summoned, keeping to his course and setting when it should; in Kahn's words, "the universe governed by law."[62] Anaximander gave this conceit its clearest surviving formulation:

ἐξ ὧν δὲ ἡ γένεσίς ἐστι τοῖς οὖσι, καὶ τὴν φθορὰν εἰς ταῦτα γίνεσθαι κατὰ τὸ χρεών· διδόναι γὰρ αὐτὰ δίκην καὶ τίσιν ἀλλήλοις τῆς ἀδικίας κατὰ τὴν τοῦ χρόνου τάξιν.

Further, the source from which existing things derive their existence is also that to which they return at their destruction, according to necessity; for they give justice and make reparation to one another for their injustice, according to the arrangement of Time.[63]

The phrase διδόναι γὰρ αὐτὰ δίκην καὶ τίσιν, "give justice and make reparation," belongs to the language of the law courts and casts the balance of the elements in terms of a cycle of offense and punishment.[64] This metaphor, which animates as well the fragment of Heraclitus discussed in chapter 1, is at work already in the *Partheneion*. Among diction sounding a note sterner than one expects on the lips of maidens, *ponōn* ("toils," 88), *irānas* ("respite," 91), and *tisis* ("reparation" or "retribution," 36) may or may not carry specific connotations. But the judicial metaphor is explicit in the remarkable *marturetai* ("summons," 42)

62. Kahn 1994, 166.
63. Anaximander 1 D–K; trans. Freeman 1948.
64. Kahn 1994, 168–69.

"commands to appear and witness" as in a court of law,[65] to say that Eos ushers in Helius.

The view of the cosmos that informs the *Partheneion* falls within mainstream traditions of archaic wisdom poetry and philosophy of nature. We should expect that it is representative of the landmark developments in the composition of choral lyrics that our sources locate in the seventh century.[66] In that respect, one of the most significant conclusions to be drawn from this study is to observe that for its dramatic nature and its exploitation of the mode of lament, for the very marginality of the persona of the chorus, the song is profoundly akin to the choral odes of tragedy. Far from illustrating the divergence of the choral performances of rituals from the choral performances of drama, the *Partheneion* documents continuity, even in the face of innovations in the late sixth century—and demonstrates that ritual is drama, and vice versa.[67]

65. On this use of *marturomai* with the infinitive, see Page 1951, 84–85; Calame 1983, 325–26. On the Sun's role as witness, see pp. 45–47 in the present text.

66. See Nagy 1990b, chap. 3.

67. Bierl 2001, 14–15.

POSTSCRIPT

The previous chapter closed with the observation that the inflections of lament in the *Partheneion* look forward to a well-known feature of the choral odes of Athenian tragedy. Unlike the tragic choruses, however, the dramatic persona of Alcman's chorus plays no part in the myths it narrates—except, of course, its own. Rather, its role is a function of the event that the festival celebrates, that is, the orderly succession of the seasons. In that its charge is to honor the gods and to commemorate the heroes and heroines of the past on a yearly recurring occasion, the chorus of Hyades is comparable to the *kourai Dēliades*, so described in the Homeric hymn to Apollo:

> πρὸς δὲ τόδε μέγα θαῦμα, ὅου κλέος οὔποτ᾽ ὀλεῖται,
> κοῦραι Δηλιάδες Ἑκατηβελέταο θεράπναι·
> αἵ τ᾽ ἐπεὶ ἂρ πρῶτον μὲν Ἀπόλλων᾽ ὑμνήσωσιν,
> αὗτις δ᾽ αὖ Λητώ τε καὶ Ἄρτεμιν ἰοχέαιραν,
> μνησάμεναι ἀνδρῶν τε παλαιῶν ἠδὲ γυναικῶν
> ὕμνον ἀείδουσιν, θέλγουσι δὲ φῦλ᾽ ἀνθρώπων.

And there is this great wonder besides—and its renown shall never perish—, the girls of Delos, hand-maidens of the Far-shooter; for when they have praised Apollo first, and also Leto and Artemis who delights in arrows, they sing a strain telling of men and women of past days, and charm the tribes of men.[1]

In the hymn, the description of the Deliades' extraordinary dance-song follows the narrative of Leto's travail and Apollo's birth on the island. It is a hypothesis of long standing—the available evidence allows no more—that the festival to which it refers celebrated the god's

---

1. *Homeric Hymns* 3.156–61; trans. Evelyn-White 1936.

127

birth.[2] The occasion perfectly suits the stage identity of the chorus, for it was then that the nymphs of Delos, the daughters of the river Inopus, sang "with far-sounding voice the holy song of Eileithyia." It is presumably this role that the historical Deliades reenacted.[3] If the analogy holds, we should ask if the recurring celebrations of the festival for which the *Partheneion* was composed included the performance of the dance of the stars.[4] With regard to this question, in the pages that follow I advance two related theses. The first proposes that the festival in question was the Karneia, the prime venue for the performances by great songwriters in the seventh century.[5] The second identifies in the representations of the so-called *kalathiskos* dance, which appear on countless monuments from the Classical period onward, images of the dance of the stars. Neither is without difficulties and both involve the reevaluation of some intractable issues and long-held assumptions.

THE SEASON OF THE KARNEIA

The astral notations that were identified in the second part of the song pinpoint a specific date in the astronomical year—in our terms, the first days of November at the latitude of Sparta in the late seventh

2. Farnell 1907, 287–91. There exists a coherent tradition, concerning the birthday of Plato, that the Delian festival celebrating the birth of Apollo fell on the Athenian calendar date of the seventh of Thargelion; Diogenes Laertius *Lives of the Philosophers* 3.2, 2.44; *Vita Platonis* p. 6 Westermann. For a review of the evidence and a skeptical appraisal of the placement of the festival in Thargelion, see Bruneau 1970, 85–91.

3. Callimachus *Hymn to Delos* 255–57; see Bruneau 1970, 216 and, in the present text, pp. 12–13.

4. The hypothesis that choral dances were, in some cases, patterned upon the movements of celestial bodies has been advanced before, albeit on the basis of sparse and late testimonies; see *Capitulum f* in Drachmann 1927, 310–11; scholium to Euripides *Hecuba* 647; *Etymologicum Magnum* 690.47, s.v. *prosōdion*. On these texts see Montanari 1989; on the dance, Lawler 1960; J. Miller 1986, 35–37. Elsewhere I have myself argued (Ferrari 2002, 170–74) that such a performance was a recurring feature of the Athenian festival of the Arkteia for Artemis Braunonia, and that in the Arktos the young daughters of the Athenians year after year reenacted the dance of the constellation of the Great Bear.

5. Hellanicus composed a list in verse and prose of the winners in the musical contests at the Karneia (*FGrHist* 4F85, via Athenaeus 14.635e); see Calame 1977, 2:35–36. From a scholium to Theocritus (5.83 Wendel) we learn that in one of his songs Alcman said that the festival was named for a Trojan called Carneus.

century—and announce that it is time to plow. The Pyanopsia, in honor of Apollo, marked this point in time in the festival calendar of Athens. The month of Pyanopsion included other important festivals directly related to the activities of plowing and sowing, namely, the Proerosia and the Thesmophoria.[6] There was, in addition, the Oschophoria, which celebrated the end of the grape harvest. Its rituals included a reenactment of the return to Athens of the children whom Theseus had rescued from the Minotaur, in a procession led by two youths bearing ōskhoi, vine branches laden with grapes. The representation of Pyanopsion on the calendar frieze, which was reused above the main entrance of the Little Metropolis church in Athens, emblematically joins a child carrying the eiresiōnē and a thesmophoros with an ōskhophoros, a youth holding the vine branch as he tramples the grapes.[7] The other major turn in the cycle of the seasons, the start of summer and the beginning of the harvest with the heliacal rising of the Pleiades and the Hyades in mid-May, was the occasion of another Athenian festival of Apollo, the Thargelia. Late sources testify that the Athenians offered sacrifices to Helius and the Horae at both the Pyanopsia and the Thargelia, thus confirming that these festivals were tied to the agricultural cycle and the astronomical calendar.[8]

We know much less about the Spartan sacred calendar.[9] On good grounds the Hyacinthia, which took place in the Spartan month of Hekatombaion, is widely considered a spring or early summer festival.[10] Of particular interest is the Karneia, because we are explicitly told that it celebrates the return of the season in the month of Karneios. Our source is the passage of Euripides' Alcestis that has been

---

6. Parke (1977, 73–94) helpfully summarizes the evidence for all festivals celebrated in Pyanopsion, while Deubner (1932, 50–60, 68–69, 198–200) and Simon (1983, 18–22, 76–77) subdivide them according to the gods each honored.

7. LIMC 6 (1992), s.v. "Menses" no. 2; Deubner 1932, 248–54. On the Oschophoria as a vintage festival, see Deubner 1932, 142–47. N. Robertson (1992, 120–24) attempts to relocate the festival in the preceding month of Boedromion. We do not know precisely when in Pyanopsion the Oschophoria fell, or which god it honored; see Mikalson 1975, 68–69.

8. Scholium to Aristophanes Knights 729; scholium to Aristophanes Wealth 1054; Suda, s.v. eiresiōnē. Porphyry On Abstinence 2.7 Bouffartigue, Patillon, and Segouds; see Deubner 1932, 190–93.

9. Overviews in Samuel 1972, 92–94 and Trümpy 1997, 135–39.

10. Nilsson 1909, 124–25n9; Farnell 1907, 265–66.

cited several times before.[11] These lines may be quoted here in their
entirety for the last time (445–52):

πολλά σε μουσοπόλοι
μέλψουσι καθ᾽ ἑπτάτονόν τ᾽ ὀρείαν
χέλυν ἔν τ᾽ ἀλύροις κλέοντες ὕμνοις,
Σπάρται κυκλὰς ἁνίκα Καρνεί-
ου περινίσεται ὥρα
μηνός, ἀειρομένας
παννύχου σελάνας,
λιπαραῖσί τ᾽ ἐν ὀλβίαις Ἀθάναις.

Poets shall sing often in your praise both on the seven-stringed
mountain tortoise-shell and in songs unaccompanied by the lyre
when at Sparta the cycle of the season of the month Karneios comes
circling round and the moon is aloft the whole night long, and also in
rich, gleaming Athens.[12]

What the chorus of the *Alcestis* predicts for its heroine perfectly suits
the circumstances of the performance of the *Partheneion*, as they were
reconstructed in the preceding chapters: a festival for the new season that included a *pannukhis* under a full moon, where songs in a
mournful vein celebrated the tragic fates of heroes. Mention in Callimachus's *Hymn to Apollo* (85) of choral dances (at Cyrene but in
direct connection to Spartan ritual) on the occasion of the coming of
the "appointed seasons of the Karneia" confirms the seasonal character of the celebration. The crucial question then is: is the season that
the Karneia inaugurates the same as that of the *Partheneion*, namely,
winter?

The sparse testimonies concerning the Karneia provide three ad-
ditional indications of its placement in the course of the year: two
of them refer to the astral calendar and are complementary to each
other, while the third refers to the festival calendars of different cities
and stands in contradiction to both. An anonymous source describes

11. See pp. 85–86, 120–22 in the present text.
12. Trans. Kovacs 1994, modified.

the rite of the *staphulodromoi*, "grape cluster runners," performed by young men (*neoi*). A man decked with garlands was set running as he prayed for the welfare of the city, with the *staphulodromoi* in pursuit. If they caught him, it meant that the city would prosper. Hesychius otherwise also links the *staphulodromoi* at the Karneia to the vintage, by defining them as "those who urge on the grape gatherers."[13] With regard to the agricultural cycle, the mentions of grape clusters and grape gatherers circumscribe a specific period, which begins when the first visible morning rising of Arcturus signals the beginning of autumn and the start of the vintage.[14] The heliacal rising of Arcturus, then, gives us a *terminus post quem* in the yearly cycle for the celebration of the Karneia. What can be said thus far, then, is the following: the festival occurred *after* the rising of Arcturus and before winter set in, and it took place at the full moon, that is, *at midmonth*. The month in question may be the one in which the rising occurs or the one following. The fact that "grape-cluster carriers," *ōskhophoroi*, figured in the festivities of the Athenian Pyanopsion, which included festivals that celebrated the beginning of winter, indicates that such references to the vintage are appropriate to the celebration of the end of the grape harvest, not just its beginning.

Thucydides unequivocally links the conclusion of the Karneia to the onset of winter in his narrative of the events following the battle of Mantinea.[15] Right after the battle, he reports, Eleans and Athenians marched to Epidaurus and began to build a fortified wall "while the Spartans conducted the Karneia" (5.75.5: ἕως οἱ Λακεδαιμόνιοι Κάρνεια ἦγον). This was the last event in the summer of the fourteenth year of the war (5.75.6: καὶ τὸ θέρος ἐτελεύτα). The Spartans took to the field again "right at the beginning of the following winter, after they had conducted the Karneia" (5.76.1: Τοῦ δ᾽ ἐπιγιγνομένου

13. Bekker, *Anecdota* 1:305.25; Hesychius, s.v. *staphulodromoi*. On the festival, see Wide 1893, 73–85; Farnell 1907, 259–63.

14. Hesiod *Works and Days* 609–14; Plato *Laws* 822e; [Hippocrates] *On Regimen* 68.10 Jones.

15. On Thucydides' method of dating by summers and winters, according to the natural calendar, see Gomme 1956, 699–715; Pritchett and van der Waerden 1961. See also Theophrastus *On Weather Signs* 6 Sider and Brunschön: "the year is divided in half by the setting and rising of the Pleiad."

χειμῶνος ἀρχομένου εὐθὺς οἱ Λακεδαιμόνιοι, ἐπειδὴ τὰ Κάρνεια ἤγαγον, ἐξεστράτευσαν). It has been pointed out that Thucydides' account of the operations of the preceding summer (5.53–55) apparently includes events that took place after the completion of the Karneia and before the end of the summer. This state of affairs would contradict what the passage just quoted implies, that winter began with the celebration of the Karneia.[16] While the difficulty needs frankly to be acknowledged, a look at the time line shows that it is far from insurmountable.

As the Argives prepared to invade Epidauros with the support of the Athenians, the Spartan army set out, coming as far as Leuctra, but returned home when the omens from the border-crossing sacrifices turned out unfavorably. This happened in the last days of the month preceding Karneios, which was "a holy month for Dorians" (5.54.2). The Spartans notified their allies that they would resume the campaign after the festival. The Argives, who were obliged to observe the holy month as well, nevertheless pressed on. With a stratagem (presumably by inserting the same intercalary day over and over again), they stopped the festival from coming by freezing their calendar on the day they had set out, the twenty-sixth of the month before Karneios.[17] They briefly withdrew at the request of a peace council held at Mantinea, then, after a second unsuccessful meeting of that council, resumed the invasion. The Spartans took to the field against Caryae apparently in response to this second Argive attack; once more, they returned home on account of an unfavorable outcome of the *diabatēria*. This event, together with the sack of Epidaurus and the return home of the Athenians, brings the summer to a close (5.55.3–4). It is possible that the expedition against Caryae was launched after the celebration of the Karneia. One cannot exclude, however, that the Spartans sent out a contingent, leaving the bulk of the army in Sparta to observe the festival, as they had done in the event of the Thermopylae (Herodotus 7.206.1). It may also be the case that Thucydides here subsumes into his account of the summer campaigns the final stages of a war that extended

16. See Nilsson 1906, 119n2; Gomme, Andrewes, and Dover 1970, 130.
17. Thucydides 5.54.3; see Pritchett 1974, 124.

marginally into winter.[18] In any case, the distance between the Karneia and the end of the summer should be measured in days, rather than weeks or months, since it is unlikely that the Argives could postpone the arrival of the month of Karneios for more than two or three weeks.[19]

The reason most commentators of Thucydides dismiss the passage at 5.76.1 as an interpolation is that it contradicts a note found in Plutarch's *Life of Nicias*, 28.1, to the effect that Karneios was the month that the Athenians called Metageitnion. We are reasonably well informed as to when the latter fell in the solar year. Since it was the second month in the Athenian lunar year, which began with the first new moon after the summer solstice,[20] its possible chronological span around 600 BCE ranged from the last week in July to the last week in September in the Julian calendar. On this basis, the notion that the Spartan Karneios is a summer month and the Karneia a summer festival has gained the status of established fact.[21]

Plutarch's passage, however, is problematic in several respects. To begin with, the statement occurs in the context of a proposal brought to the Syracusan assembly and, therefore, refers not to the Spartan month called Karneios but to a Syracusan month by the same name. The two have been equated on the assumption that months that have the same name in the calendars of different *poleis* occurred at corresponding times. That was true in some cases. Indeed, Thucydides' narrative of the campaigns of the summer of 419 (5.54.2–3), cited above, implies that the Spartan Karneios coincided with the Argive one. But such correspondences were not the rule: a given month name might occupy widely different positions in the calendars of different cities.[22] It is troubling, moreover, that we do not know on what

---

18. For other instances, see Gomme 1956, 73–75.

19. Pritchett 1974, 124.

20. Plato *Laws* 767c4–7; Aristotle *History of Animals* 543b6–13, Theophrastus *Enquiry into Plants* 4.11.4–5 Hort; see Hannah 2005, 72.

21. See, e.g., Nilsson 1906, 118; 1909, 89n2; Samuel 1972, 93; Hannah 2005, 27; Gomme, Andrewes, and Dover 1970, 130: "it seems established that the month Karneios (54.2, with n.) corresponded to the Attic Metageitnion, the second of the civil year."

22. Nilsson 1909, 132, 137; Nilsson 1962, 55–59; Pritchett 1946. Pritchett points out (1946, 359) that the most common month name, Panamos, has been assigned six different positions, which range from April to October, in the reconstructions of the civil calendars of eighteen

grounds Plutarch draws the correlation of (Syracusan) Karneios with Metageitnion, because such synchronisms are notoriously tricky to establish. The Greek *poleis* universally adopted the lunar month as the unit for the civil year, a practice that required periodic intercalations in order to keep the calendar synchronized with the cycle of the seasons. But there was no coordination among *poleis* either as regards the starting point of the year or the insertion of intercalary days and months, which occurred irregularly and might be governed by political exigencies.[23] It was precisely the disarray of the civil calendars that led Thucydides to base his chronology of the Peloponnesian War on the seasonal calendar regulated by stellar phases (5.20.3). Moreover, Plutarch's sense of chronology and the correlations he draws between events are notoriously unreliable.[24]

The equation of Spartan Karneios with Athenian Metageitnion is thus intrinsically questionable. But its fatal flaw is that it requires our ignoring what little we do know about the time of the Spartan Karneia: that it was celebrated at a plenilune and that it had something to do with the vintage, and therefore took place after the heliacal rising of Arcturus. That this event precedes by a few days the autumnal equinox, around September 21, allows one to calculate that its occurrence in the seventh century BCE fell roughly between September 15 and

cities. Samuel (1972) gives an updated list of Greek local calendars and names of months; in his preface (ix), Samuel, too, takes a strong position against drawing analogies between calendars of different cities: "as even a casual examination of the lists of months will show, colonies do not necessarily have all of or only the months which mother cities use, related cities may have quite different lists, and months with the same names may appear in quite different positions in different calendars." Samuel's position regarding Plutarch's statement, however, is unclear. He unequivocally states that the Karneios in question is a Syracusan month (137), but in his discussion of Boethius's reconstruction of the Argive calendar (90n3) he refers to it also as "Spartan Karneios," thus equating the two, as he also does at p. 93. I was unable to verify the statement in Pritchett 1974, 124n31 that "homonymous festivals, including the Karneia, did not occur at corresponding times in different Dorian calendars. . . . At Syrakuse, the Karneia was not celebrated in a month called Karneios."

23. See Samuel 1972, 10–55; West 1978, 376–81; Hannah 2005, 5–70. Pritchett (1974, 117–18) observes of Plutarch's equation of Metageitnion with Karneios (which he takes to refer to the Spartan month) that "this may have been true on the average, but we cannot be sure that it pertained for any particular year, since Athens and Sparta introduced intercalary months at different times." But the reverse may be true, that the coincidence of Syracusan Karneios and Athenian Metageitnion on a particular year was the basis for Plutarch's statement.

24. See Gomme 1956, 57, 68–69, 411n1, 444–45.

September 18.[25] The latest possible date for the end of Metageitnion, September 25, might accommodate the rising of Arcturus, although neither regularly nor frequently.[26] Even in that extreme case, however, the plenilune in Metageitnion could not be the occasion for a celebration of the grape harvest, because it would fall around September 10, well ahead of the rising.[27] All of this indicates that we should bracket Plutarch's statement and, relying instead on the authority of Thucydides, contemplate the possibility that the Karneia was the late autumn festival that inaugurated winter—precisely the occasion, I have argued, which Alcman's *Partheneion* celebrated. As to choral dances for Apollo Karneios, in addition to the passage of the *Alcestis*, cited above, we have one more piece of evidence, to which I now turn.

KALATHISKOS DANCERS

The piece in question is the large Lucanian volute-krater, the name piece of the Karneia Painter, which was found in a native tomb in Ceglie di Campo, the site of Italic Caelia.[28] A poorly understood Dionysiac scene takes up the obverse of the vase. Dionysus, seated on a rock, looks toward a maenad, who dances ecstatically to the accompaniment of a female *aulos* player. Behind the god, a female figure in

25. Ideler (1883, 247) calculated that in the late eighth century the rising took place on September 18; Ginzel (1911, 356) placed it on September 17 at 700 BCE at the latitude of Athens and Elis. Jebb's commentary on Sophocles' *Oedipus Rex* (1893, 230–32) provides a discussion of the sources attesting to the proximity of the heliacal rising of Arcturus to the autumnal equinox and arrives at a date of September 15 for Athens around 430.

26. I rely on Alan Bowen's calculation (private communication, July 5, 2007): "Suppose the New Moon occurs on the evening before the summer solstice occurs, i.e., that the solstice occurs on Skirophorion 1. Suppose also that June 29 (Julian calendar) was the day of summer solstice—as it was in 600 BC. Then, the latest Metageitnion can start is 59 days after June 29, that is, on August 27, and the latest possible date for the end of Metageitnion is September 25 (assuming another 30-day month)." Theophrastus (*Enquiry into Plants* 4.11.4 Hort) places the rising of Arcturus in Boedromion.

27. Wide (1893, 76) and N. Robertson (1992, 153n17) attempt to gloss over the difficulty, the one by suggesting that the ritual of the *staphulodromoi* refers to the beginning of the vintage, the other that it aimed at promoting the ripening of the grapes. No one, to my knowledge, has addressed the issue of seasonal change.

28. Taranto, Museo Archeologico 8263, *LCS* 55.280, plate 24; *LCS Suppl.* I 1.4; *LCS Suppl.* II 153; *LIMC* 3 (1987), s.v. "Dionysos" no. 801. On the site and the tomb, see Labellarte 1988, 312–14; Bottini 1996, 46.

huntress costume holds a torch over his head, toward the dancing figure. A satyr brings the composition to a close on the right. On the other side (plate 13) the field is subdivided into two registers. Above, a band of satyrs drop their *thyrsoi* and scatter in fright at the sight of Perseus brandishing the head of Medusa. It is highly probable that the scene refers to a satyr play and so, indirectly, to a dramatic performance in a festival of Dionysus.[29] In conjunction with the picture on the obverse, this indicates that a Dionysian frame of reference informs the decorative program of the vase.

Directly relevant to our inquiry is the subject of the second register: a choral performance, not fully under way but in its preliminary stages. What we see are members of the chorus variously holding or wearing parts of their costume, some engaging in conversation, while others try out dance figures. At the far left, a pillar inscribed *Karneios* (plate 14) identifies the setting as a sanctuary of Apollo Carneus, presumably the most famous one at Sparta—although we cannot exclude the possibility that the reference is to another of the many places where the god was worshiped under that name. There follows a group of two young, nude male dancers with short hair, who stand around a basin and face the *aulos* player. The first holds his headdress, which is of the broad, spreading type worn by two more members of the chorus. His companion, who holds an *aryballos*, wears a crown of spiky, curving elements emanating from a headband. This is similar to the one worn by a third nude youth, who is placed behind the *aulos* player and lunges to the right in dance step. He faces a fifth figure, in female dress and with locks of hair reaching the base of the neck, who performs a pirouette that sets its short costume swirling in a loop, exposing the legs. The structure of the expansive headgear is best visible in this case. It consists of an open crown that radiates outward in three concentric circles. The first is connected to the crown by a pattern of upright and inverted triangular projections; the second area consists of rounded triangular uprights, the third of a scalelike pattern suggesting openwork. From the rim arise flamelike strokes. This is also the headdress of a fifth chorus member, a nude youth

29. Trendall 1989, 22; see the recent discussion in Topper 2007, 96–100.

with locks reaching his shoulder, who stands at the far right, facing a bystander. There is little doubt that this scene represents a chorus for Apollo Carneus. The costumes identify the performance as the type conventionally labeled "*kalathiskos* dance."

The so-called *kalathiskos* is the best-loved dance of classical antiquity, the one most frequently depicted on Greek and Roman artifacts of all kinds from the fifth century to the imperial period. We recognize it by a combination of features, of which the headdress is the most telling. The best attested type has a calathoid shape, slightly flaring and more or less high, on which are drawn spearlike elements (plate 15). But there is a fair amount of variation. In the earliest extant examples, there is no "*kalathos*" (plate 16). The crown instead consists of long, thin spikes radiating from a band that encircles the figure's head.[30] The shallow, oversize version that appears on the Karneia krater from Ceglie differs from the more common "calathoid" form and only appears on Lucanian and Apulian vases. As regards dance steps, the typical position, as for the dressed dancer on our krater, is *en pointe*; in a few cases the dancer is in midair, with her toes off the ground.[31] With some notable exceptions, the performers are imagined as young women and wear a dress that is shorter than the norm, at or above the knee.

Representations of this dance are so numerous, varied, and widespread that it is difficult to draw firm conclusions as to its geographical and cultic associations. The reference to Apollo Carneus on the Karneia krater has encouraged the hypothesis that it is a specifically Laconian genre. This idea had already acquired wide currency

30. Fragment of Melian relief from the Piraeus, dated ca. 470–450, Louvre CA 592; see Stilp 2006, 110, 230–31 no. 119. Attic red-figure hydria, Naples, Museo Nazionale 3232, *ARV*[2] 1032.61; FR 3: 320–21, pl. 171. Fragment of Attic red-figure vase, Athens, Agora Museum P 1457, Moore 1997, 355–56 no. 1677, pl. 156, here plate 16. There is no comprehensive list of monuments illustrating the dance that updates those in Wuilleumier 1933, 10n1 and Cook 1940, 996–1012. Delavaud-Roux (1994, 34–47) provides an overview based on selected examples; Benda (1996, 102–7) surveys principal features; Nørskov (2004, 209–13) publishes fragments of a vase from the Mausoleum at Halicarnassus decorated with a depiction of the dance and provides a bibliographical update.

31. Fragment III.1 of the vase from the Mausoleum at Halicarnassus; see Nørskov 2004, 210, fig. 9.3.2; for the dancers of the Acanthus Column at Delphi, see pp. 139–40 in the present text.

by 1893, when Furtwängler identified the prototype of the figures of *kalathiskos* dancers on Neo-Attic reliefs and Arretine pottery in a lost masterpiece by Callimachus mentioned by Pliny: the "Spartan Dancers," *Saltantes Lacaenae*.[32] Although Furtwängler refrained from identifying the subject of Callimachus's sculpture as Spartan women (he proposed that its title was a nickname it acquired in ancient art-historical parlance), others were not so prudent.[33] The notion that the dance has its origin in Sparta has largely obscured the fact that it is at least equally at home in Athens. The earliest images all occur on objects of Athenian manufacture, and the Late Hellenistic Neo-Attic reliefs replicate Athenian fifth-century prototypes. Tiverios identified their earliest depiction in the decoration of the hem of Athena's dress on a late fifth-century Panathenaic amphora (plate 17). These figures also appear on the reverse of staters of Abdera minted at the end of the century.[34] Most remarkably, a monumental chorus of three *kalathiskos* dancers crowns the Acanthus Columns, which the Athenians dedicated at Delphi in the fourth century (plate 15).[35] It is clear that the dance is exclusively associated neither with Apollo nor with Sparta, and that visual representations of the subject are rooted in the Athenian artistic tradition.[36]

The dance owes its name to Ludolf Stephani, who in 1866 first brought together a corpus of relevant monuments.[37] The impetus for the study was the recovery of gold plaques depicting *kalathiskos* dancers in the burial mound of the Great Bliznitsa. The plaques decorated the dress of a woman, who, on other grounds, was conjecturally

32. Furtwängler 1893, 202–3; see Tiverios 1981, 28–30.

33. On that basis, Watzinger (1924, 55), for instance, interpreted an early fourth-century depiction of the dance on a fragmentary Attic oinochoe (Tübingen, University 1219, CVA Tübingen 4 [Germany 52], 86–87, pl. 38) as the choral performance of the wedding song for Menelaus and Helen. Among more recent sources, see Delavaud-Roux 1994, 34, 46; Stilp 2006, 110.

34. British Museum B 606, *ABV* 411.3; *Beazley Addenda* 107; Bentz 1998, 158 no. 5.238. See Tiverios 1981. For the issues of Abdera featuring the dancers, see May 1966, 219, pl. 17. On the derivation of the Abderan type from the Athenian prototype, see Fuchs 1959, 95; Tiverios 1981, 28.

35. On the column, see pp. 139–45 in this chapter.

36. See Tiverios 1981, 29–30. For the earliest representations see note 30 above; Stilp (2006, 51) assigns the fragment of Melian relief to an Attic workshop.

37. Stephani 1866, 21–34, 60–63.

identified as priestess of Demeter.[38] Stephani began with the observation that the characteristic headdress resembles the modius of Sera-
pis and particularly Helius's crown of rays. He then identified in the
term *kalathos*, "basket," the appropriate name for such a crown, one
that referred to its shape metaphorically, much in the way that *kalathos* might be applied to the Corinthian capital. This word allowed
Stephani to connect the crown to the name of a dance that is found in
Athenaeus (quoting the Old Comedy writer Apollophanes) and the
lexicographers: *kalathiskos*, or "little basket dance."[39] Thus identified,
this time literally, as a basket, the headdress could be brought into
connection with other performances involving baskets and reeds as
well as with the Eleusinian rites of Demeter. Finally, an explanation
could be secured for the appearance of these figures on the dress of
the "priestess."

Stephani himself acknowledged the evident slippage in his argument where he noted that in many cases it is impossible to say whether
the object in question is a "basket" or a crown of rays.[40] Subsequent
studies firmly dismissed the idea that the headdress has anything to
do with baskets, in favor of hypotheses that identify the spikes as palm
leaves or reeds. But the label "*kalathiskos* dance" is still in use, with all
that it suggests, and the basket conjecture returns with insistence in the
case of the Karneia krater and other Lucanian and Apulian representations of this feature, which can in no way be explained as crowns of
leaves.[41] Here I wish to return to the observation with which Stephani's
analysis began: that the "*kalathos*" resembles a crown of rays. I begin by
comparing, for instance, the crown in one of the earliest depictions of
a *kalathiskos* dancer (plate 16) to that of Helius on a fourth-century
Rhodian tetradrachm (plate 18). But such resemblances, however suggestive, are not conclusive. A sounder argument can be built on the

38. Ibid., 10, no. 13, f–h, pl. 3, 2–3; Artamov 1969, 74–79, figs. 266–67.

39. Athenaeus 11.467f; 14.629f; Pollux *Onomastikon* 4.105; Hesychius *Lexikon*, s.v.
kalathiskos; Stephani 1866, 23–24, 27–34.

40. Stephani 1866, 65–66. In the end, he raised other possibilities: that the two are equivalent alternatives and that the artists produced a contamination of the two.

41. Wuilleumier (1933, 12) argued that a progressive stylization of the "couronne végétale"
eventually suggested the texture of baskets and generated the deviant form that appears on
South Italian vases.

following observations: that the identification of the spiky elements as rays accounts for the variant forms of the headdress; and that at least two monuments place the dance in an astral context.

In Archaic iconography, on Attic black-figure vases the luminosity of astral figures—Eos, Nyx, and especially Helius—is signified by a disk (sometimes rendered as concentric circles [plate 10]), from which project rays, placed above or in front of the figures' heads. Although not consistently, in Classical red-figure painting and sculpture the radiant disk appears behind the head of the god and frames it, producing the familiar image of the nimbus. As on the Blacas krater (plate 8),[42] rays issue from the outer edge of the nimbus, which becomes progressively larger and more intricate. It is instructive to look at the figure of Helius on the metope from the Athenaion at Troy (plate 19).[43] The rays emanate from a narrow halo surrounding the god's head and form two superimposed tiers that define, as it were, another double nimbus. In light of this, the typical form of the "kalathiskos" may be understood as a rayed halo and an alternative equivalent rendering of the crown of freestanding upright rays, such as the ones on the Polygnotan fragment (plate 16) and the Rhodian coin (plate 18) described above. On Apulian vases the nimbus of celestial bodies conforms to the same basic structure, but it becomes more elaborate, taking the form of concentric circles, with projections connecting each to the next and rays emanating from the outermost ring. Such halos frame the heads of Eos and Helius, who follow each other on the neck of the volute-krater by the Underworld Painter—to give just one instance (plate 20).[44] This configuration corresponds in all essential features to the expansive headgear that kalathiskos dancers wear on Lucanian and Apulian vases.

The figure of the Panathenaic Athena on the amphora of the Kuban Group mentioned above (plate 17) also locates the kalathiskos dance in the sky, albeit in a different way. While the figures of dancers appear on the goddess's hem, it is apparent that the overarching decorative theme of her dress and armor is the firmament: the fabric is

42. See p. 39n54 in the present text.
43. Berlin, Staatliche Museen SK 71–72, LIMC 5 (1990), s.v. "Helios" no. 380.
44. Munich, Antikensammlung 3297, RVAp Suppl. II 533.282.

covered in large stars, with a particularly impressive one on the sleeve, and on the shield is a radiant full moon.[45] The second monument that lends itself to an interpretation in connection with the cosmic dance is the imposing Acanthus Column in the sanctuary of Pythian Apollo at Delphi, a monument that has been as much of a puzzle as Alcman's *Partheneion*, and for nearly as long.

Excavations conducted between 1893 and 1895 in the area north of the temple uncovered fragments substantial enough to allow a reconstruction of the overall structure of the column and of its sculptural decoration.[46] It consists of five drums plus the capital rising from a base of acanthus leaves, with acanthus encircling the base of each drum and entirely enveloping the capital. On top of the capital is a shaft over two meters high, also covered with acanthus, centered over the drums but narrower in diameter. Three *kalathiskos* dancers are attached to this element. Although they are broken off, it is apparent that the tips of their toes did not reach the leaves of the capital, giving the impression that the figures are suspended in the air (plate 15).[47] Three large mortises on the upper face of the leaves of the capital indicate that atop the shaft was a bronze tripod that appeared to be supported by the dancers, whose right arms are raised, palm upward.[48] Further investigations of the area in the 1960s and 1980s led

45. British Museum B 606; see n34 above. The shield device has been called a star (e.g., Bentz 1998, 158), but the central disk and "spots" in the field suggest the bright full moon among stars. For other instances of the use of astral symbols on the shield of the Panathenaic Athena and particularly for the use of small, round configurations to represent stars, see Yalouris 1980, 316. The central element on the British Museum amphora is especially comparable to the one that appears on Athena's shield on another amphora of the Kuban Group (Hermitage 17553 [*ABV* 411.2; *Beazley Addenda* 107]); there the circle of rays holds in its center the frontal face of the moon. For other depictions of the visage inscribed in the moon-disk, see *LIMC* 2 (1984), s.v. "Astra" nos. 41–44.

46. See Martinez 1997, 35–38 for the history of the discovery of the monument and of its reconstructions.

47. Homolle observed that the pillar seems "un appendice inattendu, illogique même" (1908, 225) and was appropriately puzzled by the fact that the dancers are in midair: "A défaut d'un bouche-trou sans efficacité, sans caractère et sans raison, les figures restent en l'air, situation singulière, étant suspendues si haut, sans être soutenues par des ailes, ni appuyées nulle part" (227). See also Rhomaiou 1958–59, 392: "ψηλὰ 'en plein ciel.'"

48. For the position of the arms, see Marcadé 1974. Following Marcadé, Ridgway (1990, 62n9) notes that the tripod might have been in marble; Martinez (1997, 38–39) speaks of traces of oxidation, which would confirm that the material was metal.

to the identification of the column's base, which bears an inscription indicating that the monument was dedicated by the Athenians.[49] The meaning of this assemblage of apparently disparate elements—the column, the pillar, the dancers, and the tripod—and its relevance to the cult of Pythian Apollo on the one hand and to its Athenian dedicators on the other are open questions to this day.[50] What follows is an attempt to recover the connotations of the monument by bringing into play other representations in which these features occur and by examining their connection to Delphian legends.

The image of the acanthus column topped with a tripod appears on other monuments of Classical and Hellenistic date.[51] Like the *kalathiskos* dance, this figure has a strong affinity to Apollo but ranges beyond his realm. In a few vase paintings of the late fifth century, it accompanies both Apollo and Dionysos.[52] On a fragmentary calyx-krater the column figures in the picture of Heracles' sacrifice at the altar of Chryse, and acanthus columns flank the Panathenaic Athena on the prize amphorae of 363/2.[53] The picture that reveals a connection with Delphian legends appears on a large squat lekythos of the early fourth century by the Athenian potter Xenophantos, an exceptional vase lavishly decorated in relief with polychromy and gilding (plates 21–22).[54] The subject is a hunt by men in Persian dress who bear Persian names; their prey are real beasts—boar and deer—but also mythical ones, such as the griffin. The landscape consists of laurel trees and a palm tree with dates, which is flanked on either side by an

49. Pouilloux and Roux 1963, 123–45. Debate continues over the location and the date of the column and the credibility of the epigraphic evidence offered by Vatin (1983); see Ridgway 1990, 23–25 and Martinez 1997, 44n27.

50. Martinez (1997) assigns to the monument also the marble *omphalos*, which was recovered in the same area in 1894, and reconstructs it at the very top, inside the basin of the tripod; Duguet et al. 2004 describe the project for a 3-D scan of the monument that will allow virtual manipulations of its pieces through an interactive viewer, and announce the forthcoming publication of Martinez's monograph (*La Colonne d'Acanthe de Delphes*, vol. 4 in the Collection des Fouilles de Delphes). Until such time, Homolle 1908 remains essential.

51. Monuments listed in Homolle 1908, 216–24 and Froning 1971, 112n79.

52. Calyx-krater, Athens, National Museum 12253, Bousquet 1964, 667–68, fig. 4; pelike, Barcelona, Museo Arqueológico 33, *LIMC* 7 (1994), s.v. "Paidia" no. 12.

53. St. Petersburg, Hermitage 33a, *ARV*[2] 1408.1; Froning 1971, chap. 4. On the Panathenaic amphorae of Charicleides, see Eschbach 1986, 42–45.

54. St. Petersburg, Hermitage P 1837.2, *ARV*[2] 1407.1; see Cohen 2006, 141–42.

acanthus column topped by a tripod. Such a surfeit of allusions to Apollo indicates that the land is sacred to the god, but we are neither in Delphi nor on Delos. The presence of the griffin points instead to regions imagined to lie at the end of the world, where griffins guard the gold that the earth spontaneously produces and where the Hyperboreans dwell, a people sacred to Apollo.[55] In *Olympian* 3 Pindar describes them as "servants of Apollo," from whom Heracles obtained and brought to Olympia the grove of olive trees from which the victors' crowns were made.[56]

The Hyperboreans figure prominently in the foundation legends of the cult of Apollo on Delos and, most important, at Delphi, as we learn from Alcaeus's *Hymn to Apollo*, which survives in periphrasis in an oration of Himerius:

> When Apollo was born, Zeus equipped him with golden headband and lyre and gave him also a chariot of swans to drive, and sent him to Delphi and the spring of Castalia, thence to declare justice and right for the Greeks; but when Apollo mounted the chariot he directed the swans to fly to the land of the Hyperboreans. Now when the Delphians learned this, they composed a paean and a tune and arranged dancing choirs of youths around the tripod and called on the god to come from the Hyperboreans. Apollo, however, delivered law among the men of that region for a full year; but when he thought it was time that the tripods of Delphi should ring out too, he ordered his swans to fly back again from the Hyperboreans.[57]

The role the Hyperboreans play in the cults of Apollo is tied to the significance of the region they inhabit, at the fabled sources of the Danube (Pindar *Olympian* 3.31–33). In their privileged link to the god and their untarnished and blissful way of life, the Hyperboreans constitute a northern, mirror-image counterpart to the Ethiopians. Like

55. Herodotus 4.13–16; Aeschylus *Prometheus Bound* 829–32; see Bolton 1962, 65. Franks (2008) discusses at length the Hyperborean connotations of the landscape of the Xenophantos lekythos and the nature of the hunt.

56. Pindar *Olympian* 3.13–16, 31–33. *Olympian* 10.34–44 describes the delight that Apollo takes in the Hyperboreans' sacrifices of asses and their way of life.

57. Himerius *Orations* 48.10–11 (= Alcaeus frag. 307c Voigt); trans. D. A. Campbell 1982.

the mythical land of the Aethiopes, their land is a point of juncture between the human domain and the workings of the cosmos. A fragment of Pherenicus locates them at the margin of the world (*eskhata*), "below the racecourse,"[58] that is, the path of the Sun. Strabo quotes a suggestive passage of Sophocles that deals with the abduction of Oreithya by the North Wind. Boreas carries the Athenian princess

ὑπέρ τε πόντον πάντ' ἐπ' ἔσχατα χθονὸς
νυκτός τε πηγὰς οὐρανοῦ τ' ἀναπτυχάς,
Φοίβου παλαιὸν κῆπον.

over the whole sea to the ends of the earth
and the sources of night and the unfoldings of heaven,
Phoebus' ancient garden.[59]

While the Xenophantos lekythos shows that the acanthus column has a place in the Hyperborean landscape, the imagery of another Classical Athenian vase points to the significance of the leaf-crowned column as a cosmic landmark.[60] On the lid of a pyxis (plate 6) that depicts the heavenly ride of Eos, Selene, and Nyx, the place from which Eos emerges and toward which Night advances is marked with a column. Its Corinthian capital, visible above the lower border of the picture, has elaborate volutes, partly gilded. On top, rising from a

58. Pherenicus frag. 671 Lloyd-Jones and Parsons: ἀμφί θ' Ὑπερβορέων, οἵ τ' ἔσχατα ναιετάουσι // νηῷ ὑπ' Ἀπόλλωνος, ἀπείρητοι πολέμοιο. // τοὺς μὲν ἄρα προτέρων ἐξ αἵματος ὑμνήσουσι // Τιτήνων βλαστόντας ὑπὸ δρόμον αἰθρήεντα // νάσσασθαι Βορέαο γύην Ἀριμασπὸν ἄνακτα . . . "and about the Hyperboreans, who inhabit the ends of the earth below the Temple of Apollo and know not war. Sprung from the blood of the Titans of old, hymns sing, below the racecourse they press against the clear-sky land of Boreas, the lord of the Arimaspians . . ." I retain the manuscript reading ὑπό at line 4; see O. Crusius, *ML* 1.2 (1886–90): 2824.
59. Sophocles frag. 956 *TrGF* in Strabo *Geography* 7.3.1.
60. It is worth noting that the earliest instance of a Corinthian column with its acanthus capital occurs in the Classical Temple of Apollo at Bassae, in a setting that has been conjecturally linked to the movements of the sun. The column stood before the rear chamber at the center of the northern end of the cella, where it served no structural purpose. In addition, the temple is anomalous in that it faces south and has a door opening on the eastern wall of the rear chamber, placed off center. It is clear that these peculiar features are integral to the function of the building, because they exactly repeat the plan of its Archaic predecessor, whose foundations are still visible to the south (Kelly 1995, 227–63). After observing the dramatic effect of light streaming through the door at sunrise, Cooper (1968; 1996, 182) proposed that the purpose of the opening in the eastern wall was to funnel the sun's rays into the chamber at dawn on particular days.

cluster of downward-curving leaves, is a plain, slightly tapering pillar, smaller in diameter than the column itself. There is no tripod, but this feature matches the pillar around which the *kalathiskos*-crowned figures dance atop the Delphic Acanthus Column. In the context of chariots at a gallop, however, on the Athenian pyxis the pillar is easily recognizable as a *terma*, the turning post in a chariot race.[61] The image plays on the extended metaphor of the astral bodies' trek across the sky as a racecourse by projecting the point at which they "turn" as the *terma* of a hippodrome.[62]

As an actual turning post would in a racecourse, in the celestial *dromos* the column marks the point at which the sun appears to reverse the direction of its risings along the horizon—in other words, the place of the solstices. The *Odyssey* locates the "turning around of the sun," *tropai hēliou*, in mythical Syra, whose inhabitants, much like the Hyperboreans, suffer neither hunger nor sickness and have a special tie to Apollo and Artemis.[63] A passage in Pliny the Elder's *Natural History* bears witness to a tradition that places the site of the solstices in the Hyperborean region, beyond the Rhipaean mountains:

> Behind these mountains and beyond the North Wind a fortunate people, if we can believe, called Hyperboreans, lives to a great age, renowned for its fabled wonders. There are believed to be the pivots of the universe and the extreme limits of the circuits of the stars, with six months of daylight at the turning around of the sun, not, as the ignorant affirm, from the spring equinox to autumn. The sun rises for them once a year, at the solstice, and sets once at the winter solstice.[64]

---

61. Furtwängler 1883–87, commentary to plate 63: "Vielleicht verband sich damit auch die Absicht nach Art der Meta, einer Rennbahn, dem Laufe des Helios eine Zielsäule, eine Bezeichnung des Punktes ὅθι τροπαὶ ἠελίοιο (*Odyss*. 15, 404) zu geben."

62. On another Classical vase, Vatican, Museo Gregoriano Etrusco 16531, the column itself, this time bearing a tripod, appears behind the figure of Eos; *ARV*² 1035.1, *LIMC* 3 (1986), s.v. "Eos" no. 36 (the figure tentatively identified as Nike).

63. On the *terma* of the Sun, see Macurdy 1920, 140–41.

64. Pliny *Natural History* 4.89:

> Pone eos montes ultraque Aquilonem gens felix, si credimus, quos Hyperboreos appellavere, annoso degit aevo, fabulosis celebrata miraculis. ibi creduntur esse cardines mundi extremique siderum ambitus semestri luce [et una die] solis adversi, non, ut

How old and widespread a tradition this was is impossible to say.[65] Note, however, that the conceit of a *terma* for the course of the heavenly bodies lends particular resonance to the legend that Heracles was seized by the desire to plant around the "twelve-turned *terma* for the racecourse for horses" at Olympia the olive trees at which he had marveled in the land of the Hyperboreans (Pindar *Olympian* 3.31–34).

If the Athenian pyxis is a reliable source for the connotations of the image of the acanthus column with its pillar, it opens the way for an understanding of the Delphic Column as the representation of a cosmic landmark. The underlying coherence of this assemblage of apparently disparate features emerges in light of Delphian legends and cult practices related to the seasonal movements of Apollo. The pillar on the column marks the turning point in the ethereal racecourse situated near the Hyperborean region. Around it, stars are imagined to carry Apollo's tripod aloft in their dance. They are, in the conventional sense, "caryatids" but hardly devoid of identity: the cosmic setting reveals that they perform the most harmonious of all choral dances. The fact that they are stars suspended in the sky finally explains why the dancers are aloft around the pillar, with the tips of their toes dangling well above the leaves of the capital. In this perspective, it becomes possible to explain their particular relevance not only to Apollo but also to the Athenian dedicators of the column. Looking for an answer to the puzzle of the identity of the maidens, Bousquet identified a suggestive expression in a fragment of Euripides' *Erechtheus*: ζεῦγος τριπάρθενον, "three-maiden yoke" (frag. 357 *TrGF*). Bousquet sought to apply the phrase to the daughters of Cecrops, but

---

imperiti dixere, ab aequinoctio verno in autumnum, semel in anno solstitio oriuntur iis soles brumaque semel occidunt.

"Cardo" in the sense of "turning post" for the Sun is also found in Avienus *Aratea* 653–54 Soubiran: "Hic iam Threicio veniens a cardine Phoebus vertit iter." Pliny's account of the Hyperboreans may depend on the same source as Pomponius Mela (*Chorographia* 3.36 Silberman: "Hyperborei supra aquilonem Riphaeosque montes sub ipso siderum cardine iacent" (The Hyperboreans are located beyond the north wind, above the Riphaean Mountains, and under the very pole of the stars. Trans. Romer 1998).

65. Note that Fontenrose (1943, 280–81) understands οὐρανοῦ τ᾽ ἀναπτυχάς in the fragment of Sophocles quoted at p. 142 above (frag. 956 *TrGF*) in the same sense that *cardines mundi* has in Pliny *Natural History* 4.89 — to mean "hinges of the world."

it is more likely that it refers instead to the daughters of Erechtheus, whose tragic fate was the subject of the play. From a scholium to Aratus we learn that somewhere in the *Erechtheus* it was stated that there were three Erechtheids, and that they were transformed into stars. They are the Hyades.[66] Given the nature of the evidence, the foregoing interpretation of the Acanthus Column and the argument that *kalathiskos* dancers represent astral choruses amount to a conjecture, but one that has several advantages over current ones. To begin with, it explains the meaning of the headdress as a piece of costume. Most important, it accounts for the favor that the subject enjoyed throughout the classical world, for such a long period of time. Its appeal resides in its capacity to evoke the paradigm of all choral dances, extending to the visual arts a concept that, as we have seen, runs through much poetical imagery and philosophical thought.[67] The particular connection with Apollo may be understood—not only at Sparta—in light of festivals that celebrated the cycle of the seasons, punctuated by the risings and settings of the stars. As regards the performance of Alcman's *Partheneion*, this idea allows us to contemplate the possibility that the dance that it staged was a recurring feature of the festival.

Let us return in closing to the krater from Ceglie (plate 13) and the particular view that it gives us of the composition of the chorus, to end with more questions than there are answers. Like most scholars, I too have read the scene of chorus dancers in reference to the Spartan cult of Apollo Carneus. That we recognize its subject, however, does not mean that we also understand what the picture is about. For what reason and from which perspective are the dancers at the Karneia represented here? Both the iconographic program of the krater

66. Bousquet 1964, 658–67; scholium to Aratus 172 Martin: Εὐριπίδης δὲ ἐν τῷ Φαέθοντι (frag. 780 Nauck) τρεῖς [. . .] Εὐριπίδης μὲν οὖν Ἐρεχθεῖ (Euripides frag. 357 Nauck) τὰς Ἐρεχθέως θυγατέρας Ὑάδας φησὶ γενέσθαι τρεῖς οὔσας. This tradition is recalled in Servius's commentary to Virgil *Aeneid* 1.744, in a garbled account that ends up conflating the Hyades with the Pleiades:

pluviasque Hyadas: Hyades stellae sunt in fronte tauri, quae quotiens nascuntur pluvias creant [. . .] hae autem fuerunt ut alii dicunt, Atlantis filiae, ut alii Liberi nutrices, quae se in pelagus furore praecipitaverunt. alii Erechthei filias pro patria se morti obtulisse aiunt, quas Pliadas vocant, quod Pleiones filiae esse dicantur.

67. See pp. 3–7 in the present text.

and the artistic tradition from which it issues point to the fact that we are looking at the Spartan festival through an Athenian, or philo-Athenian, lens. The piece belongs to the earliest South Italian red-figure production, vases "so closely modeled upon Attic prototypes that it seems likely that the artists responsible for them had either been trained in Athens or were immigrants from that city."[68] As we have seen, in the visual arts the *kalathiskos* dance is first and foremost an Athenian subject, for centuries and in many media. If it does illustrate a satyr play, the picture of Perseus and the satyrs on the upper register of the reverse of the Karneia krater represents a specifically Athenian dramatic genre, which belongs to the context of a festival of Dionysus. And it is Dionysus, not Apollo, who is the subject of the grand scene on the obverse.

If it matches in kind or in mode the scene in the upper register, the representation of dancers at the Karneia on our krater might be offered in a humorous vein, if not in reference to a comedy.[69] Pratinas's famous quip comes to mind: "The Spartan, that cicada made for the song and dance."[70] The figure of an old phlyax wearing the *kalathiskos* on an early Paestan bell-krater shows that the dance could indeed be the subject of farce or comedy.[71] We should then be alert to the possibility that, if the picture presents us with commonplace notions about choruses at the Karneia, it may also contain elements of exaggeration and distortions for comic effect. A few disquieting features are in plain view: the costumes, for instance, are not precisely matched and all chorus members are male, except, apparently, for one. The picture is unusual in that it is one of a handful that depict *kalathiskos* dancers as young men instead of beautiful girls. All of them, except one, appear on early South Italian vases (Lucanian and Apulian), not far in date from the Karneia krater, and they may all draw on the same

68. Trendall 1989, 17.

69. On a hydria in Naples, Museo Nazionale 3231 (Bieber 1917, 54, fig. 27), the main picture includes a *kalathiskos* dancer (at lower right) in the representation of a satyr play about the contest between Apollo and Marsyas; the dejected Marsyas wears the fleecy tights that are the stage costume of Papposilenus.

70. Pratinas frag. 4 *TrGF*; see Constantinidou 1998, 26–28.

71. London, British Museum F 188, *RVP* 68.26, plate 22 c–d.

source of inspiration.[72] The exceptions are the dancers shown in relief on either side of the southern doorway of the heroon at Trysa, under a lintel decorated with eight grotesque figures of musicians.[73] The Trysa dancers wear the short fluttering dress typical of the costume, but they are male.

What to make of the combination of nude youths and the figure in female dress on our krater? Is this a mixed chorus, comprising both male and female dancers, or is it an all-male chorus, of whom only one wears the complete female costume? The question of whether this figure is a girl or young man has been raised several times.[74] Except for the dress, it is indistinguishable from the other three, who wear the nimbus; its locks perfectly match those of the youth at the far right, and there is no indication of breasts. One might pass over this last detail, were it not for the fact that the breasts of the three female figures on the obverse of the vase are studiously outlined. The matter is clearer in the image on an early fourth-century Lucanian bell-krater in Leiden (plate 23). There the scene is set between two pillars, similar to the one that carries the inscription *Karneios* on the Karneia krater. Two nude dancing youths, each wearing the crown of rays, flank a third figure, which wears both the crown and the short, belted dress. Like its partners, the latter has short hair. Coupled with the absence of breasts, the hairstyle makes it clear that this is a youth in woman's dress.

In trying to understand what these pictures tell us about actual choral performances at the Karneia, we confront difficult choices. If the dancers were in fact maidens, the wit of these images would reside in their reversal of gender roles. But it is possible as well that the humor consists of exposing the fact that the chorus are men dressed as

72. These are the bell-kraters: (1) London, Victoria and Albert Museum 4803.1901, *APS* 9.6; *RVAp* 16.57; *RVAp Suppl.* II, 4; Moon 1929, pl. 12. (2) Zurich, Wolfensperger collection, *APS* 9.7; *RVAp* 16.58; Cook 1940, 999, fig. 809. (3) Leiden, Rijksmuseum van Oudheden Rsx 4; *LCS* 105.548; Braat and Clasens 1968, 61–62, pl. 120; here, plate 23. (4) Berlin Antikenmuseum 4520, *LCS* 78.398. (5) Calyx-krater Syracuse, Museo Archeologico 14626, Cook 1940, 997. (6) Hydria Naples, Museo Nazionale 3231, *RVAp* 401.29, Bieber 1917, 54, fig. 27.

73. Benndorf and Niemann 1889, 58, pl. 6.

74. See Moon 1929, 31; Cook 1940, 997; Bieber 1917, 55n2.

women. The effect may be gauged by looking at the explicitly comic picture of a chorus on the shoulder of an Attic hydria of the mid-sixth century, in which the dancers are bearded men in colorful female dresses.[75] That is to say, it is possible that, as on the Athenian dramatic stage, it was males who took on female roles at the Karneia, playing girls playing stars.

75. Private collection; see Green 1985, 100, fig. 5.

APPENDIX
PARTHENEION TEXT AND
TRANSLATION

The text is cited by permission of Oxford University Press from the edition of Hutchinson 2001, pp. 3–8, from which it departs at the following lines: 15 (ἀπ]έδιλος supplemented for]έδιλος); 16 (μή τις ἀν]θρώπων for ἀν]θρώπων); 17 (μηδ᾽ ὑποτ]ρήτω for μηδὲ πη]ρήτω; see p. 81); 49 († removed from entire line); 61 (ὀρθρίαι for Ὀρθρίαι, φάρος for φᾶρος); 83 (ἄνα for ἄνα); 84 ([χο]ροστάτις supplemented for . . . στατις); 86 (ἀπ᾽ [ὡ]ρανῶ supplemented for ἀπ᾽ . . ρανῶ; see p. 108); 97 (μὲν αὐδά supplemented for line ending; see p. 9 n. 21); 98 (ἀντ[ὶ δ᾽ἕνδεκα] for ἀντὶ δ᾽ ἕνδεκα).

Alcman Fragment 1 PMGF

] Πωλυδεύκης.
οὐκ ἐγω]ν Λύκαισον ἐν καμοῦσιν ἀλέγω
Ἐνα]ρσφόρον τε καὶ Σέβρον ποδώκη
]ν τε τὸν βιατὰν
] τε τὸν κορυστάν   5
Εὐτείχ]η τε ϝάνακτά τ᾽ Ἀρήϊον
]ά τ᾽ ἔξοχον ἡμισίων

]ν τὸν ἀγρόταν
] μέγαν Εὔρυτόν τε
]πώρω κλόνον   10
]ά τε τὼς ἀρίστως
] παρήσομες
]αρ Αἶσα παντῶν
] γεραιτάτοι
ἀπ]έδιλος ἀλκά.   15
μή τις ἀν]θρώπων ἐς ὡρανὸν ποτήσθω
μηδ᾽ ὑποτ]ρήτω γαμῆν τὰν Ἀφροδίταν
ϝ]άνασσαν ἤ τιν᾽

151

］ἤ παῖδα … κω
Χά]ριτες δὲ Διὸς δόμον   20
]σιν ἐρογλεφάροι

]τάτοι
]τα δαίμων
]ι φίλοις
]ωκε δῶρα   25
] ̣γαρέον
]ώλες᾽ ἤβα
]ρονον
μ]αταίας
]έβα. τῶν δ᾽ ἄλλος ἰῶι   30
] μαρμάρωι μυλάκρωι
] ̣εν Ἄιδας
] αυτοι
᾽]πον. ἄλαστα δὲ
ϝέργα πάσον κακὰ μησάμενοι.   35

ἔστι τις σιῶν τίσις·
ὁ δ᾽ ὄλβιος ὅστις εὔφρων
ἀμέραν [δι]απλέκει
ἄκλαυστος. ἐγὼν δ᾽ ἀείδω
Ἀγιδῶς τὸ φῶς· ὁρῶ   40
ϝ᾽ ὥτ᾽ ἄλιον, ὅνπερ ἄμιν
Ἀγιδὼ μαρτύρεται
φαίνην. ἐμὲ δ᾽ οὔτ᾽ ἐπαινῆν
οὔτε μωμήσθαι νιν ἀ κλεννὰ χοραγός
οὐδ᾽ ἀμῶς ἐῆι. δοκεῖ γὰρ ἤμεν αὐτά   45
ἐκπρεπὴς τὼς ὥπερ αἴ τις
    ἐν βοτοῖς στάσειεν ἵππον
παγὸν ἀεθλοφόρον καναχάποδα
    τῶν ὑποπετριδίων ὀνείρων.

ἦ οὐχ ὁρῆις; ὁ μὲν κέλης   50
Ἐνητικός, ἀ δὲ χαίτα

τᾶς ἐμᾶς ἀνεψιᾶς
Ἀγησιχόρας ἐπανθεῖ
χρυσὸς ὡς ἀκήρατος.
τό τ᾿ ἀργύριον πρόσωπον,   55
διαφάδαν τί τοι λέγω;
Ἀγησιχόρα μὲν αὔτα·
ἁ δὲ δευτέρα πεδ᾿ Ἀγιδὼ τὸ ϝεῖδος
ἵππος Ἰβηνῶι Κολαξαῖος δραμήται.
ταὶ Πεληάδες γὰρ ἇμιν   60
ὀρθρίαι φάρος φεροίσαις
νύκτα δι᾿ ἀμβροσίαν ἅτε Σήριον
ἄστρον ἀυηρομέναι μάχονται.

οὔτε γάρ τι πορφύρας
τόσσος κόρος ὥστ᾿ ἀμύναι,   65
οὔτε ποικίλος δράκων
παγχρύσιος, οὐδὲ μίτρα
Λυδία, νεανίδων
ἰανογ[λ]εφάρων ἄγαλμα,
οὐδὲ ταὶ Ναννῶς κόμαι,   70
ἀλλ᾿ οὐδ᾿ Ἀρέτα σιειδής,
οὐδὲ Συλακίς τε καὶ Κλεησισήρα.
οὐδ᾿ ἐς Αἰνησιμβρ[ό]τας ἐνθοῖσα φασεῖς
"Ἀσταφίς τέ μοι γένοιτο,
καὶ ποτιγλέποι Φίλυλλα   75
Δαμαρέτα τ᾿ ἐρατά [τ]ε ϝιανθεμίς·
ἀλλ᾿ Ἀγησιχόρα με τείρει."

οὐ γὰρ ἁ καλλίσφυρος
Ἀγησιχ[ο]ρ[α] πάρ᾿ αὐτεῖ·
Ἀγιδοῖ δὲ παρμένει   80
θωστήρια [τ᾿] ἄμ᾿ ἐπαινεῖ.
ἀλλὰ τᾶν ...... ( )ιοι
δέξασθε· σιῶν γὰρ ἄνα
καὶ τέλος· [χο]ροστάτις
ϝείποιμί κ᾿, ἐγὼν μὲν αὐτά   85

παρσένος μάταν ἀπ᾽ [ὠ]ρανῶ λέλακα
γλαύξ· ἐγὼν δὲ τᾶι μὲν Ἀώτι μάλιστα
ϝανδάνην ἐρῶ, πόνων γὰρ
ἄμιν ἰάτωρ ἔγεντο·
ἐξ Ἀγησίχορας δὲ νεάνιδες   90
ἰρ]άνας ἐρατᾶς ἐπέβαν.

τῶ]ι τε γὰρ σηραφόρωι
α[ὐ]τῶς εδ . . . . ʹ
τῶι κυβερνάται δὲ χρή
κἠν νᾶϊ μα   95
ἁ δὲ τᾶν Σηρηνίδων
ἀοιδοτέρα μὲ[ν αὐδά],
σιαὶ γάρ, ἀντ[ὶ δ᾽ ἔνδεκα]
παίδων δεκ . . . . ει
φθέγγεται δ . . . ἐπὶ Ξάνθω ῥοαῖσι   100
κύκνος. ἁ δ᾽ ἐπιμέρωι ξανθᾶι κομίσκαι
[
[
[
[105

              ] Polydeuces.
I do not count Lycaethus among the heroes
              ] and Enarsphorus and Thebrus swift of foot
              ] and mighty
              ] and the helmeted   5
and lord Euteiches and Areius
              ] and best of demigods

              ] and the hunter
              ] and mighty Eurytus
              ] battle-rout   10
              ] and the most valiant
              ] we shall [not] pass over.
              ] measure of all

                    ] most ancient
                    ] unfettered might.   15
              let no] mortal fly to the sky
              nor flee from] marrying Aphrodite
                    ] mistress or some
                    ] or child
                    ] Graces the palace of Zeus   20
                    ] love-glancing.

              [22–29]
                    ] of whom one with the arrow   30
                    ] with marble millstone
                    ] in Hades
                    ] they
                    ] things never to be forgotten
              they suffered for the evils they plotted.   35

              There is such a thing as retribution from the gods.
              Happy is he who, sound of mind,
              weaves through the day
              unwept. I sing
              the light of Agido. I see it   40
              like the sun, whom
              Agido summons to appear and
              witness for us. But the glorious chorus mistress
              forbids me to either praise
              or blame her. For she appears to be   45
              outstanding as if
                    one placed among a grazing herd
              a perfect horse, a prize-winner with resounding hooves,
                    one of the dreams that dwell below the rock.

              Don't you see? That one is an Enetic   50
              courser, while the mane
              of my cousin
              Hagesichora shines forth

like unalloyed gold.
Her face is of silver,   55
Why do I tell you explicitly?
There is Hagesichora herself.
Next will run Agido, her appearance
that of a Colaxian horse following an Ibenian.
For against us the Pleiades contend   60
    at daybreak, carried aloft
like Sirius across immortal Night,
    as we bring the season of the plow.

For surfeit of purple
does not help,   65
nor chased golden
snake-bracelet, nor Lydian
tiara, pride
of violet-eyed maids,
nor Nanno's tresses,   70
not even godlike Areta
or Thylacis and Cleesithera,
nor will you go to Ainesimbrota's house and say:
"let Astaphis stand by me,
    and let Philylla and Damareta   75
and lovely Hianthemis look upon me,
    but Hagesichora effaces me."

Nor does Hagesichora
of the beautiful ankles remain in place
to Agido . . .   80
and lauds our festival.
But [
accept. To the gods belong the fulfillment
and the end. Mistress of the chorus
I would say I myself   85
a maiden wail in vain from the sky,
an owl. But most of all I long

to please Aotis for she is ever
    the healer of our labors.
Away from Hagesichora, maidens   90
    enter upon delightful peace.

To the trace-horse
in the same way
to the steerman must
on a ship too [95
the song of the Sirens
indeed more harmonious,
for they are goddesses, instead of [eleven]
children ten [
sings . . . on the streams of Xanthus   100
the swan. She of the lovely golden hair
[
[
[
[105

ABBREVIATIONS

AbhMainz *Abhandlungen der Geistes- und Sozialwissenschaftlichen Klasse.* Akademie der Wissenschaften und der Literatur in Mainz.

ABL Haspels, C. H. E. *Attic Black-figured Lekythoi.* Paris: E. de Boccard, 1936.

ABV Beazley, J. D. *Attic Black-figure Vase-painters.* Oxford: Oxford University Press, 1956.

AE *Archaiologike Ephemeris*

AJA *American Journal of Archaeology*

AJP *American Journal of Philology*

APS Cambitoglou, A., and A. D. Trendall. *Apulian Red-figured Vase-painters of the Plain Style.* N.p. Archaeological Institute of America, 1961.

ARV² Beazley, J. D. *Attic Red-figure Vase-painters.* 2nd ed. Oxford: Oxford University Press, 1963.

Assyrian Dictionary University of Chicago, Oriental Institute. *The Assyrian Dictionary*, edited by I. J. Gelb et al. Chicago: Oriental Institute, 1964–.

BCH *Bulletin de correspondance hellénique*

Beazley Addenda Carpenter, T. H., et al. *Beazley Addenda.* 2nd ed. Oxford: Oxford University Press, 1989.

Bekker Anecdota *Anecdota graeca*, edited by E. Bekker. Berlin: G. C. Nauck, 1814–21.

BICS *Bulletin of the Institute of Classical Studies.* University of London.

BSA *Annual of the British School at Athens*

CJ *Classical Journal*

ClAnt *Classical Antiquity*

CP *Classical Philology*

CQ *Classical Quarterly*

CR *Classical Review*

CRAI *Comptes rendus de l'Academie des Inscriptions et Belles-Lettres*

CVA *Corpus Vasorum Antiquorum*

D-K Diels, H. *Die Fragmente der Vorsokratiker.* 6th ed., revised by W. Kranz. Berlin: Weidmann, 1951.

FGrHist Jacoby, F. *Die Fragmente der griechischen Historiker.* Leiden: Brill, 1923–58.

FR Furtwängler, A., and K. Reichhold. *Griechische Vasenmalerei.* Munich: F. Bruckmann, 1900–1932.

GRBS *Greek Roman and Byzantine Studies*

HSCP *Harvard Studies in Classical Philology*

JdI *Jahrbuch des Deutschen Archäologischen Instituts*

JHS *Journal of Hellenic Studies*

LCS Trendall, A. D. *The Red-figured Vases of Lucania, Campania and Sicily.* Oxford: Clarendon Press, 1967.

LCS Suppl. I Trendall, A. D. *First Supplement to The Red-figured Vases of Lucania, Campania and Sicily.* BICS Supplement 26 (1970).

LCS Suppl. II Trendall, A. D. *Second Supplement to The Red-figured Vases of Lucania, Campania and Sicily.* BICS Supplement 31 (1973).

LIMC *Lexikon Iconographicum Mythologiae Classicae.* Zurich: Artemis Verlag, 1981–99.

LSJ Liddell, H. G., R. Scott, and H. S. Jones. *A Greek-English Lexicon.* 9th ed. Oxford: Clarendon Press, 1940.

ML *Ausführliches Lexikon der griechischen und römischen*

Mythologie, edited by W. H. Roscher. Leipzig: B. G. Teubner, 1884–1937.

PCG *Poetae Comici Graeci*, edited by R. Kassel and C. Austin. Berlin: Walter de Gruyter, 1983–2001.

PMG *Poetae Melici Graeci*, edited by D. L. Page. Oxford: Clarendon Press, 1962.

PMGF *Poetarum Melicorum Graecorum Fragmenta*, edited by M. Davies. Vol. 1. Oxford: Clarendon Press, 1991.

QUCC *Quaderni urbinati di cultura classica*

RA *Revue archéologique*

RE Pauly, A. F. von. *Paulys Realencyclopädie der classischen Altertumswissenschaft*, edited by G. Wissowa. J. B. Metzler, 1894–1980.

REG *Revue des études grecques*

RFIC *Rivista di filologia e d' istruzione classica*

RhM *Rheinisches Museum*

RVAp Trendall, A. D., and A. Cambitoglou. *The Red-figured Vases of Apulia*. Oxford: Clarendon Press; New York: Oxford University Press, 1978–82.

RVAp Suppl. II Trendall, A. D., and A. Cambitoglou. *Second Supplement to The Red-figured Vases of Apulia*. BICS Supplement 60 (1992).

RVP Trendall, A. D. *The Red-figured Vases of Paestum*. London: British School at Rome, 1987.

SBBerl *Sitzungsberichte der Deutschen Akademie der Wissenschaften zu Berlin*. Klasse für Sprachen, Literatur und Kunst.

SBHeid *Sitzungsberichte der Heidelberger Akademie der Wissenschaften*. Philosophisch-historische Klasse.

SBWien *Sitzungsberichte der Akademie der Wissenschaften in Wien*. Philosophisch-historische Klasse.

SkrAth *Skrifter utgivna av Svenska Institutet i Athen*

TAPA *Transactions of the American Philological Association*

TrGF *Tragicorum Graecorum Fragmenta*, edited by B. Snell. Göttingen: Vandenhoeck & Ruprecht, 1971.

ZPE *Zeitschrift für Papyrologie und Epigraphik*

REFERENCES

Alexiou, M. 2002. *The Ritual Lament in Greek Tradition.* 2nd ed., ed. P. Roilos and D. Yatromanolakis, Lanham, MD: Rowman and Littlefield. (Orig. pub. 1974.)

Allen, A. 1993. *The Fragments of Mimnermus.* Stuttgart: Franz Steiner Verlag.

Artamov, M. I. 1969. *The Splendor of Scythian Art.* New York: Frederick A. Praeger.

Athanassakis, A. N. 2000. "The *Peléades* of Alcman's *Partheneion* and Modern Greek *Poulia*." *The Ancient World* 31:5–14.

Aujac, G. 1975. *Geminos: Introduction aux phénomènes.* Paris: Les Belles Lettres.

Austin, J. L. 1962. *How to Do Things with Words.* Oxford: Clarendon Press.

Barker, A. 1984. *Greek Musical Writings.* Vol. 1. Cambridge: Cambridge Univ. Press.

———. 1989. *Greek Musical Writings.* Vol. 2. Cambridge: Cambridge Univ. Press.

Bell, C. 1997. *Ritual: Perspectives and Dimensions.* New York: Oxford Univ. Press.

Benda, I. 1996. "Musik und Tanz in Lykien." In *Fremde Zeiten: Festschrift für Jürgen Borchhardt zum sechzigsten Geburtstag,* ed. F. Blakolmer et al., 95–109. Vienna: Phoibos Verlag.

Benndorf, O., and G. Niemann. 1889. *Das Heroon von Gjölbalschi-Trysa.* Vienna: Adolf Holzhausen.

Bentz, M. 1998. *Panathenäische Preisamphoren. Antike Kunst* Beiheft 18.

Benveniste, É. 1963. "La philosophie analytique et le langage." *Les études philosophiques* 1:3–12. Reprinted in idem, *Problèmes de la linguistique générale,* 267–76 (Paris: Gallimard, 1966).

Bieber, M. 1917. "Die Herkunft des tragischen Kostüms." *JdI* 32:15–104.

Bierl, A. F. H. 1991. *Dionysos und die griechische Tragödie: Politische und "metatheatralische" Aspekte im Text.* Tübingen: Gunter Narr.

———. 2001. *Der Chor in der alten Komödie: Ritual und Performativität.* Munich: K. G. Saur.

———. 2007. "L'uso intertestuale di Alcmane nel finale della Lisistrata di Aristofane. Coro e rito nel contesto performativo." In *Dalla lirica corale alla poesia drammatica. Forme e funzioni del canto corale nella tragedia e nella commedia greca,* ed. F. Perusino and M. Colantonio, 259–90. Pisa: Edizioni ETS.

Blass, F. 1870. "Zu Alkman, II. Das aegyptische Fragment des Alkman." *RhM* 25:177–201.

———. 1878. "Das ägyptische Fragment des Alkman." *Hermes* 13:15–32.

———. 1885. "Zu Bergk's Poetae lyrici, ed. IV vol. III. 1. Alkman." *RhM* 40:1–24.

Bloch, M. 1974. "Symbols, Song, Dance and Features of Articulation: Is Religion an Extreme Form of Traditional Authority?" *European Journal of Sociology* 15:55–81. Reprinted in idem, *Ritual, History and Power,* 19–45 (London: Athlone Press, 1989).

Bolton, J. D. P. 1962. *Aristeas of Proconnesus*. Oxford: Clarendon Press.

Bosanquet, R. C. 1905–6. "II. Excavations at Sparta, 1906." *BSA* 12:331–43.

Bottini, A. 1996. "Dioniso e Apollo: I grandi crateri di Celia." In *Studi in onore di Michele D'Elia*, ed. Clara Gelao, 46–52. Matera: R&R Editrice.

Bouffartigue, J., M. Patillon, and A. P. Segouds. 1977–95. *Porphyre: De l'abstinence*. Paris: Les Belles Lettres.

Bourdieu, P. 1982. *Ce que parler veut dire*. Paris: Fayard. Reprinted as *Language and Symbolic Power*, ed. J. B. Thompson and trans. G. Raymond and M. Adamson (Cambridge: Polity, 1991).

Bousquet, J. 1964. "Delphes et les Aglaurides d'Athènes." *BCH* 88:655–75.

Bowen, A. C. 1982. "The Foundations of Early Pythagorean Harmonic Science: Archytas, Fragment 1." *Ancient Philosophy* 2:79–104.

Bowra, C. M. 1934. "The Occasion of Alcman's *Partheneion*." *CQ* 28:35–44.

———. 1937. "The Proem of Parmenides." *CP* 32:97–112.

Braat, W. C., and A. Clasens. 1968. *Artefact: 150 jaar Rijksmuseum van Oudheden: 1818–1968*. Leiden: Rapenburg.

Brack-Bernsen, L. 2003. "The Path of the Moon, the Rising Points of the Sun, and the Oblique Great Circle on the Celestial Sphere." *Centaurus* 45:16–31.

Brink, B. ten. 1864. "Alcmanica nuper reperta." *Philologus* 21:126–39.

Brommer, F. 1979. *The Sculptures of the Parthenon*. London: Thames & Hudson.

Bruneau, P. 1970. *Recherches sur les cultes de Délos à l'époque hellénistique et à l'époque impériale*. Paris: E. de Boccard.

Bryce, T. R. 1991. "Lycian Apollo and the Authorship of the 'Rhesus.'" *CJ* 86:144–49.

Bühler, K. 1934. *Sprachtheorie: Die Darstellungsfunktion der Sprache*. Jena: Gustav Fischer. Reissued as *Theory of Language: The Representational Function of Language*, trans. D. F. Goodwin (Amsterdam: Johns Benjamins, 1990).

Burkert, W. 1963. Review of *Dichtung und Philosophie des frühen Griechentums*, by H. Fränkel (Munich: Beck, 1962). *Gnomon* 35:827–28.

———. 1969. "Das Proöimion des Parmenides und die Katabasis des Pythagoras." *Phronesis* 14:1–30.

———. 1972. *Lore and Science in Ancient Pythagoreanism*. Trans. E. L. Minar Jr. Cambridge, MA: Harvard Univ. Press.

———. 1987. "The Making of Homer in the Sixth Century B. C.: Rhapsodes versus Stesichoros." In *Papers on the Amasis Painter and His World*, 43–62. Malibu, CA: J. Paul Getty Museum.

Burnett, A. P. 1964. "The Race with the Pleiades." *CP* 59:30–34.

———. 1985. *The Art of Bacchylides*. Martin Classical Lectures. Cambridge, MA: Published for Oberlin College by Harvard Univ. Press.

Calame, C. 1977. *Les choeurs de jeunes filles en Grèce archaïque*. Vols. 1–2. Rome: Edizioni dell'Ateneo & Bizzarri.

———. 1983. *Alcman*. Rome: Edizioni dell'Ateneo.

———. 1987. "Spartan Genealogies: The Mythological Representation of a Spatial Organisation." Trans. A. Habib. In *Interpretations of Greek Mythology*, ed. J. Bremmer, 153–86. London: Croom Helm.

———. 1994–95. "From Choral Poetry to Tragic Stasimon: The Enactment of Women's Song." *Arion*, 3rd ser., 3:136–154.

———. 1997. *Choruses of Young Women in Ancient Greece.* Rev. ed. of Calame 1977, vol. 1, trans. D. Collins and J. Orion. Lanham, MD: Rowman & Littlefield.

Campbell, D. A. 1982. *Greek Lyric.* Vol. 1. Loeb Classical Library. Cambridge, MA: Harvard Univ. Press; London: William Heinemann.

———. 1983. *The Golden Lyre.* London: Duckworth.

———. 1987. "Three Notes on Alcman 1 P. (= 3 Calame)." *QUCC* 55, n.s. 26:67–72.

———. 1988. *Greek Lyric.* Vol. 2. Loeb Classical Library. Cambridge, MA: Harvard Univ. Press; London: William Heinemann.

Campbell, M. 1991. *Moschus: Europa.* Hildesheim: Olms-Weidemann.

Carlier, P. 1984. *La royauté en Grèce avant Alexandre.* Strasbourg: AECR.

Carson, A. 1982. "Wedding at Noon." *GRBS* 23:121–28.

———. 2002. *If Not, Winter: Fragments of Sappho.* New York: Alfred A. Knopf.

Carter, J. B. 1987. "The Masks of Ortheia." *AJA* 91:355–83.

———. 1988. "Masks and Poetry in Early Sparta." In *Early Greek Cult Practice,* ed. R. Hägg, N. Marinatos, and G. C. Nordquist, 89–98. *SkrAth* 40:38.

Cartledge, P. 1982. "Sparta and Samos: A Special Relationship?" *CQ* 76, n.s. 32:243–65.

———. 2001. "The Mirage of Lykourgan Sparta: Some Brazen Reflections." In idem, *Spartan Reflections,* 169–84. Berkeley and Los Angeles: Univ. of California Press.

Chantraine, P. 1999. *Dictionnaire étymologique de la langue grecque.* 2nd ed. Paris: Klincksieck.

Chapple, E. D., and C. S. Coon. 1942. *Principles of Anthropology.* New York: Henry Holt & Co.

Clark, C. A. 1996. "The Gendering of the Body in Alcman's *Partheneion* 1: Narrative, Sex, and Social Order in Archaic Sparta." *Helios* 23:143–72.

Clay, D. 1991. "Alcman's *Partheneion*." *QUCC* 68, n.s. 39:47–67.

———. 2004. *Archilochos Heros.* Washington, DC: Center for Hellenic Studies.

Clay, J. S. 1996. "The New Simonides and Homer's *Hemitheoi*." *Arethusa* 29:243–45.

Cohen, B. 2006. *The Colors of Clay.* Los Angeles: J. Paul Getty Museum.

Conacher, D. J. 1988. *Euripides: Alcestis.* Warminster, Wiltshire: Aris & Phillips.

Conche, M. 1996. *Parménide: Le poème; Fragments.* Paris: Presses Universitaires de France.

Constantinidou, S. 1998. "Dionysiac Elements in Spartan Cult Dances." *Phoenix* 52:15–30.

Cook, A. B. 1940. *Zeus: A Study in Ancient Religion.* Vol. 3. Cambridge: Cambridge Univ. Press.

Cooper, F. A. 1968. "The Temple of Apollo at Bassae: New Observations on Its Plan and Orientation." *AJA* 72:103–11.

———. 1996. *The Temple of Apollo Bassitas.* Vol. 1. Princeton, NJ: American School of Classical Studies at Athens.

Cordero, N.-L. 2004. *By Being, It Is.* Las Vegas: Parmenides Publishing.

Cornford, F. M. 1952. *Principium Sapientiae: The Origins of Greek Philosophical Thought.* Cambridge: Cambridge Univ. Press.

Cosgrove, M. R. 1974. "The ΚΟΥΡΟΣ Motif in Parmenides: B 1.24." *Phronesis* 19:81–94.

Couloubaritsis, L. 1986. *Mythe et philosophie chez Parménide*. Brussels: Ousia.

Coxon, A. H. 1968. "The Text of Parmenides fr. 1.3." *CQ* 62, n.s. 18:69.

———. 1986. *The Fragments of Parmenides. Phronesis* Suppl. vol. 3. Assen, The Netherlands: Van Gorcum.

Csapo, E. 2003. "The Dolphins of Dionysus." In *Poetry, Theory, Praxis: The Social Life of Myth, Word and Image in Ancient Greece. Essays in Honour of William J. Slater*, ed. E. Csapo and M. C. Miller, 69–98. Oxford: Oxbow.

Currie, B. 2005. *Pindar and the Cult of Heroes*. Oxford: Oxford Univ. Press.

Curtius, L. 1923. "Der Astragal des Sotades." *SBHeid* 4:5–18.

Cyrino, M. S. 2004. "The Identity of the Goddess in Alcman's Louvre *Partheneion* (PMG 1)." *CJ* 100:25–38.

Dale, A. M. 1961. *Euripides: Alcestis*. Oxford: Clarendon Press.

———. 1969. *Collected Papers*. Cambridge: Cambridge Univ. Press.

Davison, J. A. 1938. "Alcman's *Partheneion." Hermes* 73:440–58.

Deichgräber, K. 1958. *Parmenides' Auffahrt zur Göttin des Rechts. AbhMainz* 11. Wiesbaden: Franz Steiner.

Delavaud-Roux, M.-H. 1994. *Les danses pacifiques en Grèce antique*. Aix-en-Provence: Université de Provence.

Detienne, M. 1996. *The Masters of Truth in Archaic Greece*. Trans. J. Lloyd. New York: Zone Books. Orig. pub. as *Les maîtres de vérité dans la Grèce archaïque* (Paris: François Maspero, 1967).

———. 1998. *Apollon le couteau à la main*. Paris: Gallimard.

Deubner, L. 1932. *Attische Feste*. Berlin: Heinrich Keller.

Devereux, G. 1965. "The Kolaxaian Horse of Alkman's *Partheneion." CQ* 59, n.s. 15:176–84.

Dickins, G. 1929. "The Masks." In *The Sanctuary of Artemis Orthia at Sparta*, ed. R. M. Dawkins, 163–86. London: Society for the Promotion of Hellenic Studies and McMillan & Co.

Dicks, D. R. 1970. *Early Greek Astronomy to Aristotle*. Ithaca, NY: Cornell Univ. Press.

Dickson, K. 1995. *Nestor: Poetic Memory in Greek Epic*. New York: Garland.

Diels, H. 1879. *Doxographi graeci*. 4th ed. Berlin: Walter De Gruyter.

———. 1896. "Alkmans *Partheneion." Hermes* 31:339–74.

———. 1897. *Parmenides Lehrgedicht*. Berlin: Georg Reimer.

Diggle, J. 1970. *Euripides: Phaethon*. Cambridge: Cambridge Univ. Press.

———. 1994. *Euripidis fabulae*. Vol. 3. Oxford: Clarendon Press.

Dillon, J., and J. Hershbell. 1991. *Iamblichus: On the Pythagorean Way of Life*. Atlanta: Scholars Press.

Dolin, E. F. Jr. 1962. "Parmenides and Hesiod." *HSCP* 66:93–98.

Dooley, W. E. 1989. *Alexander of Aphrodisias: On Aristotle's Metaphysics I*. Ithaca, NY: Cornell Univ. Press.

Dornseiff, F. 1933. "Alkmans Mädchenlied für Orthia." *Die Antike* 9:121–29.

Drachmann, A. B. 1927. *Scholia vetera in Pindari carmina*. Vol. 3. Leipzig: B. G. Teubner.

Dué, C. 2006. *The Captive Woman's Lament in Greek Tragedy*. Austin: Univ. of Texas Press.

Duguet, F., et al. 2004. "A Point-based Approach for Capture, Display and Illustration of Very Complex Archaeological Artefacts." http://www-sop.inria.fr/reves/publications/data/2004/DDGMS04.

Ebbott, M. 2000. "The List of the War Dead in Aeschylus' *Persians*." *HSCP* 100:83–96.

———. 2003. *Imagining Illegitimacy in Classical Greek Literature*. Lanham, MD: Lexington Books.

Eisler, R. 1910. *Weltenmantel und Himmelszelt: Religionsgeschichtliche Untersuchungen zur Urgeschichte des antiken Weltbildes*. Munich: C. H. Beck.

Eschbach, N. 1986. *Statuen auf panathenäischen Preisamphoren des 4. Jhs. v. Chr.* Mainz am Rhein: Philipp von Zabern.

Evans, J. 1998. *The History and Practice of Ancient Astronomy*. New York: Oxford Univ. Press.

Evelyn-White, H. G. 1936. *Hesiod, Homeric Hymns, Epic Cycle, Homerica*. 3rd ed. Loeb Classical Library. Cambridge, MA: Harvard Univ. Press.

Fairbanks, A. 1931. *Philostratus: Imagines; Callistratus: Descriptions*. Loeb Classical Library. London: William Heinemann; New York: G. P. Putnam's Sons.

Farina, A. 1950. *Studi sul Partenio di Alcmane*. Naples: A. Caldarola.

Farnell, L. R. 1907. *The Cults of the Greek States*. Vol. 4. Oxford: Clarendon Press.

Felson, N. 2004. "Introduction." In *The Poetics of Deixis in Alcman, Pindar, and Other Lyric*, ed. N. Felson, 253–66. *Arethusa* 37.3.

Ferrari, G. 1987. "Menelas." *JHS* 107:180–82.

———. 2002. *Figures of Speech*. Chicago: Univ. of Chicago Press.

———. 2004. "The 'Anodos' of the Bride." In *Greek Ritual Poetics*, ed. D. Yatromanolakis and P. Roilos, 245–60. Washington, DC: Center for Hellenic Studies; Athens: Foundation of the Hellenic World.

Ferrari Pinney, G., and B. S. Ridgway. 1981. "Herakles at the Ends of the Earth." *JHS* 101:141–44.

Fontenrose, J. 1943. "The Garden of Phoebus." *AJP* 64:278–85.

Förtsch, R. 1998. "Spartan Art: Its Many Different Deaths." In *Sparta in Laconia*, ed. W. G. Cavanagh and S. E. C. Walker, 48–54. London: British School at Athens.

———. 2001. *Kunstverwendung und Kunstlegitimation im archaischen und frühklassischen Sparta*. Mainz am Rhein: Philipp von Zabern.

Fränkel, H. 1962. *Dichtung und Philosophie des frühen Griechentums*. Munich: C. H. Beck.

———. 1968. *Early Greek Poetry and Philosophy*. Trans. M. Hadas and J. Willis. New York: Harcourt Brace Jovanovich.

———. 1975. *Wege und Formen frühgriechischen Denkens*. Munich: C. H. Beck.

Franklin, J. C. 2004. "Structural Sympathies in Ancient Greek and South-Slavic

Heroic Song." In *Musikarchäologische Quellengruppen: Bodenurkunden, mündliche Überlieferung, Aufzeichnung*, ed. E. Hickman and R. Eichmann, 241–51. Third Symposium of the International Study Group on Music Archaeology at Monastery Michaelstein, Blankenburg (Harz), June 9–16, 2002. Rahden: M. Leidorf.

———. 2006. "Lyre Gods of the Bronze Age Musical Koine." *Journal of Ancient Near Eastern Religions* 6:39–70.

Franks, H. M. 2008. "Hunters, Heroes, Kings: The Frieze of Tomb II at Vergina." Ph.D. Diss., Harvard Univ.

Frazer, J. G. 1921. *Apollodorus: The Library*. Loeb Classical Library. Cambridge, MA: Harvard Univ. Press; London: William Heinemann.

Freeman, K. 1948. *Ancilla to the Pre-Socratic Philosophers*. Cambridge, MA: Harvard Univ. Press.

Freyburger, G. 1996. "L'harmonie des sphères calculée en stades." In *Les astres*, 283–292. Actes du colloque international de Montpellier, March 23–25, 1995. Montpellier: Université Paul Valéry.

Friedlein, G. 1867. *Boetii de institutione arithmetica libri duo, de institutione musica libri quinque*. Leipzig: B. G. Teubner.

Froning, H. 1971. *Dithyrambos und Vasenmalerei in Athen*. Würzburg: Konrad Triltsch Verlag.

Fuchs, W. 1959. *Die Vorbilder der neuattischen Reliefs. JdI* Ergänzungsheft 20.

Furtwängler, A. 1883–87. *Die Sammlung Sabouroff*. Berlin: A. Asher & Co.

———. 1893. *Meisterwerke der griechischen Plastik*. Leipzig: Giesecke & Devrient.

Gallop, D. 1984. *Parmenides of Elea: Fragments*. Toronto: Univ. of Toronto Press.

Garner, R. 1988. "Death and Victory in Euripides' *Alcestis*." *ClAnt* 7:58–71.

Garzya, A. 1954. *Alcmane: I frammenti*. Naples: Silvio Viti.

———. 1963. *Studi sulla lirica greca da Alcmane al primo impero*. Messina: D'Anna.

Gengler, O. 1995. "Les Dioscures et les Apharétides dans le Parthénée d'Alcman (Frgt 3 Calame)." *Les études classiques* 63:3–21.

Gerber, D. E. 1999. *Greek Elegiac Poetry*. Loeb Classical Library. Cambridge, MA: Harvard Univ. Press.

Gianotti, G. F. 1978. "Le Pleiadi di Alcmane." *RFIC* 106:257–71.

Gigon, O. 1968. *Der Ursprung der griechischen Philosophie*. 2nd ed. Basel: Schwabe & Co.

Gingrich, A. 1994. "Time, Ritual and Social Experience." In *Social Experience and Anthropological Knowledge*, ed. K. Hastrup and P. Hervik, 166–79. London: Routledge.

Ginzel, F. K. 1911. *Handbuch der mathematischen und technischen Chronologie*. Vol. 2. Leipzig: J. C. Hinrichs.

Goh, M. 2004. "The Poetics of Chariot Driving and Rites of Passage in Ancient Greece." Ph.D. diss., Harvard Univ.

Goldstein, B. R., and A. C. Bowen. 1983. "A New View of Early Greek Astronomy." *Isis* 74:330–40.

Gomme, A. W. 1956. *A Historical Commentary on Thucydides*. Vol. 3. Oxford: Clarendon Press.

Gomme, A. W., A. Andrewes, and K. J. Dover. 1970. *A Historical Commentary on Thucydides*. Vol. 4. Oxford: Clarendon Press.

Gostoli A. 1988. "Terpandro e la funzione etico-politica della musica nella cultura spartana del VII sec. A. C." In *La musica in Grecia*, ed. B. Gentili and R. Pretagostini, 231–37. Rome: Laterza.

Gow, A. S. F. 1953. *Greek Bucolic Poets*. Cambridge: Cambridge Univ. Press.

Green, J. R. 1985. "A Representation of the *Birds* of Aristophanes." *Greek Vases in the J. Paul Getty Museum* 2. Occasional Papers on Antiquities 3:95–118.

Guthrie, W. K. C. 1965. *A History of Greek Philosophy*. Vol. 2. Cambridge: Cambridge Univ. Press.

Hannah, R. 1994. "The Constellations on Achilles' Shield (*Iliad* 18.485–489)." *Electronic Antiquities* 2.4. http://scholar.lib.vt.edu/ejournals/ElAnt/index.html.

———. 2005. *Greek and Roman Calendars*. London: Duckworth.

Harmon, A. M. 1936. *The Works of Lucian*. Loeb Classical Library. Cambridge, MA: W. Heinemann.

Heimpel, W. 1986. "The Sun at Night and the Doors of Heaven in Babylonian Texts." *Journal of Cuneiform Studies* 38:127–51.

Henrichs, A. 1994–95. "'Why Should I Dance?': Choral Self-Referentiality in Greek Tragedy." *Arion*, 3rd ser., 3:56–111.

———. 1996a. "Dancing in Athens, Dancing on Delos: Some Patterns of Choral Projection in Euripides." *Philologus* 140:48–62.

———. 1996b. "*Warum soll ich denn tanzen?*" Lectio Teubneriana IV. Stuttgart: B. G. Teubner.

Herington, J. 1985. *Poetry into Drama*. Berkeley and Los Angeles: Univ. of California Press.

Hiller, E. 1878. *Theonis smyrnaei philosophi platonici expositio rerum mathematicarum ad legendum Platonem utilium*. Leipzig: B. G. Teubner.

Hinge, G. 2006. *Die Sprache Alkmans*. Wiesbaden: Ludwig Reichert.

Hoffmann, H. 1997. *Sotades: Mirrors of Immortality*. Oxford: Clarendon Press.

Homolle, T. 1908. "La colonne d'acanthe." *BCH* 32:205–35.

Horowitz, W. 1998. *Mesopotamian Cosmic Geography*. Winona Lake, IN: Eisenbrauns.

Hort, A. 1949. *Theophrastus: Enquiry into Plants and Minor Works on Odours and Weather Signs*. Vol. 2. Loeb Classical Library. Cambridge, MA: Harvard Univ. Press; London: William Heinemann.

How, W. W., and J. Wells 1928. *A Commentary on Herodotus*. 2nd ed. Oxford: Clarendon Press.

Huddleston, R. A. 1980. "The Wedding Songs of Ancient Greece." Ph.D. diss., Johns Hopkins Univ.

Huffman, C. A. 1993. *Philolaus of Croton*. Cambridge: Cambridge Univ. Press.

Hunger, H., and D. Pingree. 1989. *MUL.APIN: An Astronomical Compendium in Cuneiform*. Archiv für Orientforschung Beiheft 24. Horn: Ferdinand Berger & Söhne.

———. 1999. *Astral Sciences in Mesopotamia*. Leiden: Brill.

Hunter, R. 1993. *Jason and the Golden Fleece*. Oxford: Clarendon Press.

Hutchinson, G. O. 2001. *Greek Lyric Poetry: A Commentary on Selected Larger Pieces*. Oxford: Oxford Univ. Press.

Ideler, L. 1883. *Handbuch der mathematischen und technischen Chronologie*. 2nd ed. Breslau: Wilhelm Koebner.

Immerwahr, H. 1965. "Inscriptions on the Anacreon Krater in Copenhagen." *AJA* 69:152–54.

J. Paul Getty Museum and Cleveland Museum of Art. 1994. *A Passion for Antiquities: Ancient Art from the Collection of Barbara and Lawrence Fleischman*. Malibu, CA: J. Paul Getty Museum.

Janni, P. 1965. *La cultura di Sparta arcaica*. Rome: Edizioni dell'Ateneo.

Jebb, R. C. 1893. *Sophocles: The Plays and Fragments*. Vol. 1. 3rd ed. Cambridge: Cambridge Univ. Press.

Jeffery, L. H. 1949. "Comments on Some Archaic Greek Inscriptions." *JHS* 69:25–38.

Jones, W. H. S. 1953. *Hippocrates*. Vol. 4. Loeb Classical Library. Cambridge, MA: Harvard Univ. Press; London: William Heinemann.

Jowett, B. 1953. *The Dialogues of Plato*. Vol 4. 4th ed. Oxford: Clarendon Press.

Jurenka, H. 1896. "Der ägyptische Papyrus des Alkman." *SBWien* 135:1–35.

Kahn, C. H. 1994. *Anaximander and the Origins of Greek Cosmology*. 3rd ed. Indianapolis: Hackett.

Kelly, N. 1995. "The Temple of Apollo at Bassai: Correspondences to the Classical Temple." *Hesperia* 64:227–77.

Kidd, D. 1997. *Aratus: Phaenomena*. Cambridge: Cambridge Univ. Press.

Kinkel, G. 1878. *Epicorum graecorum fragmenta*. Leipzig: B. G. Teubner.

Kovacs, D. 1994. *Euripides: Cyclops, Alcestis, Medea*. Loeb Classical Library. Cambridge, MA: Harvard Univ. Press.

———. 1998. *Euripides: Suppliant Women, Electra, Heracles*. Loeb Classical Library. Cambridge, MA: Harvard Univ. Press.

———. 1999. *Euripides: Trojan Women, Iphigenia among the Taurians, Ion*. Loeb Classical Library. Cambridge, MA: Harvard Univ. Press.

———. 2002. *Euripides: Helen, Phoenician Women, Orestes*. Loeb Classical Library. Cambridge, MA: Harvard Univ. Press.

Kowalzig, B. 2004. "Changing Choral Worlds: Song-Dance and Society in Athens and Beyond." In *Music and the Muses*, ed. P. Murray and P. Wilson, 39–65. Oxford: Oxford Univ. Press.

Kranz, W. 1916. "Über Aufbau und Bedeutung des parmenideischen Gedichtes." *SBBerl* 47:1157–76.

Kretschmer, P. 1894. *Die griechischen Vaseninschriften*. Gütersloh: C. Bertelsmann.

Kukula, R. C. 1907. "Alcmans *Partheneion*." *Philologus* 66:202–30.

Kurke, L. 2005. "Choral Lyric as 'Ritualization': Poetic Sacrifice and Poetic *Ego* in Pindar's Sixth Paian." *ClAnt* 24:81–130.

Labellarte, M. 1988. "Via Giuseppe Martino." In *Archeologia di una città: Bari dalle origini al X secolo*, ed. G. Andreassi and F. Radina, 304–39. Bari: Edipuglia.

Lacroix, L. 1974. *Études d'archéologie numismatique*. Paris: Bibliothèque Salomon Reinach.

Lambert, W. G. 1960. *Babylonian Wisdom Literature*. Oxford: Clarendon Press.

Lattimore, R. 1951. *The Iliad of Homer*. Chicago: Univ. of Chicago Press.

———. 1965. *The Odyssey of Homer*. New York: Harper & Row.

Lawler, L. B. 1960. "Cosmic Dance and Dithyramb." In *Studies in Honor of Ullman*, ed. L. B. Lawler, D. M. Robathan, and W. C. Korfmacher, 12–16. Saint Louis: *Classical Bulletin*.

Lentz, A. 1870. *Grammatici graeci*. Vol. 3.2. Leipzig: Teubner.

Lesher, J. H. 1994. "The Significance of *kata pant'a<s>te* in Parmenides Fr. 1.3." *Ancient Philosophy* 14:1–20.

Lesky, A. 1932. "Zum *Phaethon* des Euripides." *Wiener Studien* 50:1–25.

Leutsch, E. L. von. 1851. *Paroemiographi graeci*. Vol. 1. Göttingen: Vandenhoeck and Ruprecht.

Lloyd-Jones, H., and P. Parsons. 1983. *Supplementum Hellenisticum*. Berlin: De Gruyter.

Lobel, E., et al. 1957. *The Oxyrhynchus Papyri* 24. London: Egypt Exploration Society.

Lonsdale, S. H. 1993. *Dance and Ritual Play in Greek Religion*. Baltimore: Johns Hopkins Univ. Press.

———. 1994–95. "*Homeric Hymn to Apollo*: Prototype and Paradigm of Choral Performance." *Arion*, 3rd ser., 3:25–40.

Loraux, N. 1995. "*Ponos*: Some Difficulties regarding the Term for 'Labor.'" In *The Experiences of Tiresias*, trans. P. Wissing, 44–58. Princeton, NJ: Princeton Univ. Press.

———. 2002. *The Mourning Voice*. Ithaca, NY: Cornell Univ. Press.

Macurdy, G. H. 1920. "The Hyperboreans Again, Abaris, and Helixoia." *CR* 34:137–41.

Mansfeld, J. 1964. *Die Offenbarung des Parmenides und die menschliche Welt*. Assen: Van Gorcum.

Marazov, I., ed. 1998. *Ancient Gold: The Wealth of the Thracians; Treasures from the Republic of Bulgaria*. New York: Harry N. Abrams.

Marcadé, J. 1974. "Les bras des danseuses." In *Mélanges helléniques offerts à Georges Daux*, 239–54. Paris: E. de Boccard.

Marcotte, D. 2000. *Les géographes grecs*. Vol. 1. Paris: Les Belles Lettres.

Marcovich, M. 1995. *Clementis Alexandrini* Protrepticus. Supplement to *Vigiliae Christianae* 34. Leiden: E. J. Brill.

———. 2001. *Heraclitus*. 2nd ed. Sankt Augustin, Germany: Academia Verlag.

Martin, J. 1974. *Scholia in Aratum vetera*. Stuttgart: B. G. Teubner.

Martinez, J.-L. 1997. "La colonne des danseuses de Delphes." *CRAI*: 35–46.

Mastronarde, D. J. 1994. *Euripides: Phoenissae*. Cambridge: Cambridge Univ. Press.

May, J. M. F. 1966. *The Coinage of Abdera*. Ed. C. M. Kraay and G. K. Jenkins. London: Royal Numismatic Society.

Meineke, A. 1849. *Stephani Byzantii Ethnicorum quae supersunt*. Berlin: G. Reimer.

Melero Bellido, A. 1972. *Athenas y el pitagorismo*. Salamanca: Universidad.

Merkelbach, R., and M. L. West. 1967. *Fragmenta Hesiodea*. Oxford: Clarendon Press.

Mikalson, J. D. 1975. *The Sacred and Civil Calendar of the Athenian Year*. Princeton, NJ: Princeton Univ. Press.

Miller, A. M. 1986. *From Delos to Delphi: A Literary Study of the Hymn to Apollo*. Leiden: Brill.

Miller, J. 1986. *Measures of Wisdom: The Cosmic Dance in Classical and Christian Antiquity*. Toronto: Univ. of Toronto Press.

Montanari, F. 1989. "Evoluzioni del coro e movimenti celesti." In *Scena e spettacolo nell'antichità*, ed. L. de Finis, 149–63. Atti del Convegno Internazionale di Studio, Trento, March 28–30, 1988. Florence: Leo S. Olschki.

Moon, N. 1929. "Some Early South Italian Vase-painters." *BSA* 11:30–49.

Moore, M. B. 1997. *Attic Red-figured and White-ground Pottery*. The Athenian Agora 30. Princeton, NJ: American School of Classical Studies at Athens.

Morris, S. P. 1984. *The Black and White Style*. Yale Classical Monographs 6. New Haven, CT: Yale Univ. Press.

Most, G. W. 1987. "Alcman's 'Cosmogonic' Fragment." *CQ* 81, n.s. 37:1–19.

Mourelatos, A. P. D. 1970. *The Route of Parmenides*. New Haven, CT: Yale Univ. Press.

Müller, K. 1855. *Geographi graeci minores*. Vol. 1. Paris: Didot.

Mynors, R. A. B. 1990. *Virgil: Georgics*. Oxford: Clarendon Press.

Naerebout, F. G. 1997. *Attractive Performances*. Amsterdam: J. C. Gieben.

Nagy, G. 1974. *Comparative Studies in Greek and Indic Meter*. Harvard Studies in Comparative Literature. Cambridge, MA: Harvard Univ. Press.

———. 1985. "Theognis and Megara: A Poet's Vision of His City." In *Theognis of Megara*, ed. T. J. Figueira and G. Nagy, 22–81. Baltimore: Johns Hopkins Univ. Press.

———. 1990a. "Phaethon, Sappho's Phaon, and the White Rock of Leukas: 'Reading' the Symbols of Greek Lyric." In *Greek Mythology and Poetics*, 223–62. Ithaca, NY: Cornell Univ. Press. Revised version of "Phaethon, Sappho's Phaon, and the White Rock of Leukas" (*HSCP* 77 [1973]:137–77).

———. 1990b. *Pindar's Homer*. Baltimore: Johns Hopkins Univ. Press.

———. 1996. *Poetry as Performance*. Cambridge: Cambridge Univ. Press.

———. 1999. *The Best of the Achaeans*. 2nd ed. Baltimore: Johns Hopkins Univ. Press.

———. 2005. "The Epic Hero." In *A Companion to Ancient Epic*, ed. J. M. Foley, 71–89. Malden, MA: Blackwell Publishing.

Nauck, A. 1889. *Tragicorum graecorum fragmenta*. 2nd ed. Leipzig: B. G. Teubner.

Nilsson, M. P. 1906. *Griechische Feste von religiöser Bedeutung mit Ausschluss der attischen*. Leipzig: B. G. Teubner.

———. 1909. *Timbres amphoriques de Lindos*. Exploration archéologique de Rhodes 5. Copenhagen: Bianco Luno.

———. 1962. *Die Entstehung und religiöse Bedeutung des griechischen Kalenders*. 2nd ed. Lund, Sweden: Gleerup.

Nørskov, V. 2004. "Finds of Red-figure Pottery." In *Subterranean and Pre-Maussollan*

Structures on the Site of the Maussolleion, ed. J. Zahle and K. Kjeldsen, 208–20. The Maussolleion at Halikarnassos 6. Copenhagen: Jutland Archaeological Society Publications and Aarhus Univ. Press.

Oakley, J. H., and R. H. Sinos. 1993. *The Wedding in Ancient Athens*. Madison: Univ. of Wisconsin Press.

Ogden, D. 1996. *Greek Bastardy*. Oxford: Clarendon Press.

Paduano, G. 1969. *Alcesti*. Florence: La Nuova Italia.

Page, D. L. 1951. *Alcman: The Partheneion*. Oxford: Clarendon Press.

———. 1959. Review of Lobel et al. 1957. *CR* 73, n.s. 9:15–23.

Papaspyridi-Karouzou, S. 1938. "A Proto-Panathenaic Amphora in the National Museum at Athens." *AJA* 42:495–505.

———. 1945–47. "Αἱ ἑπτὰ θυγατέρες τοῦ Ἄτλαντος." *AE*: 22–36.

Parke, H. W. 1945. "The Deposing of Spartan Kings." *CQ* 39:106–12.

———. 1977. *Festivals of the Athenians*. Ithaca, NY: Cornell Univ. Press.

———. 1985. *The Oracles of Apollo in Asia Minor*. London: Croom Helm.

Pelliccia, H. 1988. "The Text of Parmenides B 1.3 (D-K)." *AJP* 109:507–12.

Penwill, J. L. 1974. "Alkman's Cosmogony." *Apeiron* 8:13–39.

Peponi, A.-M. 2004. "Initiating the Viewer: Deixis and Visual Perception in Alcman's Lyric Drama." In *The Poetics of Deixis in Alcman, Pindar, and Other Lyric*, ed. N. Felson, 295–316. *Arethusa* 37.3.

Perrin, B. 1914. *Plutarch: Lives*. Vol. 1. Loeb Classical Library. Cambridge, MA: Harvard Univ. Press; London: William Heinemann.

Pettersson, M. 1992. *Cults of Apollo at Sparta*. Stockholm: Paul Åström Förlag.

Pfister, M. 1988. *The Theory and Analysis of Drama*. Trans. J. Halliday. Cambridge: Cambridge Univ. Press.

Philip, J. A. 1966. *Pythagoras and Early Pythagoreanism*. Toronto: Univ. of Toronto Press.

Phillips, J. H. 1980. "The Constellations on Achilles' Shield (*Iliad* 18.485–489)." *Liverpool Classical Monthly* 5:179–80.

Pouilloux, J., and G. Roux. 1963. *Énigmes à Delphes*. Paris: E. de Boccard.

Powell, J. U. 1925. *Collectanea Alexandrina*. Oxford: Clarendon Press.

Pretagostini, R. 1977. "Prisciano ed alcuni versi 'giambici' nella lirica greca arcaica (Alcmane, Anacreonte, Simonide e Pindaro)." *QUCC* 26:63–78.

Priestley, J. M. 2007. "The φᾶρος of Alcman's *Partheneion*." *Mnemosyne* 60:175–95.

Pritchett, W. K. 1946. "Months in Dorian Calendars." *AJA* 50:358–60.

———. 1974. *The Greek State at War, Part I*. Berkeley and Los Angeles: Univ. of California Press.

Pritchett, W. K., and B. L. van der Waerden. 1961. "Thucydidean Time-reckoning and Euctemon's Seasonal Calendar." *BCH* 85:17–52.

Prudhommeau, G. 1965. *La danse grecque antique*. Paris: Editions du CNRS.

Puelma, M. 1977. "Die Selbstbeschreibung des Chores in Alkmans grossem Partheneion-Fragment." *Museum Helveticum* 34:1–55.

Race, W. H. 1982. *The Classical Priamel from Homer to Boethius*. Leiden: E. J. Brill.

———. 1997. *Pindar: Olympian Odes, Pythian Odes*. Loeb Classical Library. Cambridge, MA: Harvard Univ. Press.

Rappaport, R. A. 1992. "Ritual." In *Folklore, Cultural Performances, and Popular Entertainments*, ed. R. Bauman, 249–60. New York: Oxford Univ. Press.

———. 1999. *Ritual and Religion in the Making of Humanity*. Cambridge: Cambridge Univ. Press.

Reckford, K. J. 1972. "Phaethon, Hippolytus, and Aphrodite." *TAPA* 103:405–32.

Rhomaiou, K. A. 1958–59. "Καρυάτιδες." *Peloponnesiaka* 3–4:376–95.

Ricciardelli Apicella, G. 1979. "La cosmogonia di Alcmane." *QUCC* 32, n.s. 3:7–27.

Richer, N. 1998. *Les éphores: Études sur l'histoire et sur l'image de Sparte (VIIIe-IIIe siècle avant Jésus Christ)*. Paris: Publications de la Sorbonne.

———. 2004. "The Hyakinthia of Sparta." In *Spartan Society*, ed. T. J. Figueira, 77–102. Swansea: Classical Press of Wales.

Ridgway, B. S. 1990. *Hellenistic Sculpture I: The Styles of ca. 331–200 B. C.* Madison: Univ. of Wisconsin Press.

Robbins, E. 1994. "Alcman's *Partheneion*: Legend and Choral Ceremony." *CQ* 88, n.s. 44:7–16.

Robert, C. 1919. *Archaeologische Hermeneutik*. Berlin: Weidmann.

Robertson, M. 1992. *The Art of Vase-painting in Classical Athens*. Cambridge: Cambridge Univ. Press.

Robertson, N. 1992. *Festivals and Legends: The Formation of Greek Cities in the Light of Public Ritual*. Toronto: Univ. of Toronto Press.

Romer, F. E. 1998. *Pomponius Mela's Description of the World*. Ann Arbor: Univ. of Michigan Press.

Rose, V. 1886. *Aristotelis qui ferebantur librorum fragmenta*. Leipzig: B. G. Teubner.

Rosenmeyer, T. G. 2002. "'Metatheater': An Essay on Overload." *Arion*, 3rd ser., 10:87–119.

Rowe, C. J. 1999: *Plato: Phaedrus*. 2nd ed. Warminster, Wiltshire: Aris & Phillips.

Rutherford, I. 1994–95. "Apollo in Ivy: The Tragic Paean." *Arion*, 3rd ser., 3:112–35.

Samuel, A. E. 1972. *Greek and Roman Chronology: Calendars and Years in Classical Antiquity*. Handbuch der Altertumswissenschaft 1, 7. Munich: C. H. Beck.

Schneidewin, F. G., and E. L. von Leutsch. 1839. *Corpus paroemiographorum graecorum*. Vol. 1. Göttingen: Vandenhoeck & Ruprecht.

Segal, C. 1982. *Dionysiac Poetics and Euripides' Bacchae*. Princeton, NJ: Princeton Univ. Press.

———. 1993. *Euripides and the Poetics of Sorrow*. Durham, NC: Duke Univ. Press.

Sider, D., and C. W. Brunschön. 2007. *Theophrastus of Eresus: On Weather Signs*. Leiden: Brill.

Silberman, A. 1998. *Pomponius Mela: Chorographie*. Paris: Les Belles Lettres.

Simon, E. 1983. *Festivals of Attica*. Madison: Univ. of Wisconsin Press.

Slatkin, L. M. 1991. *The Power of Thetis*. Berkeley and Los Angeles: Univ. of California Press.

———. 2004. "Measuring Authority, Authoritative Measures: Hesiod's *Works and Days*." In *The Moral Authority of Nature*, ed. L. Daston and F. Vidal, 25–49. Chicago: Univ. of Chicago Press.

Smyth, H. W. 1922. *Aeschylus*. Vol. 1. Loeb Classical Library. London: William Heinemann; New York: G. P. Putnam's Sons.

———. 1956. *Greek Grammar*. Cambridge, MA: Harvard Univ. Press.

Snodgrass, A. M. 1971. *The Dark Age of Greece*. Edinburgh: Edinburgh Univ. Press.

———. 1998. *Homer and the Artists*. Cambridge: Cambridge Univ. Press.

Soubiran, J. 1981. *Avienus: Les Phénomènes d'Aratos*. Paris: Les Belles Lettres.

Stackelberg, O. M. von. 1837. *Gräber der Hellenen*. Berlin: G. Reimer.

Stählin, O. 1960. *Clemens Alexandrinus*. Vol. 2. 3rd ed., rev. L. Früchtel, Berlin: Akademie Verlag.

Steele, L. D. 2002. "Mesopotamian Elements in the Proem of Parmenides? Correspondences between the Sun-Gods Helios and Shamash." *CQ* 97, n.s. 52:583–88.

Stehle, E. 1997. *Performance and Gender in Ancient Greece*. Princeton, NJ: Princeton Univ. Press.

Steiner, C. J. 2003. "Allegoresis and Alcman's 'Cosmogony': P. Oxy xxiv 2390 (Fr. 5 Page-Davies)." *ZPE* 142:21–30.

Steinhart, M. 2004. *Die Kunst der Nachahmung*. Mainz: Philipp von Zabern.

Stephani, L. 1866. "Erklärung einiger im Jahre 1864 im südlichen Russland gefundenen Gegenstände." *Compte-rendu de la Commission Impériale Archéologique pour l'année 1865*. St. Petersburg: Imprimerie de l'Académie Impériale des Sciences.

Stewart, A. 1995. "Rape?" In *Pandora*, ed. E. D. Reeder, 74–90. Baltimore: Trustees of the Walters Art Gallery in association with Princeton Univ. Press.

Stilp, F. 2006. *Die Jacobsthal-Reliefs*. Rivista di Archeologia Suppl. vol. 29. Rome: Giorgio Bretschneider.

Tambiah, S. J. 1979. "A Performative Approach to Ritual." *Proceedings of the British Academy* 65:113–69. Reprinted in idem, *Culture, Thought, and Social Action*, 123–66 (Cambridge, MA: Harvard Univ. Press, 1985).

Tarán, L. 1965. *Parmenides*. Princeton, NJ: Princeton Univ. Press.

———. 1975. *Academica: Plato, Philip of Opus, and the Pseudo-Platonic Epinomis*. Philadelphia: American Philosophical Society.

Tiverios, M. 1981. "Saltantes Lacaenae." *AE*: 25–37.

Too, Y. L. 1997. "Alcman's *Partheneion*: The Maidens Dance the City." *QUCC* 85, n.s. 56:7–29.

Topper, K. 2007. "Perseus, the Maiden Medusa, and the Imagery of Abduction." *Hesperia* 76:73–105.

Trendall, A. D. 1938. *Frühitaliotische Vasen*. Leipzig: Heinrich Keller.

———. 1989. *Red Figure Vases of South Italy and Sicily*. London: Thames & Hudson.

Trümpy, C. 1997. *Untersuchungen zu den altgriechischen Monatsnamen und Monatsfolgen*. Heidelberg: C. Winter.

Tsitsibakou-Vasalos, E. 1993. "Alcman's *Partheneion* PMG 1, 13–15. Αἶσα, Πόρος and ἀπέδιλος ἀλκά: Their Past and Present." *Materiali e discussioni per l'analisi dei testi classici* 30:129–51.

Ubersfeld, A. 1996. *L'école du spectateur: Lire le théâtre II*. Paris: Belin.

Untersteiner, M. 1958. *Parmenide: Testimonianze e frammenti*. Firenze: La Nuova Italia.

Van Gennep, A. 1960. *The Rites of Passage*. Trans. M. B. Vizedom and G. L. Caffee. Chicago: Univ. of Chicago Press. Orig. pub. as *Les rites de passage* (Paris: É. Nourry, 1909).

Van Groningen, B. A. 1936. "The Enigma of Alcman's Partheneion." *Mnemosyne*, 3rd ser., 3:241–61.

Van Otterlo, W. A. A. 1939–40. "Beitrag zur Kentniss der griechischen Priamel." *Mnemosyne*, 3rd ser., 8:145–76.

Vatin, C. 1983. "Les danseuses de Delphes." *CRAI*: 26–40.

Vernant, J.-P. 1970. "Thétis et le poème cosmogonique d'Alcman." In *Hommages à Marie Delcourt*, 38–69. *Latomus* 114.

Voelke, A.-J. 1981. "Aux origines de la philosophie grecque: La cosmogonie d'Alcman." In *Métaphysique, histoire de la philosophie: Recueil d'études offert à Fernand Brunner*, 13–24. Neuchâtel: La Baconnière.

Voigt, E.-M. 1971. *Sappho et Alcaeus*. Amsterdam: Athenaeum—Polak & Van Gennep.

Volmer, H. 1930. *De Euripidis fabula quae ΦΑΕΘΩΝ inscribitur restituenda*. Westfälische Wilhelms-Universität Münster: Aschendorff.

Von der Mühl, P. V. 1958. "Miszelle." *Museum Helveticum* 15:83.

Vos, H. 1963. "Die Bahnen von Nacht und Tag." *Mnemosyne* 16:18–34.

Wachter, R. 2001. *Non-Attic Greek Vase Inscriptions*. Oxford: Oxford Univ. Press.

Watzinger, C. 1924. *Griechische Vasen in Tübingen*. Reutlingen: Gryphius Verlag.

Webster, T. B. L. 1967. *The Tragedies of Euripides*. London: Methuen & Co.

———. 1970. *The Greek Chorus*. London: Methuen & Co.

Weil, H. 1889. "Observations sur les fragments d'Euripide." *REG* 2:322–42.

Wendel, C. 1914. *Scholia in Theocritum vetera*. Leipzig: B. G. Teubner.

West, M. L. 1963. "Three Presocratic Cosmologies." *CQ* 57, n.s. 13:154–76.

———. 1965. "Alcmanica." *CQ* 59, n.s. 15:188–202.

———. 1966. *Hesiod: Theogony*. Oxford: Oxford Univ. Press.

———. 1967. "Alcman and Pythagoras." *CQ* 61, n.s. 17:1–15.

———. 1972. *Iambi et elegi graeci ante Alexandrum cantati*. Oxford: Oxford Univ. Press.

———. 1978. *Hesiod: Works and Days*. Oxford: Oxford Univ. Press.

———. 1992. *Ancient Greek Music*. Oxford: Oxford Univ. Press.

———. 1998. *Aeschyli tragoediae*. Stuttgart: B. G. Teubner.

Westermann, A. 1862. *De clarorum philosophorum vitis, dogmatibus et apophthegmatibus libri decem*. Paris: Didot.

Wide, S. 1893. *Lakonische Kulte*. Leipzig: B. G. Teubner.

Wilamowitz-Moellendorf, U. von. 1883. "Phaethon." *Hermes* 18:396–434.

———. 1886. *Euripides: Herakles*. Part 1, *Einleitung in die attische Tragödie*. Berlin: Weidmann.

———. 1897. "Der Chor der Hagesichora." *Hermes* 32:251–63.

———. 1899. "Lesefrüchte." *Hermes* 34:203–6.

Wuilleumier, P. 1933. "Cratère inédit de Ceglie." *RA*: 3–30.

Yalouris, N. 1980. "Astral Representations in the Archaic and Classical Periods and Their Connection to Literary Sources." *AJA* 84:313–18.

Yatromanolakis, D., and P. Roilos. 2003. *Towards a Ritual Poetics*. Athens: Foundation of the Hellenic World.

INDEX OF SOURCES

Where no particular edition is specified, sources are cited after editions in the Oxford Classical Texts series. Translations are mine, unless otherwise stated.

INDEX OF MONUMENTS

GENERAL INDEX